THE **50** FUNNIEST AMERICAN WRITERS *

An **ANTHOLOGY**
of **HUMOR**
from **MARK TWAIN**
to **THE ONION**

The **50**
FUNNIEST
AMERICAN WRITERS *

* *According to*
ANDY BOROWITZ

A Special Publication of THE LIBRARY OF AMERICA

Distributed to the trade in the United States by
Penguin Group (USA) Inc.
and in Canada by Penguin Books Canada Ltd.

Library of Congress Control Number: 2011928952
ISBN 978-1-59853-107-7

Third Printing

Printed in the United States of America

CONTENTS

Introduction   *xi*

Mark Twain   *3*
A Presidential Candidate

George Ade   *6*
The Lecture Tickets That Were Bought
but Never Used

O. Henry   *11*
The Ransom of Red Chief

Sinclair Lewis   *27*
from *Babbitt*

Anita Loos   *49*
from *Gentlemen Prefer Blondes*

Ring Lardner   *52*
On Conversation

H. L. Mencken   *56*
Imperial Purple

James Thurber   *63*
More Alarms at Night

Dorothy Parker   *71*
The Waltz

S. J. Perelman   *78*
Farewell, My Lovely Appetizer

Langston Hughes   *88*
Simple Prays a Prayer

Frank Sullivan   *94*
The Night the Old Nostalgia Burned Down

E. B. White   *102*
Across the Street and into the Grill

Peter De Vries   *107*
The House of Mirth

Terry Southern   *114*
from *The Magic Christian*

Lenny Bruce   *119*
from *How to Talk Dirty and Influence People*

Tom Wolfe   *131*
The Secret Vice

Jean Shepherd   *140*
*The Counterfeit Secret Circle Member Gets
the Message,* or *The Asp Strikes Again*

Hunter S. Thompson   *150*
The Kentucky Derby Is Decadent and Depraved

Woody Allen   *177*
A Look at Organized Crime

Bruce Jay Friedman   *183*
The Tax Man

Philip Roth   *194*
Letters to Einstein

Nora Ephron *201*
A Few Words about Breasts

Henry Beard, Michael O'Donoghue, George W. S. Trow *214*
Our White Heritage

Fran Lebowitz *240*
Better Read Than Dead: A Revised Opinion

Charles Portis *246*
Your Action Line

Donald Barthelme *253*
In the Morning Post

Veronica Geng *256*
Curb Carter Policy Discord Effort Threat

John Hughes *259*
Vacation '58

Mark O'Donnell *286*
The Laws of Cartoon Motion

Garrison Keillor *289*
The Tip-Top Club

Bruce McCall *308*
Rolled in Rare Bohemian Onyx, Then
Vulcanized by Hand

Molly Ivins *313*
Tough as Bob War and Other Stuff

Calvin Trillin *319*
Corrections

Dave Barry   *323*
Tips for Women: How to Have a
Relationship with a Guy

The Onion   *335*
Clinton Deploys Vowels to Bosnia

Susan Orlean   *339*
Shiftless Little Loafers

Roy Blount Jr.   *343*
Gothic Baseball

George Carlin   *351*
If I Were in Charge of the Networks

Ian Frazier   *358*
Laws Concerning Food and Drink;
Household Principles; Lamentations of the Father

David Rakoff   *364*
The Writer's Life

Bernie Mac   *369*
from *I Ain't Scared of You*

David Sedaris   *372*
Buddy, Can You Spare a Tie?

Wanda Sykes   *386*
It's So Hard

Jack Handey   *390*
What I'd Say to the Martians

David Owen 394
Your Three Wishes: F.A.Q.

George Saunders 397
Ask the Optimist!

Jenny Allen 414
Awake

Sloane Crosley 420
The Pony Problem

Larry Wilmore 429
If Not an Apology, at Least a "My Bad"

Contributors 439

Sources and Acknowledgments 455

INTRODUCTION

Does being funny get you girls?

Growing up in Ohio, I was convinced that it did. I got this notion from sources I took to be representative of all women: *Playboy* centerfolds. Every issue, the Playmate Data Sheet would, with astonishing consistency, indicate that Miss Whenever's turn-on was "a sense of humor." (Turn-off? "Phony people.") I vowed to be a hilarious sincere person who would have sex with lots of naked people named Brandi.

I accepted this view of humor-as-pheromone despite mountains of real-world evidence to the contrary. At Shaker High, the girls mainly went for jocks whose idea of a witty retort was a wedgie. And if I had looked a little more closely at *Playboy*'s monthly "Party Pics" feature, I might have noticed that the bunnies at Hef's Mansion gravitated towards the laps of people like Lee Majors, the star of *The Six Million Dollar Man* and not, to my knowledge, a founding member of the Algonquin Round Table.

What being funny got me, mostly, was a lot of free time. While the jocks were busy having tantric romps with cheerleaders, I kept myself occupied by reading Mark Twain, Woody Allen, and *The National Lampoon*. Little did I know that over the course of a thousand dateless nights, a Library of America humor anthology was being born.

So how did I choose the fifty selections for this book? I showed the people at The Library of America my favorite humor pieces; they showed me theirs; and when we found fifty we agreed on, we stopped. To celebrate, we ordered Chinese food, using much the same process.

Based on the method I just described, you might jump to the conclusion that this anthology is a little arbitrary. Well, here's a dirty little secret about anthologies: they're *all* arbitrary. I just have the *cojones* to admit it. In college, for example, I had to read *The Norton Anthology of English Literature*. It's full of stuff like this:

> *Whan that Aprille with his shoures soote*
> *The droghte of Marche hath perced to the roote,*
> *And bathed every veyne in swich licour,*
> *Of which vertu engendred is the flour*

Say what? Not exactly sure why that gem made it in, although having just gone twelve rounds with my publisher, I know these things can get pretty political.

Trying to rank artists is a tricky business. A reporter once asked John Lennon if Ringo was the best drummer in the world. Lennon answered, "He's not even the best drummer in the Beatles." Funny people might be even harder to rank than drummers. There's probably nothing more subjective than a sense of humor, which could explain why those *Playboy* centerfolds found Lee Majors so riotous.

All I know for sure is that these fifty pieces make me laugh. I assembled this book the way I make a playlist for a party. I don't try to pick the greatest songs of all time; I just choose songs I like and hope that people have a good time — and that they won't judge me too harshly when they hear "Wake Me Up Before You Go-Go."

Now, all of this raises a legitimate question: if it's impossible to say who the fifty funniest American writers are, why did I give this anthology a title like *The 50 Funniest American Writers*? Let me answer that as honestly as I can: to sell books.

Here was my thinking. Whenever you come out with a "best of" list, you're bound to irritate people, and by "people," I mean the people you've left off the list and their relatives. They start bad-mouthing it, which forces other people (me, and my many Internet aliases) to defend it. If you're lucky, the controversy goes viral and lots of people start arguing about who deserves to be on the list and who doesn't. And all that talk "moves a shitload of units," to borrow a phrase coined by Edith Wharton.

I'm not the first to realize that lists are commercial gold. I have spent many hours on the treadmill watching those addictive countdown shows on E! ("20 Most Suspicious-looking Celebrity Cold Sores"). And while it's tempting to dismiss listmania as the province of the trashy, even the monocle-wearing Pooh-Bahs at *The New Yorker* have succumbed. In 2010 they put out their "20 Under 40" honor roll of fiction writers, the result of a mysterious selection process that seemed to be on loan from the College of Cardinals. It remains to be seen whether being on the "20 Under 40" list made anyone's career, but in the near term, it probably got somebody laid. And it sold a lot of magazines, which in the publishing world is as close as you get to sex.

Now that we've established that making lists is the road to royalties, you're probably wondering how I convinced the august gatekeepers at The Library of America to go along with such a crass scheme. I hate to shatter your illusions about the LOA, but in my entire career I have never met a more shameless cabal of publicity whores. They don't think twice about slapping a grabby title on one of their books if it'll turn a quick buck. If you don't believe me, check out their catalogue; it's larded with temptations like *History of the United States During the Administrations of James Madison (1809–1817)*.

Warning: the next two paragraphs contain actual information.

In choosing the pieces for this book, I didn't consider funny songs or poems because The Library of America already published a wonderful anthology of light verse called *American Wits* ($20.00). And I didn't consider transcripts of comedy sketches, scenes from plays or movies, or standup comedy routines, because that stuff is best enjoyed in performance. But I did find some great material in books written by standups, including George Carlin, Lenny Bruce and Bernie Mac.

Finally, I haven't written introductions to the individual pieces because I'd rather let the writing speak for itself. To get back to the playlist analogy: explaining what makes a song amazing is a pretty amazing way to wreck a song. That's why when I have a party I just put my iPod in the dock and shut my piehole.

Which is what I'll do now.

Andy Borowitz
New York 2011

THE **50 FUNNIEST** AMERICAN WRITERS *

MARK TWAIN

✳

A Presidential Candidate

I have pretty much made up my mind to run for President. What the country wants is a candidate who cannot be injured by investigation of his past history, so that the enemies of the party will be unable to rake up anything against him that nobody ever heard of before. If you know the worst about a candidate, to begin with, every attempt to spring things on him will be checkmated. Now I am going to enter the field with an open record. I am going to own up in advance to all the wickedness I have done, and if any Congressional committee is disposed to prowl around my biography in the hope of discovering any dark and deadly deed that I have secreted, why—let it prowl.

In the first place, I admit that I treed a rheumatic grandfather of mine in the winter of 1850. He was old and inexpert in climbing trees, but with the heartless brutality that is characteristic of me I ran him out of the front door in his nightshirt at the point of a shotgun, and caused him to bowl up a maple tree, where he remained all night, while I emptied shot into his legs. I did this because he snored. I will do it again if I ever have another grandfather. I am as inhuman now as I was in 1850. I candidly acknowledge that I ran away at the battle of Gettysburg. My friends have tried to smooth over this fact by asserting that I did so for the purpose of imitating Washington, who went into the woods at Valley Forge for the purpose of saying his prayers. It was a miserable subterfuge. I struck out in a straight line for the Tropic of Cancer because I was scared. I wanted my country saved, but I preferred to have somebody else save it. I entertain that preference yet. If the bubble reputation can be obtained only at the cannon's mouth, I am willing to go there for it, provided the cannon is empty. If it is loaded my immortal and inflexible purpose is to get over the fence and go home. My invariable practice in war has been to bring out of every fight two-thirds more men than when I went in. This seems to me to be Napoleonic in its grandeur.

My financial views are of the most decided character, but they are not likely, perhaps, to increase my popularity with the advocates of inflation. I do not insist upon the special supremacy of rag money or hard money. The great fundamental principle of my life is to take any kind I can get.

The rumor that I buried a dead aunt under my grapevine was correct. The vine needed fertilizing, my aunt had to be buried, and I dedicated her to this high purpose. Does that unfit me for the Presidency? The Constitution of our country does not say so. No other citizen was ever considered unworthy of this office because he enriched his grapevines with his dead relatives. Why should I be selected as the first victim of an absurd prejudice?

I admit also that I am not a friend of the poor man. I regard the poor man, in his present condition, as so much wasted raw material. Cut up and properly canned, he might be made useful to fatten the natives of the cannibal islands and to improve our export trade with that region. I shall recommend legislation upon the subject in my first message. My campaign cry will be: "Desiccate the poor workingman; stuff him into sausages."

These are about the worst parts of my record. On them I come before the country. If my country don't want me, I will go back again. But I recommend myself as a safe man—a man who starts from the basis of total depravity and proposes to be fiendish to the last.

[1879]

GEORGE ADE

✳

The Lecture Tickets That Were Bought but Never Used

Once there was a Man living in a Big Town and he had a Cousin whom he never had seen. Some people are very lucky as to their Relatives.

The Man who lived in the Wicked Metropolis was named Sanford, and the Cousin who lived out in the Woods was known as Lafe, although his real Name was Lafayette.

Every Christmas Sanford would send Lafe some kind of a stingy Gift, and then Lafe would retaliate by shipping in a fat Turkey for Thanksgiving. There was a formal Exchange of Letters about twice per Year.

Sanford was a good deal Upset one day to receive Word that Cousin Lafayette was coming to spend a Week. Whatever Joy he felt he did not show at all.

The visiting Cousin is liable to be a Fierce Proposition under the most favorable Conditions, but it is more than

Hard Luck to be saddled with one who is a Total Stranger. Sanford was hoping that the Train would run off the Track, but he wrote Cousin Lafe to be sure and come right to the House.

Sanford saw a very pink Week ahead of him. He was not very Strong for the Chaperon Game. He could see himself neglecting Business in order to lead Cousin Lafe around and show him the Sky-Scrapers, the Animals in the Park, the Éden Musée, and the big Engine in the Power-House. He had observed that the Excursionist is always keen to see a lot of Sights that are a Sealed Book to the Man who lives right in the City.

Sanford tried to get a Line on Cousin Lafe so as to frame up the right kind of a Programme. He could tell by the Picture in the Family Album that Lafe was a Pure Character and somewhat of a Rube. He wore a White Tie and had his Hair gummed down on his Forehead. He looked as if he would like to be a Preacher but could not quite make it. His open Countenance had that sweet and trusting Expression of the Hubbard Squash who is willing to give two Tens for a Five.

So far as Sanford could learn, Cousin Lafe was a kind of moral Sign-Board and snow-white Object-Lesson in the Jay Town which claimed him as its own. He was a Cemetery Trustee and Chairman of the Committee to solicit Funds for a new Y.M.C.A. Building. Also he had been prominent in the Sunday-Closing Movement and the Main Kazoo in the Citizens' Reform League.

Accordingly, Sanford had all the Drinkables removed

from the Sideboard, and he warned the Children not to
Laugh while Cousin Lafe was saying Grace at the Table.
Then he went out and bought some Tickets for a Lecture,
and got a written Permit to go through the Car-Shops.

He went to the Station to meet the rural Lamb and protect
him against the Cabmen. He saw a Hot Sport with a new Suit
of Clothes and a Red Tie come through the Gate, but he did
not spot anything that resembled a Cemetery Trustee. While
he was still waiting, the Hot Sport came up and walloped him
on the Back and introduced himself.

"What do you think?" asked the President of the Yapville
Citizens' Reform League. "I got into a Poker Game with
two of them Ikey Drummers on the Train and trimmed them
for 87 Samoleons. If the Train had been a half-hour late I'd
have got their Sample-Cases. I've got a Roll here that would
choke a Horse, and I have a Feeling that I am about to Buy.
We drank up everything in the Dining-Car except the Cat-
sup before we got to Springfield, and I wouldn't take $7 for
my Thirst. By the way, I want to tell you that I've left my
Pajamas at Home, and you might as well move the Bed out
of my Room, because I won't need it. If you have any Word
to send to your Folks before we cut loose, step into the Box
and telephone while you're still able to talk."

"What do you wish to see first of all, the Parks or the
Power-House?" asked Sanford.

"If it's all the same to you," said the Cemetery Trustee, "I
should like to begin my Vacation by putting a tall Crimp in
the Guy that spins the little Ivory Ball. Then you can send

home for your Low-Neck and we will have a little Dinner-Party. I have engaged the Louis XIV Room up at the Hotel. I have in my Suit-Case no less than 17 Letters of Introduction to well-known Society Ladies who are always Hungry. This Afternoon I expect to have all the Messenger Boys in Town busy. When we sit down this Evening there will be $8 worth of Violets and four Cocktails at every Plate. I'll show these Tessies that I'm no Piker. After the Eats we are going over and sit in all of the Boxes at that Rough-House Show that I've been reading about. After that we are going to a nice, quiet all-night Restaurant, where they have the Hungarian Orchestra, and any one that passes away before 6 A.M. will be called a Quitter."

"Are you Cousin Lafe or a Ringer?" asked Sanford.

"I am the Cemetery Trustee all right, all right," was the reply. "A Cemetery Trustee breaks over only about once in Three Years, but when he does hit the Track he makes a Mile in 2.00 look like a Funeral Procession. For many Months I have been drinking Milk and posing as an Example for the Young. I live in one of those Towns where every living Soul knows how much I pay for my Clothes and how many Lumps of Sugar I put in my Coffee. If I took a Drink out there everybody would know about it in twenty Minutes. If I smoked a Cigarette I would be hanged in Effigy. I might as well go out and kill an Aged Woman with a Hatchet as mix up in any Poker Games. So I do the Straight and Narrow. But now I'm up here among the Electric Lights with no one to keep Cases on me. I am long on Sleep, and I have Money in every Pocket. I'm up here to play a short Engagement as the Village Indian. If you care to follow me, I think I can put you in right and probably show you a good many Places that you never saw before, even if you do live right in Town."

Sanford tried to be Game, but in two Days Cousin Lafe had him Down and Out. He fell back and took the Count. Cousin Lafe took him Home in a Hack and roasted him, and told him he was a Rhinestone Sport and a Mackerel.

"I'm all in," said the Wreck. " I admit everything you say. The Man who lives in Town and thinks he is a Gay Dog isn't a Marker alongside of the Respectable Citizen from down the Road. I am supposed to be a dissolute Clubman, but I take off my Hat to a Cemetery Trustee."

Cousin Lafe went back to the Country and reported that Sanford was a Nice Man but seemed to be a little Wild.

MORAL: Don't try to keep up with any Pillar of Society.

[1904]

O. HENRY

✳

The Ransom of Red Chief

It looked like a good thing: but wait till I tell you. We were down South, in Alabama—Bill Driscoll and myself—when this kidnapping idea struck us. It was, as Bill afterward expressed it, "during a moment of temporary mental apparition"; but we didn't find that out till later.

There was a town down there, as flat as a flannel-cake, and called Summit, of course. It contained inhabitants of as undeleterious and self-satisfied a class of peasantry as ever clustered around a Maypole.

Bill and me had a joint capital of about six hundred dollars, and we needed just two thousand dollars more to pull off a fraudulent town-lot scheme in Western Illinois with. We talked it over on the front steps of the hotel. Philoprogenitiveness, says we, is strong in semi-rural communities; therefore, and for other reasons, a kidnapping project ought to do better there than in the radius of newspapers that send reporters out in plain clothes to stir up talk about such things.

We knew that Summit couldn't get after us with anything stronger than constables and, maybe, some lackadaisical bloodhounds and a diatribe or two in the *Weekly Farmers' Budget*. So, it looked good.

We selected for our victim the only child of a prominent citizen named Ebenezer Dorset. The father was respectable and tight, a mortgage fancier and a stern, upright collection-plate passer and forecloser. The kid was a boy of ten, with bas-relief freckles, and hair the colour of the cover of the magazine you buy at the news-stand when you want to catch a train. Bill and me figured that Ebenezer would melt down for a ransom of two thousand dollars to a cent. But wait till I tell you.

About two miles from Summit was a little mountain, covered with a dense cedar brake. On the rear elevation of this mountain was a cave. There we stored provisions.

One evening after sundown, we drove in a buggy past old Dorset's house. The kid was in the street, throwing rocks at a kitten on the opposite fence.

"Hey, little boy!" says Bill, "would you like to have a bag of candy and a nice ride?"

The boy catches Bill neatly in the eye with a piece of brick.

"That will cost the old man an extra five hundred dollars," says Bill, climbing over the wheel.

That boy put up a fight like a welter-weight cinnamon bear; but, at last, we got him down in the bottom of the buggy and drove away. We took him up to the cave, and I hitched the horse in the cedar brake. After dark I drove the buggy to the little village, three miles away, where we had hired it, and walked back to the mountain.

Bill was pasting court-plaster over the scratches and bruises on his features. There was a fire burning behind the big rock at the entrance of the cave, and the boy was watching a pot of boiling coffee, with two buzzard tail-feathers stuck in his red hair. He points a stick at me when I come up, and says:

"Ha! cursed paleface, do you dare to enter the camp of Red Chief, the terror of the plains?"

"He's all right now," says Bill, rolling up his trousers and examining some bruises on his shins. "We're playing Indian. We're making Buffalo Bill's show look like magic-lantern views of Palestine in the town hall. I'm Old Hank, the Trapper, Red Chief's captive, and I'm to be scalped at daybreak. By Geronimo! that kid can kick hard."

Yes, sir, that boy seemed to be having the time of his life. The fun of camping out in a cave had made him forget that he was a captive himself. He immediately christened me Snake-eye, the Spy, and announced that, when his braves returned from the warpath, I was to be broiled at the stake at the rising of the sun.

Then we had supper; and he filled his mouth full of bacon and bread and gravy, and began to talk. He made a during-dinner speech something like this:

"I like this fine. I never camped out before; but I had a pet 'possum once, and I was nine last birthday. I hate to go to school. Rats ate up sixteen of Jimmy Talbot's aunt's speckled hen's eggs. Are there any real Indians in these woods? I want some more gravy. Does the trees moving make the wind blow? We had five puppies. What makes your nose so red, Hank? My father has lots of money. Are the stars hot? I whipped Ed Walker twice, Saturday. I don't like girls. You dassent catch toads unless with a string. Do oxen make any noise? Why are oranges round? Have you got beds to sleep on in this cave? Amos Murray has got six toes. A parrot can talk, but a monkey or a fish can't. How many does it take to make twelve?"

Every few minutes he would remember that he was a pesky redskin, and pick up his stick rifle and tiptoe to the mouth of the cave to rubber for the scouts of the hated paleface. Now and then he would let out a war-whoop that made Old Hank the Trapper, shiver. That boy had Bill terrorized from the start.

"Red Chief," says I to the kid, "would you like to go home?"

"Aw, what for?" says he. "I don't have any fun at home. I hate to go to school. I like to camp out. You won't take me back home again, Snake-eye, will you?"

"Not right away," says I. "We'll stay here in the cave a while."

"All right!" says he. "That'll be fine. I never had such fun in all my life."

We went to bed about eleven o'clock. We spread down some wide blankets and quilts and put Red Chief between us.

We weren't afraid he'd run away. He kept us awake for three hours, jumping up and reaching for his rifle and screeching: "Hist! pard," in mine and Bill's ears, as the fancied crackle of a twig or the rustle of a leaf revealed to his young imagination the stealthy approach of the outlaw band. At last, I fell into a troubled sleep, and dreamed that I had been kidnapped and chained to a tree by a ferocious pirate with red hair.

Just at daybreak, I was awakened by a series of awful screams from Bill. They weren't yells, or howls, or shouts, or whoops, or yawps, such as you'd expect from a manly set of vocal organs—they were simply indecent, terrifying, humiliating screams, such as women emit when they see ghosts or caterpillars. It's an awful thing to hear a strong, desperate, fat man scream incontinently in a cave at daybreak.

I jumped up to see what the matter was. Red Chief was sitting on Bill's chest, with one hand twined in Bill's hair. In the other he had the sharp case-knife we used for slicing bacon; and he was industriously and realistically trying to take Bill's scalp, according to the sentence that had been pronounced upon him the evening before.

I got the knife away from the kid and made him lie down again. But, from that moment, Bill's spirit was broken. He laid down on his side of the bed, but he never closed an eye again in sleep as long as that boy was with us. I dozed off for a while, but along toward sun-up I remembered that Red Chief had said I was to be burned at the stake at the rising of the sun. I wasn't nervous or afraid; but I sat up and lit my pipe and leaned against a rock.

"What you getting up so soon for, Sam?" asked Bill.

"Me?" says I. "Oh, I got a kind of a pain in my shoulder. I thought sitting up would rest it."

"You're a liar!" says Bill. "You're afraid. You was to be burned at sunrise, and you was afraid he'd do it. And he would, too, if he could find a match. Ain't it awful, Sam? Do you think anybody will pay out money to get a little imp like that back home?"

"Sure," said I. "A rowdy kid like that is just the kind that parents dote on. Now, you and the Chief get up and cook breakfast, while I go up on the top of this mountain and reconnoitre."

I went up on the peak of the little mountain and ran my eye over the contiguous vicinity. Over toward Summit I expected to see the sturdy yeomanry of the village armed with scythes and pitchforks beating the countryside for the dastardly kidnappers. But what I saw was a peaceful landscape dotted with one man ploughing with a dun mule. Nobody was dragging the creek; no couriers dashed hither and yon, bringing tidings of no news to the distracted parents. There was a sylvan attitude of somnolent sleepiness pervading that section of the external outward surface of Alabama that lay exposed to my view. "Perhaps," says I to myself, "it has not yet been discovered that the wolves have borne away the tender lambkin from the fold. Heaven help the wolves!" says I, and I went down the mountain to breakfast.

When I got to the cave I found Bill backed up against the side of it, breathing hard, and the boy threatening to smash him with a rock half as big as a cocoanut.

"He put a red-hot boiled potato down my back," explained Bill, "and then mashed it with his foot; and I boxed his ears. Have you got a gun about you, Sam?"

I took the rock away from the boy and kind of patched up the argument. "I'll fix you," says the kid to Bill. "No man ever yet struck the Red Chief but what he got paid for it. You better beware!"

After breakfast the kid takes a piece of leather with strings wrapped around it out of his pocket and goes outside the cave unwinding it.

"What's he up to now?" says Bill, anxiously. "You don't think he'll run away, do you, Sam?"

"No fear of it," says I. "He don't seem to be much of a home body. But we've got to fix up some plan about the ransom. There don't seem to be much excitement around Summit on account of his disappearance; but maybe they haven't realized yet that he's gone. His folks may think he's spending the night with Aunt Jane or one of the neighbours. Anyhow, he'll be missed to-day. To-night we must get a message to his father demanding the two thousand dollars for his return."

Just then we heard a kind of war-whoop, such as David might have emitted when he knocked out the champion Goliath. It was a sling that Red Chief had pulled out of his pocket, and he was whirling it around his head.

I dodged, and heard a heavy thud and a kind of a sigh from Bill, like a horse gives out when you take his saddle off. A niggerhead rock the size of an egg had caught Bill just behind his left ear. He loosened himself all over and fell in the fire across the frying pan of hot water for washing the dishes. I dragged him out and poured cold water on his head for half an hour.

By and by, Bill sits up and feels behind his ear and says: "Sam, do you know who my favourite Biblical character is?"

"Take it easy," says I. "You'll come to your senses presently."

"King Herod," says he. "You won't go away and leave me here alone, will you, Sam?"

I went out and caught that boy and shook him until his freckles rattled.

"If you don't behave," says I, "I'll take you straight home. Now, are you going to be good, or not?"

"I was only funning," says he sullenly. "I didn't mean to hurt Old Hank. But what did he hit me for? I'll behave, Snake-eye, if you won't send me home, and if you'll let me play the Black Scout to-day."

"I don't know the game," says I. "That's for you and Mr. Bill to decide. He's your playmate for the day. I'm going away for a while, on business. Now, you come in and make friends with him and say you are sorry for hurting him, or home you go, at once."

I made him and Bill shake hands, and then I took Bill aside and told him I was going to Poplar Cove, a little village three miles from the cave, and find out what I could about how the kidnapping had been regarded in Summit. Also, I thought it best to send a peremptory letter to old man Dorset that day, demanding the ransom and dictating how it should be paid.

"You know, Sam," says Bill, "I've stood by you without

batting an eye in earthquakes, fire and flood—in poker games, dynamite outrages, police raids, train robberies and cyclones. I never lost my nerve yet till we kidnapped that two-legged skyrocket of a kid. He's got me going. You won't leave me long with him, will you, Sam?"

"I'll be back some time this afternoon," says I. "You must keep the boy amused and quiet till I return. And now we'll write the letter to old Dorset."

Bill and I got paper and pencil and worked on the letter while Red Chief, with a blanket wrapped around him, strutted up and down, guarding the mouth of the cave. Bill begged me tearfully to make the ransom fifteen hundred dollars instead of two thousand. "I ain't attempting," says he, "to decry the celebrated moral aspect of parental affection, but we're dealing with humans, and it ain't human for anybody to give up two thousand dollars for that forty-pound chunk of freckled wildcat. I'm willing to take a chance at fifteen hundred dollars. You can charge the difference up to me."

So, to relieve Bill, I acceded, and we collaborated a letter that ran this way:

Ebenezer Dorset, Esq.:

We have your boy concealed in a place far from Summit. It is useless for you or the most skilful detectives to attempt to find him. Absolutely, the only terms on which you can have him restored to you are these: We demand fifteen hundred dollars in large bills for his return; the money to be left at midnight to-night at the same spot and in the same box as your reply—as hereinafter described. If you agree to these terms, send your answer in writing by a solitary messenger to-night at half-past eight o'clock. After crossing Owl Creek, on the road to Poplar Cove, there are three large trees about a hundred yards apart, close to the fence of the wheat field on the right-hand side. At the bottom of the fence-post, opposite the third tree, will be found a small pasteboard box.

The messenger will place the answer in this box and return immediately to Summit.

If you attempt any treachery or fail to comply with our demand as stated, you will never see your boy again.

If you pay the money as demanded, he will be returned to you safe and well within three hours. These terms are final, and if you do not accede to them no further communication will be attempted.

Two Desperate Men.

I addressed this letter to Dorset, and put it in my pocket. As I was about to start, the kid comes up to me and says:

"Aw, Snake-eye, you said I could play the Black Scout while you was gone."

"Play it, of course," says I. "Mr. Bill will play with you. What kind of a game is it?"

"I'm the Black Scout," says Red Chief, "and I have to ride to the stockade to warn the settlers that the Indians are coming. I'm tired of playing Indian myself. I want to be the Black Scout."

"All right," says I. "It sounds harmless to me. I guess Mr. Bill will help you foil the pesky savages."

"What am I to do?" asks Bill, looking at the kid suspiciously.

"You are the hoss," says Black Scout. "Get down on your hands and knees. How can I ride to the stockade without a hoss?"

"You'd better keep him interested," said I, "till we get the scheme going. Loosen up."

Bill gets down on his all fours, and a look comes in his eye like a rabbit's when you catch it in a trap.

"How far is it to the stockade, kid?" he asks, in a husky manner of voice.

"Ninety miles," says the Black Scout. "And you have to hump yourself to get there on time. Whoa, now!"

The Black Scout jumps on Bill's back and digs his heels in his side.

"For Heaven's sake," says Bill, "hurry back, Sam, as soon as you can. I wish we hadn't made the ransom more than a thousand. Say, you quit kicking me or I'll get up and warm you good."

I walked over to Poplar Cove and sat around the post-office and store, talking with the chawbacons that came in to trade. One whiskerando says that he hears Summit is all upset on account of Elder Ebenezer Dorset's boy having been lost or stolen. That was all I wanted to know. I bought some smoking tobacco, referred casually to the price of black-eyed peas, posted my letter surreptitiously and came away. The postmaster said the mail-carrier would come by in an hour to take the mail on to Summit.

When I got back to the cave Bill and the boy were not to be found. I explored the vicinity of the cave, and risked a yodel or two, but there was no response.

So I lighted my pipe and sat down on a mossy bank to await developments.

In about half an hour I heard the bushes rustle, and Bill wabbled out into the little glade in front of the cave. Behind him was the kid, stepping softly like a scout, with a broad grin on his face. Bill stopped, took off his hat and wiped his face with a red handkerchief. The kid stopped about eight feet behind him.

"Sam," says Bill, "I suppose you'll think I'm a renegade, but I couldn't help it. I'm a grown person with masculine proclivities and habits of self-defense, but there is a time when all systems of egotism and predominance fail. The boy is gone. I have sent him home. All is off. There was martyrs in old times," goes on Bill, "that suffered death rather than give up the particular graft they enjoyed. None of 'em ever was subjugated to such supernatural tortures as I have been. I tried to be faithful to our articles of depredation; but there came a limit."

"What's the trouble, Bill?" I asks him.

"I was rode," says Bill, "the ninety miles to the stockade, not barring an inch. Then, when the settlers was rescued, I was given oats. Sand ain't a palatable substitute. And then, for an hour I had to try to explain to him why there was nothin' in holes, how a road can run both ways and what makes the grass green. I tell you, Sam, a human can only stand so much. I takes him by the neck of his clothes and drags him down the mountain. On the way he kicks my legs black-and-blue from the knees down; and I've got to have two or three bites on my thumb and hand cauterized.

"But he's gone"—continues Bill—"gone home. I showed him the road to Summit and kicked him about eight feet nearer there at one kick. I'm sorry we lose the ransom; but it was either that or Bill Driscoll to the madhouse."

Bill is puffing and blowing, but there is a look of ineffable peace and growing content on his rose-pink features.

"Bill," says I, "there isn't any heart disease in your family, is there?"

"No," says Bill, "nothing chronic except malaria and accidents. Why?"

"Then you might turn around," says I, "and have a look behind you."

Bill turns and sees the boy, and loses his complexion and sits down plump on the ground and begins to pluck aimlessly at grass and little sticks. For an hour I was afraid for his mind. And then I told him that my scheme was to put the whole job through immediately and that we would get the ransom and be off with it by midnight if old Dorset fell in with our proposition. So Bill braced up enough to give the kid a weak sort of a smile and a promise to play the Russian in a Japanese war with him as soon as he felt a little better.

I had a scheme for collecting that ransom without danger of being caught by counterplots that ought to commend itself to professional kidnappers. The tree under which the answer was to be left—and the money later on—was close to the road fence with big, bare fields on all sides. If a gang of constables should be watching for any one to come for the note they could see him a long way off crossing the fields or in the road. But no, sirree! At half-past eight I was up in that tree as well hidden as a tree toad, waiting for the messenger to arrive.

Exactly on time, a half-grown boy rides up the road on a bicycle, locates the pasteboard box at the foot of the fence-post, slips a folded piece of paper into it and pedals away again back toward Summit.

I waited an hour and then concluded the thing was square. I slid down the tree, got the note, slipped along the fence till I struck the woods, and was back at the cave in another half an hour. I opened the note, got near the lantern and read it to Bill. It was written with a pen in a crabbed hand, and the sum and substance of it was this:

Two Desperate Men.

Gentlemen: I received your letter to-day by post, in regard to the ransom you ask for the return of my son. I think you are a little high in your demands, and I hereby make you a counter-proposition, which I am inclined to believe you will accept. You bring Johnny home and pay me two hundred and fifty dollars in cash, and I agree to take him off your hands. You had better come at night, for the neighbours believe he is lost, and I couldn't be responsible for what they would do to anybody they saw bringing him back.

Very respectfully,

EBENEZER DORSET.

"Great pirates of Penzance!" says I; "of all the impu-dent—"

But I glanced at Bill, and hesitated. He had the most

appealing look in his eyes I ever saw on the face of a dumb or a talking brute.

"Sam," says he, "what's two hundred and fifty dollars, after all? We've got the money. One more night of this kid will send me to a bed in Bedlam. Besides being a thorough gentleman, I think Mr. Dorset is a spendthrift for making us such a liberal offer. You ain't going to let the chance go, are you?"

"Tell you the truth, Bill," says I, "this little he ewe lamb has somewhat got on my nerves too. We'll take him home, pay the ransom and make our get-away."

We took him home that night. We got him to go by telling him that his father had bought a silver-mounted rifle and a pair of moccasins for him, and we were going to hunt bears the next day.

It was just twelve o'clock when we knocked at Ebenezer's front door. Just at the moment when I should have been abstracting the fifteen hundred dollars from the box under the tree, according to the original proposition, Bill was counting out two hundred and fifty dollars into Dorset's hand.

When the kid found out we were going to leave him at home he started up a howl like a calliope and fastened himself as tight as a leech to Bill's leg. His father peeled him away gradually, like a porous plaster.

"How long can you hold him?" asks Bill.

"I'm not as strong as I used to be," says old Dorset, "but I think I can promise you ten minutes."

"Enough," says Bill. "In ten minutes I shall cross the Central, Southern and Middle Western States, and be legging it trippingly for the Canadian border."

And, as dark as it was, and as fat as Bill was, and as good a runner as I am, he was a good mile and a half out of Summit before I could catch up with him.

[1910]

SINCLAIR LEWIS

✳

from **Babbitt**

I

Babbitt's preparations for leaving the office to its feeble self during the hour and a half of his lunch-period were somewhat less elaborate than the plans for a general European war.

He fretted to Miss McGoun, "What time you going to lunch? Well, make sure Miss Bannigan is in then. Explain to her that if Wiedenfeldt calls up, she's to tell him I'm already having the title traced. And oh, b' the way, remind me tomorrow to have Penniman trace it. Now if anybody comes in looking for a cheap house, remember we got to shove that Bangor Road place off onto somebody. If you need me, I'll be at the Athletic Club. And—uh— And—uh— I'll be back by two."

He dusted the cigar-ashes off his vest. He placed a difficult unanswered letter on the pile of unfinished work, that he might not fail to attend to it that afternoon. (For three noons, now, he had placed the same letter on the unfinished pile.) He scrawled on a sheet of yellow backing-paper the memorandum: "See abt apt h drs," which gave him an agreeable feeling of having already seen about the apartment-house doors.

He discovered that he was smoking another cigar. He threw it away, protesting, "Darn it, I thought you'd quit this darn smoking!" He courageously returned the cigar-box to the correspondence-file, locked it up, hid the key in a more difficult place, and raged, "Ought to take care of myself. And need more exercise—walk to the club, every single noon— just what I'll do—every noon—cut out this motoring all the time."

The resolution made him feel exemplary. Immediately after it he decided that this noon it was too late to walk. It took but little more time to start his car and edge it into the traffic than it would have taken to walk the three and a half blocks to the club.

II

As he drove he glanced with the fondness of familiarity at the buildings.

A stranger suddenly dropped into the business-center of Zenith could not have told whether he was in a city of Oregon or Georgia, Ohio or Maine, Oklahoma or Manitoba. But to Babbitt every inch was individual and stirring. As always he noted that the California Building across the way was three stories lower, therefore three stories less beautiful, than his own Reeves Building. As always when he passed the Parthenon Shoe Shine Parlor, a one-story hut which beside the granite and red-brick ponderousness of the old California Building resembled a bath-house under a cliff, he commented, "Gosh, ought to get my shoes shined this afternoon. Keep forgetting it." At the Simplex Office Furniture Shop, the National Cash Register Agency, he yearned for a dictaphone, for a typewriter which would add and multiply, as a poet yearns for quartos or a physician for radium.

At the Nobby Men's Wear Shop he took his left hand off the steering-wheel to touch his scarf, and thought well of himself as one who bought expensive ties "and could pay cash for 'em, too, by golly"; and at the United Cigar Store, with its crimson and gold alertness, he reflected, "Wonder if I need some cigars—idiot—plumb forgot—going t' cut down my fool smoking." He looked at his bank, the Miners' and Drovers' National, and considered how clever and solid he was to bank with so marbled an establishment. His high moment came in the clash of traffic when he was halted at the corner beneath the lofty Second National Tower. His car was banked with four others in a line of steel restless as cavalry, while the crosstown traffic, limousines and enormous moving-vans and insistent motor-cycles, poured by; on the farther corner, pneumatic riveters rang on the sun-plated skeleton of a new building; and out of this tornado flashed the inspiration of a familiar face, and a fellow Booster shouted, "H' are you, George!" Babbitt waved in neighborly affection, and slid on with the traffic as the policeman lifted his hand. He noted how quickly his car picked up. He felt superior and powerful, like a shuttle of polished steel darting in a vast machine.

As always he ignored the next two blocks, decayed blocks
not yet reclaimed from the grime and shabbiness of the Zenith
of 1885. While he was passing the five-and-ten-cent store,
the Dakota Lodging House, Concordia Hall with its lodge-
rooms and the offices of fortune-tellers and chiropractors,
he thought of how much money he made, and he boasted a
little and worried a little and did old familiar sums:

"Four hundred fifty plunks this morning from the Lyte
deal. But taxes due. Let's see: I ought to pull out eight thousand net this year, and save fifteen hundred of that — no, not
if I put up garage and — Let's see: six hundred and forty clear
last month, and twelve times six-forty makes — makes — let
see: six times twelve is seventy-two hundred and — Oh rats,
anyway, I'll make eight thousand — gee now, that's not so
bad; mighty few fellows pulling down eight thousand dollars
a year — eight thousand good hard iron dollars — bet there
isn't more than five per cent. of the people in the whole
United States that make more than Uncle George does, by
golly! Right up at the top of the heap! But — Way expenses
are — Family wasting gasoline, and always dressed like mil-
lionaires, and sending that eighty a month to Mother — And
these stenographers and salesmen gouging me for every cent
they can get — "

The effect of his scientific budget-planning was that he felt
at once triumphantly wealthy and perilously poor, and in the
midst of these dissertations he stopped his car, rushed into
a small news-and-miscellany shop, and bought the electric
cigar-lighter which he had coveted for a week. He dodged his

conscience by being jerky and noisy, and by shouting at the clerk, "Guess this will prett' near pay for itself in matches, eh?"

It was a pretty thing, a nickeled cylinder with an almost silvery socket, to be attached to the dashboard of his car. It was not only, as the placard on the counter observed, "a handy little refinement, lending the last touch of class to a gentleman's auto," but a priceless time-saver. By freeing him from halting the car to light a match, it would in a month or two easily save ten minutes.

As he drove on he glanced at it. "Pretty nice. Always wanted one," he said wistfully. "The one thing a smoker needs, too."

Then he remembered that he had given up smoking.

"Darn it!" he mourned. "Oh well, I suppose I'll hit a cigar once in a while. And— Be a great convenience for other folks. Might make just the difference in getting chummy with some fellow that would put over a sale. And— Certainly looks nice there. Certainly is a mighty clever little jigger. Gives the last touch of refinement and class. I— By golly, I guess I can afford it if I want to! Not going to be the only member of this family that never has a single doggone luxury!"

Thus, laden with treasure, after three and a half blocks of romantic adventure, he drove up to the club.

III

The Zenith Athletic Club is not athletic and it isn't exactly a club, but it is Zenith in perfection. It has an active and smoke-misted billiard room, it is represented by baseball and football teams, and in the pool and the gymnasium a tenth of the members sporadically try to reduce. But most of its three thousand members use it as a café in which to lunch, play cards, tell stories, meet customers, and entertain out-of-town uncles at dinner. It is the largest club in the city, and its chief hatred is the conservative Union Club, which all sound members of the Athletic call "a rotten, snobbish, dull, expensive old hole — not one Good Mixer in the place — you couldn't hire me to join." Statistics show that no member of the Athletic has ever refused election to the Union, and of those who are elected, sixty-seven per cent. resign from the Athletic and are thereafter heard to say, in the drowsy sanctity of the Union lounge, "The Athletic would be a pretty good hotel, if it were more exclusive."

The Athletic Club building is nine stories high, yellow brick with glassy roof-garden above and portico of huge limestone columns below. The lobby, with its thick pillars of porous Caen stone, its pointed vaulting, and a brown glazed-tile floor like well-baked bread-crust, is a combination of cathedral-crypt and rathskellar. The members rush into the lobby as though they were shopping and hadn't much time for it. Thus did Babbitt enter, and to the group standing by the cigar-counter he whooped, "How's the boys? How's the boys? Well, well, fine day!"

Jovially they whooped back — Vergil Gunch, the coal-dealer, Sidney Finkelstein, the ladies'-ready-to-wear buyer for Parcher & Stein's department-store, and Professor Joseph

K. Pumphrey, owner of the Riteway Business College and
instructor in Public Speaking, Business English, Scenario
Writing, and Commercial Law. Though Babbitt admired this
savant, and appreciated Sidney Finkelstein as "a mighty smart
Buyer and a good liberal spender," it was to Vergil Gunch
that he turned with enthusiasm. Mr. Gunch was president of
the Boosters' Club, a weekly lunch-club, local chapter of a
national organization which promoted sound business and
friendliness among Regular Fellows. He was also no less an
official than Esteemed Leading Knight in the Benevolent and
Protective Order of Elks, and it was rumored that at the next
election he would be a candidate for Exalted Ruler. He was a
jolly man, given to oratory and to chumminess with the arts.
He called on the famous actors and vaudeville artists when
they came to town, gave them cigars, addressed them by their
first names, and—sometimes—succeeded in bringing them
to the Boosters' lunches to give The Boys a Free Entertainment. He was a large man with hair *en brosse*, and he knew
the latest jokes, but he played poker close to the chest. It was
at his party that Babbitt had sucked in the virus of to-day's
restlessness.

Gunch shouted, "How's the old Bolsheviki? How do you
feel, the morning after the night before?"

"Oh, boy! Some head! That was a regular party you
threw, Verg! Hope you haven't forgotten I took that last
cute little jack-pot!" Babbitt bellowed. (He was three feet
from Gunch.)

"That's all right now! What I'll hand you next time,

Georgie! Say, juh notice in the paper the way the New York Assembly stood up to the Reds?"

"You bet I did. That was fine, eh? Nice day to-day."

"Yes, it's one mighty fine spring day, but nights still cold."

"Yeh, you're right they are! Had to have coupla blankets last night, out on the sleeping-porch. Say, Sid," Babbitt turned to Finkelstein, the buyer, "got something wanta ask you about. I went out and bought me an electric cigar-lighter for the car, this noon, and—"

"Good hunch!" said Finkelstein, while even the learned Professor Pumphrey, a bulbous man with a pepper-and-salt cutaway and a pipe-organ voice, commented, "That makes a dandy accessory. Cigar-lighter gives tone to the dashboard."

"Yep, finally decided I'd buy me one. Got the best on the market, the clerk said it was. Paid five bucks for it. Just wondering if I got stuck. What do they charge for 'em at the store, Sid?"

Finkelstein asserted that five dollars was not too great a sum, not for a really high-class lighter which was suitably nickeled and provided with connections of the very best quality. "I always say—and believe me, I base it on a pretty fairly extensive mercantile experience—the best is the cheapest in the long run. Of course if a fellow wants to be a Jew about it, he can get cheap junk, but in the long *run*, the cheapest thing is—the best you can get! Now you take here just th' other day: I got a new top for my old boat and some upholstery, and I paid out a hundred and twenty-six fifty, and of course a lot of fellows would say that was too much—Lord, if the Old Folks—they live in one of these hick towns up-state and they simply can't get onto the way a city fellow's mind works, and then, of course, they're Jews, and they'd lie right down and die if they knew Sid had anted up a hundred and twenty-six bones. But I don't figure I was stuck, George, not a bit. Machine looks brand new now—not that it's so darned old, of course; had it less 'n three years, but I give it hard service; never drive less 'n a hundred miles on Sunday and, uh— Oh, I don't really think you got stuck, George. In the *long* run, the best is, you might say, it's unquestionably the cheapest."

"That's right," said Vergil Gunch. "That's the way I look at it. If a fellow is keyed up to what you might call intensive living, the way you get it here in Zenith—all the hustle and mental activity that's going on with a bunch of live-wires like the Boosters and here in the Z.A.C., why, he's got to save his nerves by having the best."

Babbitt nodded his head at every fifth word in the roaring rhythm; and by the conclusion, in Gunch's renowned humorous vein, he was enchanted:

"Still, at that, George, don't know's you can afford it. I've heard your business has been kind of under the eye of the gov'ment since you stole the tail of Eathorne Park and sold it!"

"Oh, you're a great little josher, Verg. But when it comes to kidding, how about this report that you stole the black marble steps off the post-office and sold 'em for high-grade coal!" In delight Babbitt patted Gunch's back, stroked his arm.

"That's all right, but what I want to know is: who's the real-estate shark that bought that coal for his apartment-houses?"

"I guess that'll hold you for a while, George!" said Finkelstein. "I'll tell you, though, boys, what I did hear: George's missus went into the gents' wear department at Parcher's to buy him some collars, and before she could give his neck-size the clerk slips her some thirteens. 'How juh know the size?' says Mrs. Babbitt, and the clerk says, 'Men that let their wives buy collars for 'em always wear thirteen, madam.' How's that! That's pretty good, eh? How's that, eh? I guess that'll about fix you, George!"

"I—I—" Babbitt sought for amiable insults in answer. He stopped, stared at the door. Paul Riesling was coming in. Babbitt cried, "See you later, boys," and hastened across the lobby. He was, just then, neither the sulky child of the sleeping-porch, the domestic tyrant of the breakfast table, the crafty money-changer of the Lyte-Purdy conference, nor the blaring Good Fellow, the Josher and Regular Guy, of the Athletic Club. He was an older brother to Paul Riesling, swift to defend him, admiring him with a proud and credulous love passing the love of women. Paul and he shook hands solemnly; they smiled as shyly as though they had been parted three years, not three days—and they said:

"How's the old horse-thief?"

"All right, I guess. How're you, you poor shrimp?"

"I'm first-rate, you second-hand hunk o' cheese."

Reassured thus of their high fondness, Babbitt grunted, "You're a fine guy, you are! Ten minutes late!" Riesling snapped, "Well, you're lucky to have a chance to lunch with a gentleman!" They grinned and went into the Neronian washroom, where a line of men bent over the bowls inset along a prodigious slab of marble as in religious prostration before their own images in the massy mirror. Voices thick, satisfied, authoritative, hurtled along the marble walls, bounded from the ceiling of lavender-bordered milky tiles, while the lords of the city, the barons of insurance and law and fertilizers and motor tires, laid down the law for Zenith; announced that the day was warm—indeed, indisputably of spring; that wages were too high and the interest on mortgages too low; that Babe Ruth, the eminent player of baseball, was a noble man; and that "those two nuts at the Climax Vaudeville Theater this week certainly are a slick pair of actors." Babbitt, though ordinarily his voice was the surest and most episcopal of all, was silent. In the presence of the slight dark reticence of Paul Riesling, he was awkward, he desired to be quiet and firm and deft.

The entrance lobby of the Athletic Club was Gothic, the washroom Roman Imperial, the lounge Spanish Mission, and the reading-room in Chinese Chippendale, but the gem of the club was the dining-room, the masterpiece of Ferdinand Reitman, Zenith's busiest architect. It was lofty and half-timbered, with Tudor leaded casements, an oriel, a somewhat musicianless musicians'-gallery, and tapestries believed to illustrate the granting of Magna Charta. The open beams had been hand-adzed at Jake Offutt's car-body works, the hinges were of hand-wrought iron, the wainscot studded with handmade wooden pegs, and at one end of the room was a heraldic and hooded stone fireplace which the club's advertising-pamphlet asserted to be not only larger than any of the fireplaces in European castles but of a draught incomparably more scientific. It was also much cleaner, as no fire had ever been built in it.

Half of the tables were mammoth slabs which seated twenty or thirty men. Babbitt usually sat at the one near the door, with a group including Gunch, Finkelstein, Professor Pumphrey, Howard Littlefield, his neighbor, T. Cholmondeley Frink, the poet and advertising-agent, and Orville Jones, whose laundry was in many ways the best in Zenith. They composed a club within the club, and merrily called themselves "The Roughnecks." To-day as he passed their table the Roughnecks greeted him, "Come on, sit in! You 'n' Paul too proud to feed with poor folks? Afraid somebody might stick you for a bottle of Bevo, George? Strikes me you swells are getting awful darn exclusive!"

He thundered, "You bet! We can't afford to have our reps ruined by being seen with you tightwads!" and guided Paul to one of the small tables beneath the musicians'-gallery. He felt guilty. At the Zenith Athletic Club, privacy was very bad form. But he wanted Paul to himself.

That morning he had advocated lighter lunches and now

he ordered nothing but English mutton chop, radishes, peas, deep-dish apple pie, a bit of cheese, and a pot of coffee with cream, adding, as he did invariably, "And uh— Oh, and you might give me an order of French fried potatoes." When the chop came he vigorously peppered it and salted it. He always peppered and salted his meat, and vigorously, before tasting it.

Paul and he took up the spring-like quality of the spring, the virtues of the electric cigar-lighter, and the action of the New York State Assembly. It was not till Babbitt was thick and disconsolate with mutton grease that he flung out:

"I wound up a nice little deal with Conrad Lyte this morning that put five hundred good round plunks in my pocket. Pretty nice—pretty nice! And yet— I don't know what's the matter with me to-day. Maybe it's an attack of spring fever, or staying up too late at Verg Gunch's, or maybe it's just the Winter's work piling up, but I've felt kind of down in the mouth all day long. Course I wouldn't beef about it to the fellows at the Roughnecks' Table there, but you— Ever feel that way, Paul? Kind of comes over me: here I've pretty much done all the things I ought to; supported my family, and got a good house and a six-cylinder car, and built up a nice little business, and I haven't any vices 'specially, except smoking— and I'm practically cutting that out, by the way. And I belong to the church, and play enough golf to keep in trim, and I only associate with good decent fellows. And yet, even so, I don't know that I'm entirely satisfied!"

It was drawled out, broken by shouts from the neighboring tables, by mechanical love-making to the waitress, by stertorous grunts as the coffee filled him with dizziness and indigestion. He was apologetic and doubtful, and it was Paul, with his thin voice, who pierced the fog:

"Good Lord, George, you don't suppose it's any novelty to me to find that we hustlers, that think we're so all-fired successful, aren't getting much out of it? You look as if you expected me to report you as seditious! You know what my own life's been."

"I know, old man."

"I ought to have been a fiddler, and I'm a pedler of tar-roofing! And Zilla— Oh, I don't want to squeal, but you know as well as I do about how inspiring a wife she is. . . . Typical instance last evening: We went to the movies. There was a big crowd waiting in the lobby, us at the tail-end. She began to push right through it with her 'Sir, how dare you?' manner— Honestly, sometimes when I look at her and see how she's always so made up and stinking of perfume and looking for trouble and kind of always yelping, 'I tell yuh I'm a lady, damn yuh!'—why, I want to kill her! Well, she keeps elbowing through the crowd, me after her, feeling good and ashamed, till she's almost up to the velvet rope and ready to be the next let in. But there was a little squirt of a man there—probably been waiting half an hour—I kind of admired the little cuss—and he turns on Zilla and says, perfectly polite, 'Madam, why are you trying to push past me?' And she simply—God, I was so ashamed!—she rips out at him, 'You're no gentleman,' and she drags me into it and

able she is, and when I get sore and try to have it out with her she plays the Perfect Lady so well that even I get fooled and get all tangled up in a lot of 'Why did you say's' and 'I didn't mean's.' I'll tell you, Georgie: You know my tastes are pretty fairly simple—in the matter of food, at least. Course, as you're always complaining, I do like decent cigars—not those Flor de Cabagos you're smoking—"

"That's all right now! That's a good two-for. By the way, Paul, did I tell you I decided to practically cut out smok—"

"Yes you— At the same time, if I can't get what I like, why, I can do without it. I don't mind sitting down to burnt steak, with canned peaches and store cake for a thrilling little dessert afterwards, but I do draw the line at having to sympathize with Zilla because she's so rotten bad-tempered that the cook has quit, and she's been so busy sitting in a dirty lace negligée all afternoon, reading about some brave manly Western hero, that she hasn't had time to do any cooking. You're always talking about 'morals'—meaning monogamy, I suppose. You've been the rock of ages to me, all right, but you're essentially a simp. You—"

"Where d' you get that 'simp,' little man? Let me tell you—"

"—love to look earnest and inform the world that it's the duty of responsible business men to be strictly moral, as an example to the community.' In fact you're so earnest about morality, old Georgie, that I hate to think how essentially immoral you must be underneath. All right, you can—"

"Wait, wait now! What's—"

"—talk about morals all you want to, old thing, but believe me, if it hadn't been for you and an occasional evening playing the violin to Terrill O'Farrell's cello, and three or four darling girls that let me forget this beastly joke they call 'respectable life,' I'd 've killed myself years ago.

"And business! The roofing business! Roofs for cowsheds! Oh, I don't mean I haven't had a lot of fun out of the Game; out of putting it over on the labor unions, and seeing a big check coming in, and the business increasing. But what's the use of it? You know, my business isn't distributing roofing—it's principally keeping my competitors from distributing roofing. Same with you. All we do is cut each other's throats and make the public pay for it!"

"Look here now, Paul! You're pretty darn near talking socialism!"

"Oh yes, of course I don't really exactly mean that—I s'pose. Course—competition—brings out the best—survival of the fittest—but— But I mean: Take all these fellows we know, the kind right here in the club now, that seem to be perfectly content with their home-life and their businesses, and that boost Zenith and the Chamber of Commerce and holler for a million population. I bet if you could cut into their heads you'd find that one-third of 'em are sure-enough satisfied with their wives and kids and friends and their offices; and one-third feel kind of restless but won't admit it; and one-third are miserable and know it. They hate the whole peppy, boosting, go-ahead game, and they're bored by their lives and think their families are fools—at least when they come to forty or forty-five they're bored — and they hate business, and they'd go — Why do you suppose there's so many 'mysterious' suicides? Why do you suppose so many Substantial Citizens jumped right into the war? Think it was patriotism?"

Babbitt snorted, "What do you expect? Think we were sent into the world to have a soft time and — what is it? — 'float on flowery beds of ease'? Think Man was just made to be happy?"

"Why not? Though I've never discovered anybody that knew what the deuce Man really was made for!"

"Well we know — not just in the Bible alone, but it stands to reason — a man who doesn't buckle down and do his duty, even if it does bore him sometimes, is nothing but a — well, he's simply a weakling. Mollycoddle, in fact! And what do you advocate? Come down to cases! If a man is bored by his wife, do you seriously mean he has a right to chuck her and take a sneak, or even kill himself?"

"Good Lord, I don't know what 'rights' a man has! And I don't know the solution of boredom. If I did, I'd be the one philosopher that had the cure for living. But I do know that about ten times as many people find their lives dull, and unnecessarily dull, as ever admit it; and I do believe that if we busted out and admitted it sometimes, instead of being nice and patient and loyal for sixty years, and then nice and patient and dead for the rest of eternity, why, maybe, possibly, we might make life more fun."

They drifted into a maze of speculation. Babbitt was

elephantishly uneasy. Paul was bold, but not quite sure about what he was being bold. Now and then Babbitt suddenly agreed with Paul in an admission which contradicted all his defense of duty and Christian patience, and at each admission he had a curious reckless joy. He said at last:

"Look here, old Paul, you do a lot of talking about kicking things in the face, but you never kick. Why don't you?"

"Nobody does. Habit too strong. But— Georgie, I've been thinking of one mild bat—oh, don't worry, old pillar of monogamy; it's highly proper. It seems to be settled now, isn't it—though of course Zilla keeps rooting for a nice expensive vacation in New York and Atlantic City, with the bright lights and the bootlegged cocktails and a bunch of lounge-lizards to dance with—but the Babbitts and the Rieslings are sure-enough going to Lake Sunasquam, aren't we? Why couldn't you and I make some excuse—say business in New York—and get up to Maine four or five days before they do, and just loaf by ourselves and smoke and cuss and be natural?"

"Great! Great idea!" Babbitt admired.

Not for fourteen years had he taken a holiday without his wife, and neither of them quite believed they could commit this audacity. Many members of the Athletic Club did go camping without their wives, but they were officially dedicated to fishing and hunting, whereas the sacred and unchangeable sports of Babbitt and Paul Riesling were golfing, motoring, and bridge. For either the fishermen or the golfers to have changed their habits would have been an infraction of their self-imposed discipline which would have shocked all right-thinking and regularized citizens.

Babbitt blustered, "Why don't we just put our foot down and say, 'We're going on ahead of you, and that's all there is to it!' Nothing criminal in it. Simply say to Zilla—"

"You don't say anything to Zilla simply. Why, Georgie, she's almost as much of a moralist as you are, and if I told her the truth she'd believe we were going to meet some dames in New York. And even Myra—she never nags you, the way Zilla does, but she'd worry. She'd say, 'Don't you *want* me to go to Maine with you? I shouldn't dream of going unless you wanted me'; and you'd give in to save her feelings. Oh, the devil! Let's have a shot at duck-pins."

During the game of duck-pins, a juvenile form of bowling, Paul was silent. As they came down the steps of the club, not more than half an hour after the time at which Babbitt had sternly told Miss McGoun he would be back, Paul sighed, "Look here, old man, oughtn't to talked about Zilla way I did."

"Rats, old man, it lets off steam."

"Oh, I know! After spending all noon sneering at the conventional stuff, I'm conventional enough to be ashamed of saving my life by busting out with my fool troubles!"

"Old Paul, your nerves are kind of on the bum. I'm going to take you away. I'm going to rig this thing. I'm going to have an important deal in New York and—and sure, of course!—I'll need you to advise me on the roof of the building! And the ole deal will fall through, and there'll be nothing for us but to go on ahead to Maine. I—Paul, when it comes right down to it, I don't care whether you bust loose or not. I do like having a rep for being one of the Bunch, but if you ever needed me I'd chuck it and come out for you every time! Not of course but what you're—course I don't mean you'd ever do anything that would put—that would put a decent position on the fritz but— See how I mean? I'm kind of a clumsy old codger, and I need your fine Eyetalian hand. We— Oh, hell, I can't stand here gassing all day! On the job! S' long! Don't take any wooden money, Paulibus! See you soon! S' long!"

[1922]

ANITA LOOS

*

from Gentlemen Prefer Blondes

March 22nd:
Well my birthday has come and gone but it was really quite depressing. I mean it seems to me a gentleman who has a friendly interest in educating a girl like Gus Eisman, would want her to have the biggest square cut diamond in New York. I mean I must say I was quite disappointed when he came to the apartment with a little thing you could hardly see. So I told him I thought it was quite cute, but I had quite a headache and I had better stay in a dark room all day and I told him I would see him the next day, perhaps. Because even Lulu thought it was quite small and she said, if she was I, she really would do something definite and she said she always believed in the old addage, "Leave them while you're looking good." But he came in at dinner time with really a very very beautiful bracelet of square cut diamonds so I was quite cheered up. So then we had dinner at the Colony and we went to a show and supper at the Trocadero as usual

whenever he is in town. But I will give him credit that he
realized how small it was. I mean he kept talking about how
bad business was and the button profession was full of bolshevicks who make nothing but trouble. Because Mr. Eisman
feels that the country is really on the verge of the bolshevicks
and I become quite worried. I mean if the bolshevicks do get
in, there is only one gentleman who could handle them and
that is Mr. D. W. Griffith. Because I will never forget when
Mr. Griffith was directing Intolerance. I mean it was my last
cinema just before Mr. Eisman made me give up my career
and I was playing one of the girls that fainted at the battle
when all of the gentlemen fell off the tower. And when I saw
how Mr. Griffith handled all of those mobs in Intolerance I
realized that he could do anything, and I really think that the
government of America ought to tell Mr. Griffith to get all
ready if the bolshevicks start to do it.

Well I forgot to mention that the English gentleman who
writes novels seems to have taken quite an interest in me,
as soon as he found out that I was literary. I mean he has
called up every day and I went to tea twice with him. So he
has sent me a whole complete set of books for my birthday by a gentleman called Mr. Conrad. They all seem to be
about ocean travel although I have not had time to more than
glance through them. I have always liked novels about ocean
travel ever since I posed for Mr. Christie for the front cover
of a novel about ocean travel by McGrath because I always
say that a girl never really looks as well as she does on board
a steamship, or even a yacht.

So the English gentleman's name is Mr. Gerald Lamson as those who have read his novels would know. And he also sent me some of his own novels and they all seem to be about middle age English gentlemen who live in the country over in London and seem to ride bicycles, which seems quite different from America, except at Palm Beach. So I told Mr. Lamson how I write down all of my thoughts and he said he knew I had something to me from the first minute he saw me and when we become better acquainted I am going to let him read my diary. I mean I even told Mr. Eisman about him and he is quite pleased. Because of course Mr. Lamson is quite famous and it seems Mr. Eisman has read all of his novels going to and fro on the trains and Mr. Eisman is always anxious to meet famous people and take them to the Ritz to dinner on Saturday night. But of course I did not tell Mr. Eisman that I am really getting quite a little crush on Mr. Lamson, which I really believe I am, but Mr. Eisman thinks my interest in him is more literary.

[1925]

RING LARDNER

✳

On Conversation

The other night I happened to be comeing back from Wilmington, Del. to wherever I was going and was setting in the smokeing compartment or whatever they now call the wash room and overheard a conversation between two fellows who we will call Mr. Butler and Mr. Hawkes. Both of them seemed to be from the same town and I only wished I could repeat the conversation verbatim but the best I can do is report it from memory. The fellows evidently had not met for some three to fifteen years as the judges say.

"Well," said Mr. Hawkes, "if this isn't Dick Butler!"

"Well," said Mr. Butler, "if it isn't Dale Hawkes."

"Well, Dick," said Hawkes, "I never expected to meet you on this train."

"No," replied Butler. "I genally always take Number 28. I just took this train this evening because I had to be in Wilmington today."

"Where are you headed for?" asked Hawkes.

"Well I am going to the big town," said Butler.

"So am I, and I am certainly glad we happened to be in the same car."

"I am glad too, but it is funny we happened to be in the same car."

It seemed funny to both of them but they successfully concealed it so far as facial expression was conserned. After a pause Hawkes spoke again:

"How long since you been back in Lansing?"

"Me?" replied Butler. "I ain't been back there for 12 years."

"I ain't been back there either myself for ten years. How long since you been back there?"

"I ain't been back there for twelve years."

"I ain't been back there myself for ten years. Where are you headed for?"

"New York," replied Butler. "I have got to get there about once a year. Where are you going?"

"Me?" asked Hawkes. "I am going to New York too. I have got to go down there every little while for the firm."

"Do you have to go there very often?"

"Me? Every little while. How often do you have to go there?"

"About once a year. How often do you get back to Lansing?"

"Last time I was there was ten years ago. How long since you was back?"

"About twelve years ago. Lot of changes there since we left there."

"That's the way I figured it. It makes a man seem kind of old to go back there and not see nobody you know."

"You said something. I go along the streets there now and don't see nobody I know."

"How long since you was there?"

"Me?" said Hawkes. "I only get back there about once every ten years. By the way what become of old man Kelsey?"

"Who do you mean, Kelsey?"

"Yes, what become of him?"

"Old Kelsey? Why he has been dead for ten years."

"Oh, I didn't know that. And what become of his daughter? I mean Eleanor."

"Why Eleanor married a man named Forster or Jennings or something like that from Flint."

"Yes, but I mean the other daughter, Louise."

"Oh, she's married."

"Where are you going now?"

"I am headed for New York on business for the firm."

"I have to go there about once a year myself—for the firm."

"Do you get back to Lansing very often?"

"About once in ten or twelve years. I hardly know anybody there now. It seems funny to go down the street and not know nobody."

"That the way I always feel. It seems like it was not my old home town at all. I go up and down the street and don't know anybody and nobody speaks to you. I guess I know more people in New York now than I do in Lansing."

"Do you get to New York often?"

"Only about once a year. I have to go there for the firm."

"New York isn't the same town it used to be neither."

"No, it is changeing all the time. Just like Lansing, I guess they all change."

"I don't know much about Lansing any more. I only get there about once in ten or twelve years."

"What are you reading there?"

"Oh, it is just a little article in Asia. They's a good many interesting articles in Asia."

"I only seen a couple copies of it. This thing I am reading is a little article on 'Application' in the American."

"Well, go ahead and read and don't let me disturb you."

"Well I just wanted to finish it up. Go ahead and finish what you're reading yourself."

"All right. We will talk things over later. It is funny we happened to get on the same car."

[1925]

H. L. MENCKEN

*

Imperial Purple

Most of the rewards of the Presidency, in these degenerate days, have come to be very trashy. The President continues, of course, to be an eminent man, but only in the sense that Jack Dempsey, Lindbergh, Babe Ruth and Henry Ford are eminent men. He sees little of the really intelligent and amusing people of the country: most of them, in fact, make it a sort of point of honor to scorn him and avoid him. His time is put in mainly with shabby politicians and other such designing fellows—in brief, with rogues and ignoramuses. When he takes a little holiday his customary companions are vermin that no fastidious man would consort with—dry Senators with panting thirsts, the proprietors of bad newspapers in worse towns, grafters preying on the suffering farmers, power and movie magnates, prehensile labor leaders, the more pliable sort of journalists, and so on. They must be pretty dreadful company. Dr. Harding, forced to entertain them, resorted to poteen as an analgesic; Dr. Coolidge loaded them aboard the *Mayflower*, and then fled to his cabin, took off his vest and shirt, and went to sleep; Dr. Hoover hauls them to the Rapidan at 60 miles per hour, and back at 80 or 90.

The honors that are heaped upon a President in this one hundred and fifty-sixth year of the Republic are seldom of a kind to impress and content a civilized man. People send him turkeys, possums, pieces of wood from the Constitution, goldfish, carved peach-kernels, models of the State capitols of Wyoming and Arkansas, and pressed flowers from the Holy Land. His predecessors before 1917 got demijohns of 12-year-old rye, baskets of champagne, and cases of Moselle and Burgundy, but them times ain't no more. Once a year some hunter in Montana or Idaho sends him 20 pounds of bear-steak, usually collect. It arrives in a high state, and has to be fed to the White House dog. He receives 20 or 30 chain-prayer letters every day, and fair copies of 40 or 50 sets of verse. Colored clergymen send him illustrated Bibles, mad-stones and boxes of lucky powders, usually accompanied by applications for appointment as collectors of customs at New Orleans, or Register of the Treasury.

His public rewards come in the form of LL.D.'s from colleges eager for the publicity — and on the same day others precisely like it are given to a champion lawn-tennis player, a banker known to be without heirs of his body, and a general in the Army. No one ever thinks to give him any other academic honor; he is never made a Litt.D., a D.D., an S.T.D., a D.D.S, or a J.U.D., but always an LL.D. Dr. Hoover, to date, has 30 or 40 such degrees. After he leaves office they will continue to fall upon him. He apparently knows as little about law as a policeman, but he is already more solidly *legum doctor* than Blackstone or Pufendorf, and the end is not yet.

The health of a President is watched very carefully, not only by the Vice-President but also by medical men detailed for the purpose by the Army or Navy. These medical men have high-sounding titles, and perform the duties of their office in full uniform, with swords on one side and stethoscopes on the other. The diet of their imperial patient is rigidly scrutinized. If he eats a few peanuts they make a pother; if he goes for a dozen steamed hard crabs at night, washed down by what passes in Washington for malt liquor, they complain to the newspapers. Every morning they look at his tongue, take his pulse and temperature, determine his blood pressure, and examine his eye-grounds and his knee-jerks. The instant he shows the slightest sign of being upset they clap him into bed, post Marines to guard him, put him on a regimen fit for a Trappist, and issue bulletins to the newspapers.

When a President goes traveling he never goes alone, but always with a huge staff of secretaries, Secret Service agents, doctors, nurses, and newspaper reporters. Even so stingy a fellow as Dr. Coolidge had to hire two whole Pullman cars to carry his entourage. The cost, to be sure, is borne by the taxpayers, but the President has to put up with the company. As he rolls along thousands of boys rush out to put pennies on the track, and now and then one of them loses a finger or a toe, and the train has to be backed up to comfort his mother, who, it usually turns out, cannot speak English and voted for Al in 1928. When the train arrives anywhere all the town bores and scoundrels gather to greet the Chief Magistrate, and that night he has to eat a bad dinner, with only ginger-ale to wash it down, and to listen to three hours of bad speeches.

The President has less privacy than any other American. Thousands of persons have the right of access to him, beginning with the British Ambassador and running down to the secretary of the Republican country committee of Ziebach County, South Dakota. Among them are the 96 members of the United States Senate, perhaps the windiest and most tedious group of men in Christendom. If a Senator were denied admission to the White House, even though he were a Progressive, the whole Senate would rise in indignation, even though it were 80% stand-pat Republican. Such is Senatorial courtesy. And if the minister from Albania were kicked out even the French and German Ambassadors would join in protesting.

Many of these gentlemen drop in, not because they have anything to say, but simply to prove to their employers or customers that they can do it. How long they stay is only partly determined by the President himself. Dr. Coolidge used to get rid of them by falling asleep in their faces, but that device is impossible to Presidents with a more active interest in the visible world. It would not do to have them heaved out by the Secret Service men or by the White House police, or to insult and affront them otherwise, for many of them have wicked tongues. On two occasions within historic times Presidents who were irritable with such bores were reported in Washington to be patronizing the jug, and it took a lot of fine work to put down the scandal.

All day long the right hon. lord of us all sits listening solemnly to quacks who pretend to know what the farmers are thinking about in Nebraska and South Carolina, how the Swedes of Minnesota are taking the German moratorium, and how much it would cost in actual votes to let fall a word for beer and light wines. Anon a secretary rushes in with the news that some eminent movie actor or football coach has died, and the President must seize a pen and write a telegram of condolence to the widow. Once a year he is repaid by receiving a cable on his birthday from King George V. These autographs are cherished by Presidents, and they leave them, *post mortem*, to the Library of Congress.

There comes a day of public ceremonial, and a chance to make a speech. Alas, it must be made at the annual banquet of some organization that is discovered, at the last minute, to be made up mainly of gentlemen under indictment, or at the tomb of some statesman who escaped impeachment by a hair. A million voters with IQs below 60 have their ears glued to the radio: it takes four days' hard work to concoct a speech without a sensible word in it. Next day a dam must be opened somewhere. Four dry Senators get drunk and make a painful scene. The Presidential automobile runs over a dog. It rains.

––––––

The life seems dull and unpleasant. A bootlegger has a better time, in jail or out. Yet it must have its charms, for no man who has experienced it is ever unwilling to endure it again. On the contrary, all ex-Presidents try their level damndest to get back, even at the expense of their dignity, their sense of humor, and their immortal souls. The struggles of the late Major-General Roosevelt will be recalled by connoisseurs. He was a melancholy spectacle from the moment the White House doors closed upon him, and he passed out of this life a disappointed and even embittered man. You and I can scarcely imagine any such blow as that he suffered in 1912. It shook him profoundly, and left him a wreck.

Long ago I proposed that unsuccessful candidates for the Presidency be quietly hanged, as a matter of public sanitation and decorum. The sight of their grief must have a very evil effect upon the young. We have enough hobgoblins in America without putting up with downright ghosts. Perhaps it might be a good idea to hand over ex-Presidents to the hangman in the same way. As they complete their terms their consciences are clear, and their chances of going to Heaven are excellent. But a few years of longing and repining are enough to imperil the souls of even the most philosophical of them. I point to Dr. Coolidge. He pretends to like the insurance business, but who really believes it? Who can be unaware that his secret thoughts have to do, not with 20-year endowment policies, but with 1600 Pennsylvania Avenue? Who can fail to mark the tragedy that marks his countenance, otherwise so beautifully smooth and vacant, so virginally bare of signs? If you say that he does not suffer, then you say also that a man with *cholera morbus* does not suffer.

On second thoughts, I withdraw my suggestion. It is probably illegal, and maybe even immoral. But certainly something ought to be done. Maybe it would be a good idea to make every ex-President a Methodist bishop.

[1931]

JAMES THURBER

＊

More Alarms at Night

One of the incidents that I always think of first when I cast back over my youth is what happened the night that my father "threatened to get Buck." This, as you will see, is not precisely a fair or accurate description of what actually occurred, but it is the way in which I and the other members of my family invariably allude to the occasion. We were living at the time in an old house at 77 Lexington Avenue, in Columbus, Ohio. In the early years of the nineteenth century, Columbus won out, as state capital, by only one vote over Lancaster, and ever since then has had the hallucination that it is being followed, a curious municipal state of mind which affects, in some way or other, all those who live there. Columbus is a town in which almost anything is likely to happen and in which almost everything has.

My father was sleeping in the front room on the second floor next to that of my brother Roy, who was then about sixteen. Father was usually in bed by nine-thirty and up again by ten-thirty to protest bitterly against a Victrola record we three boys were in the habit of playing over and over, namely, "No News, or What Killed the Dog," a recitation by Nat Wills. The record had been played so many times that its grooves were deeply cut and the needle often kept revolving in the same groove, repeating over and over the same words. Thus: "ate some burnt hoss flesh, ate some burnt hoss flesh, ate some burnt hoss flesh." It was this reiteration that generally got father out of bed.

On the night in question, however, we had all gone to bed at about the same time, without much fuss. Roy, as a matter of fact, had been in bed all day with a kind of mild fever. It wasn't severe enough to cause delirium and my brother was the last person in the world to give way to delirium. Nevertheless, he had warned father when father went to bed, that he *might* become delirious.

About three o'clock in the morning, Roy, who was wakeful, decided to pretend that delirium was on him, in order to have, as he later explained it, some "fun." He got out of bed and, going to my father's room, shook him and said, "Buck, your time has come!" My father's name was not Buck but Charles, nor had he ever been called Buck. He was a tall, mildly nervous, peaceable gentleman, given to quiet pleasures, and eager that everything should run smoothly. "Hmm?" he said, with drowsy bewilderment. "Get up, Buck," said my brother, coldly, but with a certain gleam in his eyes. My father leaped out of bed, on the side away from his son, rushed from the room, locked the door behind him, and shouted us all up.

We were naturally enough reluctant to believe that Roy, who was quiet and self-contained, had threatened his father with any such abracadabra as father said he had. My older brother, Herman, went back to bed without any comment. "You've had a bad dream," my mother said. This vexed my father. "I tell you he called me Buck and told me my time had come," he said. We went to the door of his room, unlocked it, and tiptoed through it to Roy's room. He lay in his bed, breathing easily, as if he were fast asleep. It was apparent at a glance that he did not have a high fever. My mother gave my father a look. "I tell you he did," whispered father.

Our presence in the room finally seemed to awaken Roy and he was (or rather, as we found out long afterward, pretended to be) astonished and bewildered. "What's the matter?" he asked. "Nothing," said my mother. "Just your father had a nightmare." "I did not have a nightmare," said father, slowly and firmly. He wore an old-fashioned, "side-slit" nightgown which looked rather odd on his tall, spare figure. The situation, before we let it drop and everybody went back to bed again, became, as such situations in our family usually did, rather more complicated than ironed out. Roy demanded to know what had happened, and my mother told him, in considerably garbled fashion, what father had told her. At this a light dawned in Roy's eyes. "Dad's got it backward," he said. He then explained that he had heard father get out of bed and had called to him. "I'll handle this," his father had answered. "Buck is downstairs." "Who is this Buck?" my mother demanded of father. "I don't know any Buck and I never said that," father contended, irritably.

None of us (except Roy, of course) believed him. "You had a dream," said mother. "People have these dreams." "I did not have a dream," father said. He was pretty well nettled by this time, and he stood in front of a bureau mirror, brushing his hair with a pair of military brushes; it always seemed to calm father to brush his hair. My mother declared that it was "a sin and a shame" for a grown man to wake up a sick boy simply because he (the grown man: father) had got on his back and had a bad dream. My father, as a matter of fact, *had* been known to have nightmares, usually about Lillian Russell and President Cleveland, who chased him.

We argued the thing for perhaps another half-hour, after which mother made father sleep in her room. "You're all safe now, boys," she said, firmly, as she shut her door. I could hear father grumbling for a long time, with an occasional monosyllable of doubt from mother.

It was some six months after this that father went through a similar experience with me. He was at that time sleeping in the room next to mine. I had been trying all afternoon, in vain, to think of the name Perth Amboy. It seems now like a very simple name to recall and yet on the day in question I thought of every other town in the country, as well as such words and names and phrases as terra cotta, Walla-Walla, bill of lading, vice versa, hoity-toity, Pall Mall, Bodley Head, Schumann-Heink, etc., without even coming close to Perth Amboy. I suppose terra cotta was the closest I came, although it was not very close.

Long after I had gone to bed, I was struggling with the

problem. I began to indulge in the wildest fancies as I lay there in the dark, such as that there was no such town, and even that there was no such state as New Jersey. I fell to repeating the word "Jersey" over and over again, until it became idiotic and meaningless. If you have ever lain awake at night and repeated one word over and over, thousands and millions and hundreds of thousands of millions of times, you know the disturbing mental state you can get into. I got to thinking that there was nobody else in the world but me, and various other wild imaginings of that nature. Eventually, lying there thinking these outlandish thoughts, I grew slightly alarmed. I began to suspect that one might lose one's mind over some such trivial mental tic as a futile search for terra firma Piggly Wiggly Gorgonzola Prester John Arc de Triomphe Holy Moses Lares and Penates. I began to feel the imperative necessity of human contact. This silly and alarming tangle of thought and fancy had gone far enough. I might get into some kind of mental aberrancy unless I found out the name of that Jersey town and could go to sleep. Therefore, I got out of bed, walked into the room where father was sleeping, and shook him. "Um?" he mumbled. I shook him more fiercely and he finally woke up, with a glaze of dream and apprehension in his eyes. "What's matter?" he asked, thickly. I must, indeed, have been rather wild of eye, and my hair, which is unruly, becomes monstrously tousled and snarled at night. "Wha's it?" said my father, sitting up, in readiness to spring out of bed on the far side. The thought must have been going through his mind that all his sons were crazy, or on the verge of going crazy. I see that now, but I didn't then, for I had forgotten the Buck incident and did not realize how similar my appearance must have been to Roy's the night he called father Buck and told him his time had come. "Listen," I said. "Name some towns in New Jersey quick!" It must have been around three in the morning. Father got up, keeping the bed between him and me, and started to pull his trousers on. "Don't bother about dressing," I said. "Just name some towns in New Jersey." While he hastily pulled on his clothes— I remember he left his socks off and put his shoes on his bare feet—father began to name, in a shaky voice, various New Jersey cities. I can still see him reaching for his coat without taking his eyes off me. "Newark," he said, "Jersey City, Atlantic City, Elizabeth, Paterson, Passaic, Trenton, Jersey City, Trenton, Paterson—" "It has two names," I snapped. "Elizabeth and Paterson," he said. "No, no!" I told him, irritably. "This is one town with one name, but there are two words in it, like helter-skelter." "Helter-skelter," said my father, moving slowly toward the bedroom door and smiling in a faint, strained way which I understand now—but didn't then—was meant to humor me. When he was within a few paces of the door, he fairly leaped for it and ran out into the hall, his coat-tails and shoelaces flying. The exit stunned me. I had no notion that he thought I had gone out of my senses; I could only believe that he had gone out of *his* or that, only partially awake, he was engaged in some form of running in his sleep. I ran after him and I caught him at the door of mother's room and grabbed him, in order to reason with him. I shook him a little, thinking to wake him completely. "Mary! Roy! Herman!" he shouted. I, too, began to shout for my brothers and my mother. My mother opened her door instantly, and there we were at 3:30 in the morning grappling and shouting, father partly dressed, but without socks or shirt, and I in pajamas.

"*Now*, what?" demanded my mother, grimly, pulling us apart. She was capable, fortunately, of handling any two of us and she never in her life was alarmed by the words or actions of any one of us.

"Look out for Jamie!" said father. (He always called me Jamie when excited.) My mother looked at me.

"What's the matter with your father?" she demanded. I said I didn't know; I said he had got up suddenly and dressed and ran out of the room.

"Where did you think you were going?" mother asked him, coolly. He looked at me. We looked at each other, breathing hard, but somewhat calmer.

"He was babbling about New Jersey at this infernal hour of the night," said father. "He came to my room and asked me to name towns in New Jersey." Mother looked at me.

"I just asked him," I said. "I was trying to think of one and couldn't sleep."

"You see?" said father, triumphantly. Mother didn't look at him.

"Get to bed, both of you," she said. "I don't want to hear any more out of you tonight. Dressing and tearing up and down the hall at this hour in the morning!" She went back into the room and shut her door. Father and I went back to bed. "Are you all right?" he called to me. "Are you?" I asked. "Well, good night," he said. "Good night," I said.

Mother would not let the rest of us discuss the affair next morning at breakfast. Herman asked what the hell had been the matter. "We'll go on to something more elevating," said mother.

[1933]

DOROTHY PARKER

✳

The Waltz

Why, thank you so much. I'd adore to.

I don't want to dance with him. I don't want to dance with anybody. And even if I did, it wouldn't be him. He'd be well down among the last ten. I've seen the way he dances; it looks like something you do on Saint Walpurgis Night. Just think, not a quarter of an hour ago, here I was sitting, feeling so sorry for the poor girl he was dancing with. And now *I'm* going to be the poor girl. Well, well. Isn't it a small world?

And a peach of a world, too. A true little corker. Its events are so fascinatingly unpredictable, are not they? Here I was, minding my own business, not doing a stitch of harm to any living soul. And then he comes into my life, all smiles and city manners, to sue me for the favor of one memorable mazurka. Why, he scarcely knows my name, let alone what it stands for. It stands for Despair, Bewilderment, Futility, Degradation, and Premeditated Murder, but little does he wot. I don't wot his name, either; I haven't any idea what it is. Jukes, would be my guess from the look in his eyes. How do you do, Mr. Jukes? And how is that dear little brother of yours, with the two heads?

Ah, now why did he have to come around me, with his low requests? Why can't he let me lead my own life? I ask so little—just to be left alone in my quiet corner of the table, to do my evening brooding over all my sorrows. And he must come, with his bows and his scrapes and his may-I-have-this-ones. And I had to go and tell him that I'd adore to dance with him. I cannot understand why I wasn't struck right down dead. Yes, and being struck dead would look like a day in the country, compared to struggling out a dance with this boy. But what could I do? Everyone else at the table had got up to dance, except him and me. There was I, trapped. Trapped like a trap in a trap.

What can you say, when a man asks you to dance with him? I most certainly will *not* dance with you, I'll see you in hell first. Why, thank you, I'd like to awfully, but I'm having labor pains. Oh, yes, *do* let's dance together—it's so nice to meet a man who isn't a scaredy-cat about catching my beri-beri. No. There was nothing for me to do, but say I'd adore to. Well, we might as well get it over with. All right, Cannonball, let's run out on the field. You won the toss; you can lead.

Why, I think it's more of a waltz, really. Isn't it? We might just listen to the music a second. Shall we? Oh, yes, it's a waltz. Mind? Why, I'm simply thrilled. I'd love to waltz with you.

I'd love to waltz with you. I'd love to waltz with you. I'd

love to have my tonsils out, I'd love to be in a midnight fire at sea. Well, it's too late now. We're getting under way. *Oh. Oh, dear. Oh, dear, dear, dear.* Oh, this is even worse than I thought it would be. I suppose that's the one dependable law of life—everything is always worse than you thought it was going to be. Oh, if I had any real grasp of what this dance would be like, I'd have held out for sitting it out. Well, it will probably amount to the same thing in the end. We'll be sitting it out on the floor in a minute, if he keeps this up.

I'm so glad I brought it to his attention that this is a waltz they're playing. Heaven knows what might have happened, if he had thought it was something fast; we'd have blown the sides right out of the building. Why does he always want to be somewhere that he isn't? Why can't we stay in one place just long enough to get acclimated? It's this constant rush, rush, rush, that's the curse of American life. That's the reason that we're all of us so—*Ow!* For God's sake, don't *kick*, you idiot; this is only second down. Oh, my shin. My poor, poor shin, that I've had ever since I was a little girl!

Oh, no, no, no. Goodness, no. It didn't hurt the least little bit. And anyway it was my fault. Really it was. Truly. Well, you're just being sweet, to say that. It really was all my fault.

I wonder what I'd better do—kill him this instant, with my naked hands, or wait and let him drop in his traces. Maybe it's best not to make a scene. I guess I'll just lie low, and watch the pace get him. He can't keep this up indefinitely—he's only flesh and blood. Die he must, and die he shall, for what he did to me. I don't want to be of the over-sensitive type, but you can't tell me that kick was unpremeditated. Freud says there are no accidents. I've led no cloistered life, I've known dancing partners who have spoiled my slippers and torn my dress; but when it comes to kicking, I am Outraged Womanhood. When you kick me in the shin, *smile*.

Maybe he didn't do it maliciously. Maybe it's just his way of showing his high spirits. I suppose I ought to be glad that one of us is having such a good time. I suppose I ought to think myself lucky if he brings me back alive. Maybe it's captious to demand of a practically strange man that he leave your shins as he found them. After all, the poor boy's doing the best he can. Probably he grew up in the hill country, and never had no larnin'. I bet they had to throw him on his back to get shoes on him.

Yes, it's lovely, isn't it? It's simply lovely. It's the loveliest waltz. Isn't it? Oh, I think it's lovely, too.

Why, I'm getting positively drawn to the Triple Threat here. He's my hero. He has the heart of a lion, and the sinews of a buffalo. Look at him—never a thought of the consequences, never afraid of his face, hurling himself into every scrimmage, eyes shining, cheeks ablaze. And shall it be said that I hung back? No, a thousand times no. What's it to me if I have to spend the next couple of years in a plaster cast? Come on, Butch, right through them! Who wants to live forever?

Oh. Oh, dear. Oh, he's all right, thank goodness. For a while I thought they'd have to carry him off the field. Ah,

I couldn't bear to have anything happen to him. I love him. I love him better than anybody in the world. Look at the spirit he gets into a dreary, commonplace waltz; how effete the other dancers seem, beside him. He is youth and vigor and courage, he is strength and gaiety and—*Ow!* Get off my instep, you hulking peasant! What do you think I am, anyway—a gangplank? *Ow!*

No, of course it didn't hurt. Why, it didn't a bit. Honestly. And it was all my fault. You see, that little step of yours—well, it's perfectly lovely, but it's just a tiny bit tricky to follow at first. Oh, did you work it up yourself? You really did? Well, aren't you amazing! Oh, now I think I've got it. Oh, I think it's lovely. I was watching you do it when you were dancing before. It's awfully effective when you look at it.

It's awfully effective when you look at it. I bet I'm awfully effective when you look at me. My hair is hanging along my cheeks, my skirt is swaddled about me, I can feel the cold damp of my brow. I must look like something out of the "Fall of the House of Usher." This sort of thing takes a fearful toll of a woman my age. And he worked up his little step himself, he with his degenerate cunning. And it was just a tiny bit tricky at first, but now I think I've got it. Two stumbles, slip, and a twenty-yard dash; yes. I've got it. I've got several other things, too, including a split shin and a bitter heart. I hate this creature I'm chained to. I hated him the moment I saw his leering, bestial face. And here I've been locked in his noxious embrace for the thirty-five years this waltz has lasted. Is that orchestra never going to stop playing?

Or must this obscene travesty of a dance go on until hell burns out?

Oh, they're going to play another encore. Oh, goody. Oh, that's lovely. Tired? I should say I'm not tired. I'd like to go on like this forever.

I should say I'm not tired. I'm dead, that's all I am. Dead, and in what a cause! And the music is never going to stop playing, and we're going on like this, Double-Time Charlie and I, throughout eternity. I suppose I won't care any more, after the first hundred thousand years. I suppose nothing will matter then, not heat nor pain nor broken heart nor cruel, aching weariness. Well. It can't come too soon for me.

I wonder why I didn't tell him I was tired. I wonder why I didn't suggest going back to the table. I could have said let's just listen to the music. Yes, and if he would, that would be the first bit of attention he has given it all evening. George Jean Nathan said that the lovely rhythms of the waltz should be listened to in stillness and not be accompanied by strange gyrations of the human body. I think that's what he said. I think it was George Jean Nathan. Anyhow, whatever he said and whoever he was and whatever he's doing now, he's better off than I am. That's safe. Anybody who isn't waltzing with this Mrs. O'Leary's cow I've got here is having a good time.

Still if we were back at the table, I'd probably have to talk to him. Look at him—what could you say to a thing like that! Did you go to the circus this year, what's your favorite kind of ice cream, how do you spell cat? I guess I'm as well off here. As well off as if I were in a cement mixer in full action.

I'm past all feeling now. The only way I can tell when he steps on me is that I can hear the splintering of bones. And all the events of my life are passing before my eyes. There was the time I was in a hurricane in the West Indies, there was the day I got my head cut open in the taxi smash, there was the night the drunken lady threw a bronze ash-tray at her own true love and got me instead, there was that summer that the sailboat kept capsizing. Ah, what an easy, peaceful time was mine, until I fell in with Swifty, here. I didn't know what trouble was, before I got drawn into this *danse macabre*. I think my mind is beginning to wander. It almost seems to me as if the orchestra were stopping. It couldn't be, of course; it could never, never be. And yet in my ears there is a silence like the sound of angel voices. . . .

Oh, they've stopped, the mean things. They're not going to play any more. Oh, darn. Oh, do you think they would? Do you really think so, if you gave them twenty dollars? Oh, that would be lovely. And look, do tell them to play this same thing. I'd simply adore to go on waltzing.

[1933]

S. J. PERELMAN

*

Farewell, My Lovely Appetizer

Add Smorgasbits to your ought-to-know department, the newest of the three Betty Lee products. What in the world! Just small mouth-size pieces of herring and of pinkish tones. We crossed our heart and promised not to tell the secret of their tinting.

Clementine Paddleford's
food column in the Herald Tribune.

The "Hush-Hush" Blouse. We're very hush-hush about his name, but the celebrated shirtmaker who did it for us is famous on two continents for blouses with details like those deep yoke folds, the wonderful shoulder pads, the shirtband bow!

Russeks adv. in the Times.

I came down the sixth-floor corridor of the Arbogast Building, past the World Wide Noodle Corporation, Zwinger & Rumsey, Accountants, and the Ace Secretarial Service, Mimeographing Our Specialty. The legend on the ground-glass

panel next door said, "Atlas Detective Agency, Noonan &
Driscoll," but Snapper Driscoll had retired two years before
with a .38 slug between the shoulders, donated by a snow-
bird in Tacoma, and I owned what good will the firm had.
I let myself into the crummy anteroom we kept to impress
clients, growled good morning at Birdie Claflin.

"Well, you certainly look like something the cat dragged
in," she said. She had a quick tongue. She also had eyes like
dusty lapis lazuli, taffy hair, and a figure that did things to
me. I kicked open the bottom drawer of her desk, let two
inches of rye trickle down my craw, kissed Birdie square on
her lush red mouth, and set fire to a cigarette.

"I could go for you, sugar," I said slowly. Her face was
veiled, watchful. I stared at her ears, liking the way they were
joined to her head. There was something complete about
them; you knew they were there for keeps. When you're a
private eye, you want things to stay put.

"Any customers?"

"A woman by the name of Sigrid Bjornsterne said she'd
be back. A looker."

"Swede?"

"She'd like you to think so."

I nodded toward the inner office to indicate that I was
going in there, and went in there. I lay down on the daven-
port, took off my shoes, and bought myself a shot from the
bottle I kept underneath. Four minutes later, an ash blonde
with eyes the color of unset opals, in a Nettie Rosenstein
basic black dress and a baum-marten stole, burst in. Her

bosom was heaving and it looked even better that way. With a gasp she circled the desk, hunting for some place to hide, and then, spotting the wardrobe where I keep a change of bourbon, ran into it. I got up and wandered out into the anteroom. Birdie was deep in a crossword puzzle.

"See anyone come in here?"

"Nope." There was a thoughtful line between her brows. "Say, what's a five-letter word meaning 'trouble'?"

"Swede," I told her, and went back inside. I waited the length of time it would take a small, not very bright boy to recite *Ozymandias*, and, inching carefully along the wall, took a quick gander out the window. A thin galoot with stooping shoulders was being very busy reading a paper outside the Gristede store two blocks away. He hadn't been there an hour ago, but then, of course, neither had I. He wore a size seven dove-colored hat from Browning King, a tan Wilson Brothers shirt with pale-blue stripes, a J. Press foulard with a mixed-red-and-white figure, dark blue Interwoven socks, and an unshined pair of ox-blood London Character shoes. I let a cigarette burn down between my fingers until it made a small red mark, and then I opened the wardrobe.

"Hi," the blonde said lazily. "You Mike Noonan?" I made a noise that could have been "Yes," and waited. She yawned. I thought things over, decided to play it safe. I yawned. She yawned back, then, settling into a corner of the wardrobe, went to sleep. I let another cigarette burn down until it made a second red mark beside the first one, and then I woke her up. She sank into a chair, crossing a pair of gams that tightened my throat as I peered under the desk at them.

"Mr. Noonan," she said, "you — you've got to help me."

"My few friends call me Mike," I said pleasantly.

"Mike." She rolled the syllable on her tongue. "I don't believe I've ever heard that name before. Irish?"

"Enough to know the difference between a gossoon and a bassoon."

"What *is* the difference?" she asked. I dummied up; I figured I wasn't giving anything away for free. Her eyes narrowed. I shifted my two hundred pounds slightly, lazily set fire to a finger, and watched it burn down. I could see she was admiring the interplay of muscles in my shoulders. There wasn't any extra fat on Mike Noonan, but I wasn't telling *her* that: I was playing it safe until I knew where we stood.

When she spoke again, it came with a rush. "Mr. Noonan, he thinks I'm trying to poison him. But I swear the herring was pink — I took it out of the jar myself. If I could only find out how they tinted it. I offered them money, but they wouldn't tell."

"Suppose you take it from the beginning," I suggested.

She drew a deep breath. "You've heard of the golden spintria of Hadrian?" I shook my head. "It's a tremendously valuable coin believed to have been given by the Emperor Hadrian to one of his proconsuls, Caius Vitellius. It disappeared about 150 A.D., and eventually passed into the possession of Hucbald the Fat. After the sack of Adrianople by the Turks, it was loaned by a man named Shapiro to the court physician, or hakim, of Abdul Mahmoud. Then it dropped out of sight for nearly five hundred years, until last August, when a dealer in second-hand books named Lloyd Thursday sold it to my husband."

"And now it's gone again," I finished.

"No," she said. "At least, it was lying on the dresser when I left, an hour ago." I leaned back, pretending to fumble a carbon out of the desk, and studied her legs again. This was going to be a lot more intricate than I had thought. Her voice got huskier. "Last night I brought home a jar of Smorgasbits for Walter's dinner. You know them?"

"Small mouth-size pieces of herring and of pinkish tones, aren't they?"

Her eyes darkened, lightened, got darker again. "How did you know?"

"I haven't been a private op nine years for nothing, sister. Go on."

"I—I knew right away something was wrong when Walter screamed and upset his plate. I tried to tell him the herring was supposed to be pink, but he carried on like a madman. He's been suspicious of me since—well, ever since I made him take out that life insurance."

"What was the face amount of the policy?"

"A hundred thousand. But it carried a triple indemnity clause in case he died by sea food. Mr. Noonan—Mike"—her tone caressed me—"I've got to win back his confidence. You could find out how they tinted that herring."

"What's in it for me?"

"Anything you want." The words were a whisper. I leaned over, poked open her handbag, counted off five grand.

"This'll hold me for a while," I said. "If I need any more, I'll beat my spoon on the high chair." She got up. "Oh, while I think of it, how does this golden spintria of yours tie in with the herring?"

"It doesn't," she said calmly. "I just threw it in for glamour." She trailed past me in a cloud of scent that retailed at ninety rugs the ounce. I caught her wrist, pulled her up to me.

"I go for girls named Sigrid with opal eyes," I said.

"Where'd you learn my name?"

"I haven't been a private snoop twelve years for nothing, sister."

"It was nine last time."

"It seemed like twelve till *you* came along." I held the clinch until a faint wisp of smoke curled out of her ears, pushed her through the door. Then I slipped a pint of rye into my stomach and a heater into my kick and went looking for a bookdealer named Lloyd Thursday. I knew he had no connection with the herring caper, but in my business you don't overlook anything.

The thin galoot outside Gristede's had taken a powder when I got there; that meant we were no longer playing girls' rules. I hired a hack to Wanamaker's, cut over to Third, walked up toward Fourteenth. At Twelfth a mink-faced jasper made up as a street cleaner tailed me for a block, drifted into a dairy restaurant. At Thirteenth somebody dropped a sour tomato out of a third-story window, missing me by inches. I doubled back to Wanamaker's, hopped a bus up Fifth to Madison Square, and switched to a cab down Fourth, where the second-hand bookshops elbow each other like dirty urchins.

A flabby hombre in a Joe Carbondale rope-knit sweater, whose jowl could have used a shave, quit giggling over the Heptameron long enough to tell me he was Lloyd Thursday. His shoe-button eyes became opaque when I asked to see any first editions or incunabula relative to the *Clupea harengus*, or common herring.

"You got the wrong pitch, copper," he snarled. "That stuff is hotter than Pee Wee Russell's clarinet."

"Maybe a sawbuck'll smarten you up," I said. I folded one to the size of a postage stamp, scratched my chin with it. "There's five yards around for anyone who knows why those Smorgasbits of Sigrid Bjornsterne's happened to be pink." His eyes got crafty.

"I might talk for a grand."

"Start dealing." He motioned toward the back. I took a step forward. A second later a Roman candle exploded inside my head and I went away from there. When I came to, I was on the floor with a lump on my sconce the size of a lapwing's egg and big Terry Tremaine of Homicide was bending over me.

"Someone sapped me," I said thickly. "His name was—"

"Webster," grunted Terry. He held up a dog-eared copy of Merriam's Unabridged. "You tripped on a loose board and this fell off a shelf on your think tank."

"Yeah?" I said skeptically. "Then where's Thursday?" He pointed to the fat man lying across a pile of erotica. "He passed out cold when he saw you cave." I covered up, let Terry figure it any way he wanted. I wasn't telling him what cards I held. I was playing it safe until I knew all the angles.

In a seedy pharmacy off Astor Place, a stale Armenian whose name might have been Vulgarian but wasn't dressed my head and started asking questions. I put my knee in his groin and he lost interest. Jerking my head toward the coffee urn, I spent a nickel and the next forty minutes doing some heavy thinking. Then I holed up in a phone booth and dialled a clerk I knew called Little Farvel in a delicatessen store on Amsterdam Avenue. It took a while to get the dope I wanted because the connection was bad and Little Farvel had been dead two years, but we Noonans don't let go easily.

By the time I worked back to the Arbogast Building, via the Weehawken ferry and the George Washington Bridge to cover my tracks, all the pieces were in place. Or so I thought up to the point she came out of the wardrobe holding me between the sights of her ice-blue automatic.

"Reach for the stratosphere, gumshoe." Sigrid Bjornsterne's voice was colder than Horace Greeley and Little Farvel put together, but her clothes were plenty calorific. She wore a forest-green suit of Hockanum woollens, a Knox Wayfarer, and baby crocodile pumps. It was her blouse, though, that made tiny red hairs stand up on my knuckles. Its deep yoke folds, shoulder pads, and shirtband bow could only have been designed by some master craftsman, some Cézanne of the shears.

"Well, Nosy Parker," she sneered, "so you found out how they tinted the herring."

"Sure—grenadine," I said easily. "You knew it all along. And you planned to add a few grains of oxylbutane-cheriphosphate, which turns the same shade of pink in solution, to your husband's portion, knowing it wouldn't show in the post-mortem. Then you'd collect the three hundred g's and join Harry Pestalozzi in Nogales till the heat died down. But you didn't count on me."

"You?" Mockery nicked her full-throated laugh. "What are you going to do about it?"

"This." I snaked the rug out from under her and she went down in a swirl of silken ankles. The bullet whined by me into the ceiling as I vaulted over the desk, pinioned her against the wardrobe.

"Mike." Suddenly all the hatred had drained away and her body yielded to mine. "Don't turn me in. You cared for me—once."

"It's no good, Sigrid. You'd only double-time me again."

"Try me."

"O.K. The shirtmaker who designed your blouse—what's his name?" A shudder of fear went over her; she averted her head. "He's famous on two continents. Come on Sigrid, they're your dice."

"I won't tell you. I can't. It's a secret between this—this department store and me."

"They wouldn't be loyal to *you*. They'd sell you out fast enough."

"Oh, Mike, you mustn't. You don't know what you're asking."

"For the last time."

"Oh, sweetheart, don't you see?" Her eyes were tragic
pools, a cenotaph to lost illusions. "I've got so little. Don't
take that away from me. I—I'd never be able to hold up my
head in Russeks again."

"Well, if that's the way you want to play it . . ." There
was silence in the room, broken only by Sigrid's choked sob.
Then, with a strangely empty feeling, I uncradled the phone
and dialled Spring 7-3100.

For an hour after they took her away, I sat alone in the
taupe-colored dusk, watching lights come on and a woman
in the hotel opposite adjusting a garter. Then I treated my
tonsils to five fingers of firewater, jammed on my hat, and
made for the anteroom. Birdie was still scowling over her
crossword puzzle. She looked up crookedly at me.

"Need me any more tonight?"

"No." I dropped a grand or two in her lap. "Here, buy
yourself some stardust."

"Thanks, I've got my quota." For the first time I caught a
shadow of pain behind her eyes. "Mike, would—would you
tell me something?"

"As long as it isn't clean," I flipped to conceal my bitter-
ness.

"What's an eight-letter word meaning 'sentimental'?"

"Flatfoot, darling," I said, and went out into the rain.

[1944]

LANGSTON HUGHES

*

Simple Prays a Prayer

It was a hot night. Simple was sitting on his landlady's stoop reading a newspaper by streetlight. When he saw me coming, he threw the paper down.

"Good evening," I said.

"Good evening nothing," he answered. "It's too hot to be any good evening. Besides, this paper's full of nothing but atom bombs and bad news, wars and rumors of wars, airplane crashes, murders, fightings, wife-whippings, and killings from the Balkans to Brooklyn. Do you know one thing? If I was a praying man, I would pray a prayer for this world right now."

"What kind of prayer would you pray, friend?"

"I would pray a don't-want-to-have-no-more-wars prayer, and it would go like this: 'Lord,' I would say, I would ask Him, 'Lord, kindly please, take the blood off of my hands and off of my brothers' hands, and make us shake hands *clean* and not be afraid. Neither let me nor them have no knives behind our backs, Lord, nor up our sleeves, nor no bombs piled out yonder in a desert. Let's forget about bygones. Too many mens and womens are dead. The fault is mine and theirs, too. So teach us *all* to do right, Lord, *please*, and to get along together with that atom bomb on this earth—because I do not want it to fall on me—nor Thee— nor anybody living. Amen!'"

"I didn't know you could pray like that," I said.

"It ain't much," said Simple, "but that girl friend of mine, Joyce, drug me to church last Sunday where the man was preaching and praying about peace, so I don't see why I shouldn't make myself up a prayer, too. I figure God will listen to me as well as the next one."

"You certainly don't have to be a minister to pray," I said, "and you have composed a good prayer. But now it's up to you to help God bring it into being, since God is created in your image."

"I thought it was the other way around," said Simple.

"However that may be," I said, "according to the Bible, God can bring things about on this earth only through man. You are a man, so you must help God make a good world."

"I am willing to help Him," said Simple, "but I do not know much what to do. The folks who run this world are going to run it in the ground in spite of all, throwing people out of work and then saying, 'Peace, it's wonderful!' Peace ain't wonderful when folks ain't got no job."

"Certainly a good job is essential to one's well-being," I said.

"It is essential to me," said Simple, "if I do not want to live off of Joyce. And I do *not* want to live off of no woman. A woman will take advantage of you, if you live off of her."

"If a woman loves you, she does not mind sharing with you," I said. "Share and share alike."

"Until times get hard!" said Simple. "But when there is not much to share, *loving* is one thing, and *sharing* is another. Often they parts company. I know because I have both loved and shared. As long as I shared *mine*, all was well, but when my wife started sharing, skippy!

"My wife said, 'Baby, when is you going to work?'

"I said, 'When I find a job.'

"She said, 'Well, it better be soon because I'm giving out.'

"And, man, I felt bad. You know how long and how hard it took to get on WPA. Many a good man lost his woman in them dark days when that stuff about 'I can't give you anything but love' didn't go far. Now it looks like love is all I am going to have to share again. Do you reckon depression days is coming back?"

"I don't know," I said. "I am not a sociologist."

"You's colleged," said Simple. "Anyhow, it looks like every time I gets a little start, something happens. I was doing right well pulling down that *fine* defense check all during the war, then all of a sudden the war had to jump up and end!"

"If you wanted the war to continue just on your account, you are certainly looking at things from a selfish view-point."

"Selfish!" said Simple. "You may *think* I am selfish when

the facts is *I am just hongry* if I didn't have a job. It looks like in peace time nobody works as much or gets paid as much as in a war. Is that clear?"

"Clear, but not right," I said.

"Of course, it's not right to be out of work and hongry," said Simple, "just like it's not right to want to fight. That's why I prayed my prayer. I prayed for white folks, too, even though a lot of them don't believe in religion. If they did, they couldn't act the way they do.

"Last Sunday morning when I was laying in bed drowsing and resting, I turned on the radio on my dresser and got a church—by accident. I was trying to get the Duke on records, but I turned into the wrong station. I got some white man preaching a sermon. He was talking about peace on earth, good will to men, and all such things, and he said Christ was born to bring this peace he was talking about. He said mankind has sinned! But that we have got to get ready for the Second Coming of Christ—because Christ will be back! That is what started me to wondering."

"Wondering what?" I asked.

"Wondering what all these prejudiced white folks would do if Christ did come back. I always thought Christ believed in folks treating people right."

"He did," I said.

"Well, if He did," said Simple, "what will all these white folks do who believe in Jim Crow? Jesus said, 'Love one another,' didn't He? But they don't love me, do they?"

"Some do not," I said.

"Jesus said, 'Do unto others as you would have others do unto you.' But they don't do that way unto me, do they?"

"I suppose not," I said.

"You know not," said Simple. "They Jim Crow me and lynch me any time they want to. Suppose I was to do unto them as they does unto me? Suppose I was to lynch and Jim Crow white folks, where would I be? Huh?"

"In jail."

"You can bet your boots I would! But these are *Christian* white folks that does such things to me. At least, they call themselves Christians in my home. They got more churches down South than they got up North. They read more Bibles and sing more hymns. I hope when Christ comes back, He comes back down South. My folks need Him down there to tell them Ku Kluxers where to head in. But I'll bet you if Christ does come back, not only in the South but all over America, there would be such another running and shutting and slamming of white folks' doors in His face as you never saw! And I'll bet the Southerners couldn't get inside their Jim Crow churches fast enough to lock the gates and keep Christ out. Christ said, 'Such as ye do unto the least of these, ye do it unto me.' And Christ *knows* what these white folks have been doing to old colored me all these years."

"Of course, He knows," I said. "When Christ was here on earth, He fought for the poor and the oppressed. But some people called Him an agitator. They cursed Him and reviled Him and sent soldiers to lock Him up. They killed Him on the cross."

"At Calvary," said Simple, "way back in B.C. I know the Bible, too. My Aunt Lucy read it to me. She read how He drove the money-changers out of the Temple. Also how He changed the loaves and fishes into many and fed the poor — which made the rulers in their high places mad because they didn't want the poor to eat. Well, when Christ comes back this time, I hope He comes back *mad* His own self. I hope He drives the Jim Crowers out of their high places, every living last one of them from Washington to Texas! I hope He smites white folks down!"

"You don't mean *all* white folks, do you?"

"No," said Simple. "I hope He lets Mrs. Roosevelt alone."

[1944]

FRANK SULLIVAN

✳

The Night the Old Nostalgia Burned Down

When I was a boy, Fourteenth Street was where Twenty-third Street is now, and Samuel J. Tilden and I used to play marbles on the lot where the Grand Opera House still stood. Governor Lovelace brought the first marble from England to this country on August 17, 1668, and gave it to my Great-Aunt Amelia van Santvoort, of whom he was enamored. She had several copies made, and Sam Tilden and I used to amuse ourselves with them.

I remember the Sunday afternoons when Governor Lovelace would come to tea at our house, although I could not have been much more than a tad at the time. I can hear the rich clanking of the silver harness as his magnificent equipage, with its twelve ebony outriders in cerise bombazine, rolled up to our house at No. 239 East 174th Street. I was the envy of all the kids on the block because I was allowed to sit in the carriage while the Governor went in to take tea with Great-Aunt Amelia. I always chose Ada Rehan to sit beside me. She was a little golden-haired thing at the time and none of us dreamed she would one day go out from East 174th Street and shoot President Garfield.

Great-Aunt Amelia was a dowager of the old school. You don't see many of her kind around New York today, probably because the old school was torn down a good many years ago; its site is now occupied by Central Park. People used to say that the Queen, as they called Great-Aunt Amelia, looked more like my Aunt Theodosia than my Aunt Theodosia did.

But Aunt Caroline was really the great lady of our family. I can still see her descending the staircase, dressed for the opera in silk hat, satin-lined cape, immaculate shirt, white tie, and that magnificent, purple-black beard.

"Well, boy!" she would boom at me. "Well!"

"Well, Aunt Caroline!" I would say, doing my best to boom back at her.

She would chuckle and say, "Boy, I like your spirit! Tell Grimson I said to add an extra tot of brandy to your bedtime milk."

Oh, those lollipops at Preem's, just around the corner from the corner! Mm-m-m, I can still taste them! After school, we kids would rush home and shout, "Ma, gimme a penny for a lollipop at Preem's, willya, Ma? Hey, Ma, willya?" Then we would go tease Jake Astor, the second-hand-fur dealer around the corner. I shall never forget the day Minnie Maddern Fiske swiped the mink pelt from Jake's cart and stuffed it under Bishop Potter's cope.

Miss Hattie Pumplebutt was our teacher at P.S. 67. She was a demure wisp of a woman, with white hair parted in the middle, pince-nez that were forever dropping off her nose, always some lacy collar high around her throat, and paper cuffs. We adored her. Every once in a while she would climb up on her desk, flap her arms, shout "Whee-e-e! I'm a bobolink!," and start crowing. Or she would take off suddenly and go skipping about the tops of our desks with a dexterity and sure-footedness truly marvellous in one of her age. When we grew old enough, we were told about Miss Pumplebutt. She took dope. Well, she made history and geography far more interesting than a lot of non-sniffing teachers I have known.

One day, Jim Fisk and I played hooky from school and went to the old Haymarket on Sixth Avenue, which was then between Fifth and Seventh. We had two beers apiece and thought we were quite men about town. I dared Jim to go over and shoot Stanford White, never dreaming the chump would do it. I didn't know he was loaded. I got Hail Columbia from Father for that escapade.

Father was very strict about the aristocratic old New York ritual of the Saturday-night bath. Every Saturday night at eight sharp we would line up: Father, Mother, Diamond Jim Brady; Mrs. Dalrymple, the housekeeper; Absentweather, the butler; Aggie, the second girl; Aggie, the third girl; Aggie, the fourth girl; and twelve of us youngsters, each one equipped with soap and a towel. At a command from Father, we would leave our mansion on East Thirtieth Street and proceed solemnly up Fifth Avenue in single file to the old reservoir, keeping a sharp eye out for Indians. Then, at a signal from Papa, in we'd go. Everyone who was anyone in New York in those days had his Saturday-night bath in the reservoir, and it was there that I first saw and fell in love with the little girl whom I later made Duchess of Marlborough.

My Grandmamma Satterthwaite was a remarkable old lady. At the age of eighty-seven she could skip rope four hundred and twenty-two consecutive times without stopping, and every boy on the block was madly in love with her. Then her father failed in the crash of '87 and in no time she was out of pigtails, had her hair up, and was quite the young lady. I never did hear what became of her.

It rather amuses me to hear the youngsters of today enthusing about the croissants, etc., at Spodetti's and the other fashionable Fifth Avenue patisseries. Why, they aren't a patch on Horan's!

Mike Horan's place was at Minetta Lane and Washington Mews, and I clearly remember my father telling a somewhat startled Walt Whitman that old Mike Horan could bend a banana in two — with his bare hands! But I never saw him do it. We kids used to stand in front of his shop for hours after school waiting for Mike to bend a banana, but he never did. I can still hear the cheerful clang of his hammer on the anvil and the acrid smell of burning hoofs from the Loveland Dance Palace, across the way on Delancey Street, which was then Grand. Then the Civil War came and the property of the Loyalists was confiscated. I still have some old Loyalist property I confiscated on that occasion. I use it for a paperweight. Old Gammer Wilberforce was a Loyalist. We used to chase her down the street, shouting "Tory!" at her. Then she would chase us up the street, shouting:

> *"Blaine, Blaine, James G. Blaine!*
> *Continental liar from the State of Maine!"*

or:

> *"Ma! Ma! Where's my Pa?"*
> *"Gone to the White House, ha, ha ha!"*

Of course, very few white people ever went to Chinatown in those days. It was not until the Honorah Totweiler case that people became aware of Chinatown. I venture to say that few persons today would recall Honorah Totweiler, yet in 1832 the Honorah Totweiler case was the sensation of the country. In one day the circulation of the elder James Gordon Bennett jumped seventy-four thousand as a result of the Totweiler case.

One sunny afternoon in the autumn of September 23, 1832, a lovely and innocent girl, twelfth of eighteen daughters of Isaac Totweiler, a mercer, and Sapphira, his wife, set out from her home in Washington Mews to return a cup of sugar—but let the elder Bennett tell the story:

> It is high time [Bennett wrote] that the people of these United States were awakened to the menace in which the old liberties for which our forefathers fought and bled, in buff and blue, by day and night, at Lexington and Concord, in '75 and '76, have been placed as a result of the waste, the orgy of spending, the deliberate falsifications, the betrayal of public trust, and the attempt to set up a bureaucratic and unconstitutional dictatorship, of the current Administration in Washington. Murphy must go, and Tammany with him!

After dinner on Sundays, my Grandpa Bemis would take a nap, with the *Times,* or something, thrown over his face to keep out the glare. If he was in a good humor when he awoke, he would take us youngsters up to Dick Canfield's to play games, but as he was never in a good humor when he awoke, we never went to Dick Canfield's to play games.

Sometimes, when we kids came home from school, Mrs. Rossiter, the housekeeper, would meet us in the hall and place a warning finger on her lips. We knew what that meant. We must be on our good behavior. The wealthy Mrs. Murgatroyd was calling on Mother. We would be ushered into the Presence, Mother would tell us to stop using our sleeves as a handkerchief, and then Mrs. Murgatroyd would laugh and say, "Oh, Annie, let the poor children alone. Sure, you're only young once." Then she would lift up her skirt to the knee, fish out a huge wallet from under her stocking, and give us each $2,000,000. We loved her. Not only did she have a pair of d——d shapely stems for an old lady her age, but she was reputed to be able to carry six schooners of beer in each hand.

I shall never forget the night of the fire. It was about three o'clock in the morning when it started, in an old distaff factory on West Twelfth Street. I was awakened by the crackling. I shivered, for my brother, as usual, had all the bedclothes, and there I was, with fully three inches of snow (one inch powder, two inches crust) on my bare back. The next morning there were seven feet of snow on West Twenty-seventh Street alone. You don't get that sort of winter nowadays. That was the winter the elder John D. Rockefeller was frozen over solid from November to May.

On Saturdays we used to go with Great-Aunt Tib to the Eden Musee to see the wax figure of Lillian Russell. There was a woman! They don't build girls like her nowadays. You can't get the material, and even if you could, the contractors and the plumbers would gyp you and substitute shoddy.

I was six when the riots occurred. No, I was *thirty*-six. I remember because it was the year of the famous Horace Greeley hoax, and I used to hear my parents laughing about it. It was commonly believed that Mark Twain was the perpetrator of the hoax, although Charles A. Dana insisted to his dying day that it was Lawrence Godkin. At any rate, the hoax, or "sell," originated one night at the Union League Club when Horace chanced to remark to Boss Tweed that his (Horace's) wife was entertaining that night. The town was agog for days, no one having the faintest notion that the story was not on the level. Greeley even threatened Berry Wall with a libel suit.

Well, that was New York, the old New York, the New York of gaslit streets, and sparrows (and, of course, horses), and cobblestones. The newsboy rolled the *Youth's Companion* into a missile and threw it on your front stoop and the postmen wore uniforms of pink velvet and made a point of bringing everybody a letter every day.

Eheu, fugaces! —

[1946]

E. B. WHITE

*

Across the Street and into the Grill
(With my respects to Ernest Hemingway)

This is my last and best and true and only meal, thought Mr. Perley as he descended at noon and swung east on the beat-up sidewalk of Forty-fifth Street. Just ahead of him was the girl from the reception desk. I am a little fleshed up around the crook of the elbow, thought Perley, but I commute good.

He quickened his step to overtake her and felt the pain again. What a stinking trade it is, he thought. But after what I've done to other assistant treasurers, I can't hate anybody. Sixteen deads, and I don't know how many possibles.

The girl was near enough now so he could smell her fresh receptiveness, and the lint in her hair. Her skin was light blue, like the sides of horses.

"I love you," he said, "and we are going to lunch together for the first and only time, and I love you very much."

"Hello, Mr. Perley," she said, overtaken. "Let's not think of anything."

A pair of fantails flew over from the sad old Guaranty Trust Company, their wings set for a landing. A lovely double, thought Perley, as he pulled. "Shall we go to the Hotel Biltmore, on Vanderbilt Avenue, which is merely a feeder lane for the great streets, or shall we go to Schrafft's, where my old friend Botticelli is captain of girls and where they have the mayonnaise in fiascos?"

"Let's go to Schrafft's," said the girl, low. "But first I must phone Mummy." She stepped into a public booth and dialled true and well, using her finger. Then she telephoned.

As they walked on, she smelled good. She smells good, thought Perley. But that's all right, I add good. And when we get to Schrafft's, I'll order from the menu, which I like very much indeed.

They entered the restaurant. The wind was still west, ruffling the edges of the cookies. In the elevator, Perley took the controls. "I'll run it," he said to the operator. "I checked out long ago." He stopped true at the third floor, and they stepped off into the men's grill.

"Good morning, my Assistant Treasurer," said Botticelli, coming forward with a fiasco in each hand. He nodded at the girl, who he knew was from the West Seventies and whom he desired.

"Can you drink the water here?" asked Perley. He had the fur trapper's eye and took in the room at a glance, noting that there was one empty table and three pretty waitresses.

Botticelli led the way to the table in the corner, where Perley's flanks would be covered.

"Alexanders," said Perley. "Eighty-six to one. The way Chris mixes them. Is this table all right, Daughter?"

Botticelli disappeared and returned soon, carrying the old Indian blanket.

"That's the same blanket, isn't it?" asked Perley.

"Yes. To keep the wind off," said the Captain, smiling from the backs of his eyes. "It's still west. It should bring the ducks in tomorrow, the chef thinks."

Mr. Perley and the girl from the reception desk crawled down under the table and pulled the Indian blanket over them so it was solid and good and covered them right. The girl put her hand on his wallet. It was cracked and old and held his commutation book. "We are having fun, aren't we?" she asked.

"Yes, Sister," he said.

"I have here the soft-shelled crabs, my Assistant Treasurer," said Botticelli. "And another fiasco of the 1926. This one is cold."

"Dee the soft-shelled crabs," said Perley from under the blanket. He put his arm around the receptionist good.

"Do you think we should have a green pokeweed salad?" she asked. "Or shall we not think of anything for a while?"

"We shall not think of anything for a while, and Botticelli would bring the pokeweed if there was any," said Perley. "It isn't the season." Then he spoke to the Captain. "Botticelli, do you remember when we took all the mailing envelopes from the stockroom, spit on the flaps, and then drank rubber cement till the foot soldiers arrived?"

"I remember, my Assistant Treasurer," said the Captain. It was a little joke they had.

"He used to mimeograph pretty good," said Perley to the girl. "But that was another war. Do I bore you, Mother?"

"Please keep telling me about your business experiences, but not the rough parts." She touched his hand where the knuckles were scarred and stained by so many old mimeographings. "Are both your flanks covered, my dearest?" she asked, plucking at the blanket. They felt the Alexanders in their eyeballs. Eighty-six to one.

"Schrafft's is a good place and we're having fun and I love you," Perley said. He took another swallow of the 1926, and it was a good and careful swallow. "The stockroom men were very brave," he said, "but it is a position where it is extremely difficult to stay alive. Just outside that room there is a little bare-assed highboy and it is in the way of the stuff that is being brought up. The hell with it. When you make a breakthrough, Daughter, first you clean out the baskets and the half-wits, and all the time they have the fire escapes taped. They also shell you with old production orders, many of them approved by the general manager in charge of sales. I am boring you and I will not at this time discuss the general manager in charge of sales as we are unquestionably being listened to by that waitress over there who is setting out the decoys."

"I am going to give you my piano," the girl said, "so that

when you look at it you can think of me. It will be something between us."

"Call up and have them bring the piano to the restaurant," said Perley. "Another fiasco, Botticelli!"

They drank the sauce. When the piano came, it wouldn't play. The keys were stuck good. "Never mind, we'll leave it here, Cousin," said Perley.

They came out from under the blanket and Perley tipped their waitress exactly fifteen per cent minus withholding. They left the piano in the restaurant, and when they went down the elevator and out and turned in to the old, hard, beat-up pavement of Fifth Avenue and headed south toward Forty-fifth Street, where the pigeons were, the air was as clean as your grandfather's howitzer. The wind was still west.

I commute good, thought Perley, looking at his watch. And he felt the old pain of going back to Scarsdale again.

[1950]

PETER DE VRIES

*

The House of Mirth

The collaboration known as marriage could, I think, be profitably extended from the domestic to the social sphere, where a man and wife might brighten their contribution to, say, the give-and-take of dinner-table conversation by preparing a few exchanges in advance. "It's simply the principle of teamwork," I told my wife in partially describing the idea to her one evening as we were dressing to go to dinner at the home of some friends named Anthem. "For instance, tonight, Sue Anthem being as hipped as she is on family trees, we're bound to talk relatives at some point. Well, I'm going to tell about my seagoing grandfather who's so wonderful. In the middle of it, I'll pause and take up my napkin, and then I'd appreciate it if you'd ask me, 'Was he on your mother's side?'" (I planned to answer, "Yes, except in money matters, when he usually stuck up for my father." This wasn't much, but I was feeling my way around in the form, trying to get the hang of it before going on to something more nearly certifiable as wit.)

Dinner ran along the lines I had foreseen. Sue Anthem got off on kinship, and I launched my little account of this wonderful grandfather. I paused at the appointed moment and, glancing at my wife, reached for my napkin.

"I keep forgetting," she came in brightly. "Was he your maternal grandfather?"

"Yes, except in money matters, when he usually stuck up for my father," I replied.

A circle of blank looks met my gaze. I coughed into my napkin, and Sue picked up the thread of the discussion while I reviewed in my mind a couple of other gambits I had worked out with my wife, on the way over. One of these concerned a female friend, not present that evening, whom I will cut corners by calling a gay divorcée. She had just announced her engagement to a man so staid that news of the match took everyone who knew her by surprise. "Now, if the thing comes up, as it probably will," I had coached my wife, "say something about how you've only met him a few times but he seems a man of considerable reserve." I intended then to adroitly add, "Which Monica will get her hands on in short order." I expected that to go over big, the divorcée being a notorious gold-digger.

The gossip did get around to her soon after it left the subject of relatives, and my wife came in on cue punctually enough, but her exact words were "He's such a quiet, unassuming chap."

This time, I had the presence of mind to realize the quip was useless, and check myself. Another misfire followed almost immediately. In preparation for possible discussion of Italy, where Monica and her fiancé planned to honeymoon, I had primed my wife to tell about her own visit to the Gulf of Spezia, where the drowned Shelley had been washed up. "In a way, you know, he was lucky," I had planned to comment. "Most poets are washed up *before* they're dead." She told her story, but used the words "where Shelley was found," thus washing up *that* mot.

It was clear that I would have to explain the system to my wife in detail if I was ever to get the thc bugs out of it. I decided, in, fact, that I had better reveal in each case what the capper was to be, so that she would realize the importance of delivering her line exactly as prearranged. I did this while we were driving to our next party, several evenings later. I had ducked her questions about the failures at the Anthems', preferring to wait till I had some new material worked up to hammer my point home with before I laid the whole thing on the line.

"At the Spiggetts' tonight," I said, "there's certain to be the usual talk about art. Here's a chance for you to get in those licks of yours about abstract painting—isn't it high time painters got back to nature, and so on. The sort of thing you said at the Fentons'. You might cite a few of the more traditional paintings, like the portraits of Mrs. Jack Gardner and Henry Marquand. Then turn to me and ask—now, get this, it's important—ask, 'Why can't we have portraits like that any more?'"

"Then what will you say?" she asked.

I slowed to make a left turn, after glancing in the rear-view mirror to make sure nobody was behind me. "It's no time for Sargents, my dear."

My wife reached over and pushed in the dash lighter, then sat waiting for it to pop, a cigarette in her hand.

"Of course I'll throw it away," I said. "Just sort of murmur it."

She lit the cigarette and put the lighter back in its socket. "Isn't this a little shabby?" she asked.

"Why? What's shabby about it? Isn't it better than the conversation you have to put up with normally — doesn't it make for something at least a cut above that?" I said. "What's wrong with trying to brighten life up? We can turn it around if you like. You can take the cappers while I feed you the straight lines — "

"Lord, no, leave it as it is."

"Can I count on you, then?"

"I suppose," she said, heaving a sigh. "But step on it. We're supposed to eat early and then go to that Shakespearean little theatre in Norwalk."

My wife and I parted on entering the Spiggetts' house. I made off to where a new television comedienne, named Mary Cobble, was holding court with a dozen or so males. She was a small blonde, cute as a chipmunk and bright as a dollar. The men around her laughed heartily at everything she said. It was well known in Westport that her writers, of whom she kept a sizable stable, formed a loyal claque who followed her to every party, but it didn't seem to me that *all* the men around her could be writers. I knocked back a few quick Martinis and soon felt myself a gay part of the group. Once, I glanced around and saw my wife looking stonily my way over the shoulder of a man whose fame as a bore was so great that he was known around town as the Sandman. Matters weren't helped, I suppose, when, presently returning from the buffet with two plates of food, I carried one to Mary Cobble and sat down on the floor in front of her to eat the other. At the same time, I saw the Sandman fetching my wife a bite.

Midway through this lap dinner, there was one of those moments when all conversation suddenly stops at once. Lester Spiggett threw in a comment about a current show at a local art gallery. I saw my wife put down her fork and clear her throat. "Well, if there are any portraits in it I hope the things on the canvases are faces," she said. She looked squarely at me. "Why is it we no longer have portraits that *portray*—that give you pictures of *people*? Like, oh, the 'Mona Lisa,' or 'The Man with the Hoe,' or even that 'American Gothic' thing? Why is that?"

Everybody turned to regard me, as the one to whom the query had obviously been put. "That's a hard question for me to answer," I said, frowning into my plate. I nibbled thoughtfully on a fragment of cold salmon. "Your basic point is, of course, well taken—that the portraits we get are not deserving of the name. Look like somebody threw an egg at the canvas."

Fuming, I became lost in the ensuing free-for-all. Not so

my wife, whom annoyance renders articulate. She more than held her own in the argument, which was cut short when Mary Cobble upset a glass of iced tea. She made some cheery remark to smooth over the incident. The remark wasn't funny, nor was it intended to be funny, but to a man her retinue threw back their heads and laughed.

Meaning to be nice, I laughed, too, and said, "Well, it goes to show you. A good comedienne has her wits about her."

"And pays them well," my wife remarked, in her corner. (Luckily, Mary Cobble didn't hear it, but two or three others did, and they repeated it until it achieved wide circulation, with a resulting increase in our dinner invitations. That, however, was later. The present problem was to get through the rest of the evening.)

We had to bolt our dessert and rush to the theatre, where they were doing "King Lear" in Bermuda shorts, or something, and my wife and I took another couple in our car, so I didn't get a chance to speak to her alone until after the show. Then I let her have it.

"That was a waspish remark," I said. "And do you know why you made it? Resentment. A feeling of being out of the swim. It's because you're not good at repartee that you say things like that, and are bitter."

"Things like what?" my wife asked.

I explained what, and repeated my charge.

In the wrangle, quite heated, that followed her denial of it, she gave me nothing but proof of its truth. I submitted that the idea of mine that had given rise to this hassle, and of which the hassle could safely be taken to be the corpse, had been a cozy and even a tender one: the idea that a man and wife could operate as a team in public. "What could be more domestic?" I said.

"Domesticity begins at home," she rather dryly returned.

I met this with a withering silence.

[1956]

TERRY SOUTHERN

*

from The Magic Christian

Grand's theatre was one of the city's largest and had first-run rights on the most publicized films. In the manager's absence, things proceeded normally for a while; until one night when the house was packed for the opening of the smart new musical, *Main Street, U.S.A.*

First there was an annoying half-hour delay while extra camp-stool seats were sold and set up in the aisles; then, when the house lights finally dimmed into blackness, and the audience settled back to enjoy the musical, Grand gave them something they weren't expecting: a cheap foreign film.

The moment the film began, people started leaving. In the darkness, however, with seats two-abreast choking the aisles, most of them were forced back. So the film rolled on; and while the minutes gathered into quarter-hours, and each quarter-hour cut cripplingly deep into the evening, Grand, locked in the projection room high above, stumbled from wall to wall, choking with laughter.

After forty-five minutes, the film was taken off and it was announced over the public-address system, and at a volume strength never before used anywhere, that a mistake had been made, that this was *not* the new musical.

Shouts of "*And how!*" came from the crowd, and "*I'll say it's not!*" and "*You're telling me! God!*"

Then after another delay for rewinding, the cheap foreign film was put on again, upside down.

By ten thirty the house was seething towards angry panic, and Grand gave the order to refund the money of everyone who wished to pass by the box office. At eleven o'clock there was a line outside the theatre two blocks long.

From his office above, Grand kept delaying the cashier's work by phoning every few minutes to ask: "How's it going?" or "What's up?"

The next day there was a notice on the central bulletin board:

"Rocks on the green! All hands alert!"

It also announced another fat pay-hike.

Into certain films such as *Mrs. Miniver*, Grand made eccentric inserts.

In one scene in *Mrs. Miniver*, Walter Pidgeon was sitting at evening in his fire-lit study and writing in his journal. He had just that afternoon made the acquaintance of Mrs. Miniver and was no doubt thinking about her now as he paused reflectively and looked towards the open fire. In the original version of this film, he took a small penknife from the desk drawer and meditatively sharpened the pencil he had been writing with. During this scene the camera remained on his *face*, which was filled with quiet reflection and modest hopefulness, so that the intended emphasis of the scene was quite clear: his genteel and wistfully ambitious thoughts about Mrs. Miniver.

The insert Grand made into this film, was, like those he made into others, professionally done, and as such, was technically indiscernable. It was introduced just at the moment where Pidgeon opened the knife, and it was a three-second close shot of the fire-glint blade.

This simple insert misplaced the emphasis of the scene; the fire-glint blade seemed to portend dire evil, and occurring as it did early in the story, simply "spoiled" the film.

Grand would hang around the lobby after the show to overhear the remarks of those leaving, and often he would join in himself:

"What was that part about the *knife?*" he would demand querulously, stalking up and down the lobby, striking his fist into his open hand, ". . . he *had* that knife . . . I thought he was going to try and *kill* her! Christ, I don't *get* it!"

In some cases, Grand's theatre had to have two copies of the film on hand, because his alterations were so flagrant that he did not deem it wise to project the altered copy twice in succession. This was the case with a popular film called *The Best Years of Our Lives*. This film was mainly concerned, in its attempt at an odd kind of realism, with a young veteran of war, who was an amputee and had metal hooks instead of hands. It was a story told quite seriously and one which depended for much of its drama upon a straight-faced identification with the amputee's situation and attitude. Grand's insert occurred in the middle of the film's big scene. This original scene was a seven-second pan of the two principal characters, the amputee and his pretty home-town fiancée while they were sitting on the family porch swing one summer evening. The hero was courting her, in his quiet way — and this consisted of a brave smile, more or less in apology, it would seem, for having the metal hooks instead of hands — while the young girl's eyes shone with tolerance and understanding . . . a scene which was interrupted by Grand's insert: a cut to below the girl's waist where the hooks were seen to hover for an instant and then disappear, grappling urgently beneath her skirt. The duration of this cut was less than one-half second, but was unmistakably seen by anyone not on the brink of sleep.

It brought some of the audience bolt upright. Others the scene affected in a sort of double-take way, reacting to it as they did only minutes later. The rest, that is to say about one-third of the audience, failed to notice it at all; and the film rolled on. No one could believe his eyes; those who were positive they had seen something funny in the realism there, sat through the film again to make certain — though, of course, the altered version was never run twice in succession — but *all* who had seen were so obsessed by what they had seen, or what they imagined they had seen, that they could no longer follow the story line, though it was, from that point on, quite as it was intended, without incongruity or surprise.

Grand had a good deal of trouble about his alterations of certain films and was eventually sued by several of the big studios. You can bet it cost him a pretty to keep clear in the end.

[1959]

LENNY BRUCE

*

from **How to Talk Dirty and Influence People**

"Are you a sick comic?"

"Why do they call you a sick comic?"

"Do you mind being called a sick comic?"

It is impossible to label me. I develop, on the average, four minutes of new material a night, constantly growing and changing my point of view; I am heinously guilty of the paradoxes I assail in our society.

The reason for the label "sick comic" is the lack of creativity among journalists and critics. There is a comedy actor from England with a definite Chaplinesque quality. "Mr. Guinness, do you mind being called a Chaplinesque comic?" There is a comedian by the name of Peter Sellers who has a definite Guinnessesque quality. "Mr. Sellers, why do they say you have a Guinnessesque quality?"

The motivation of the interviewer is not to get a terse, accurate answer but rather to write an interesting, slanted article within the boundaries of the editorial outlook of his particular publication, so that he will be given the wherewithal to make the payment on his MG. Therefore this writer prostitutes his integrity by asking questions, the answers to which he already has, much like a cook who follows a recipe and mixes the ingredients properly.

The way I speak, the words with which I relate are much more correct in effect than those of a previous pedantic generation.

If I talk about a chick onstage and say, "She was a hooker," an uncontemporary person would say, "Lenny Bruce, you are course and crude."

"What should I have said?"

"If you must be specific, you should have said 'prostitute.'"

"But wait a minute; shouldn't the purpose of a word be to get close to the object the user is describing?

"Yes, and correct English can do this; 'hooker' is incorrect."

The word has become too general. He *prostituted* his art. He *prostituted* the very thing he loved. Can he write anymore? Not like he used to—he has *prostituted* his work.

So the word "prostitute" doesn't mean anymore what the word "hooker" does. If a man were to send out for a $100 prostitute, a writer with a beard might show up.

Concomitant with the "sick comic" label is the carbon cry, "What happened to the healthy comedian who just got up there and showed everybody a good time and didn't preach, didn't have to resort to knocking religion, mocking physical handicaps and telling dirty toilet jokes?"

Yes, what *did* happen to the wholesome trauma of the 1930s and 1940s—the honeymoon jokes, concerned not only with what they did but also with how many times they did it; the distorted wedding-night tales, supported visually by the trite vacationland postcards of an elephant with his trunk searching through the opening of a pup tent, and a woman's head straining out the other end, hysterically screaming, "George!"—whatever happened to all this wholesomeness?

What happened to the healthy comedian who at least had good taste? . . . Ask the comedians who used to do the harelip jokes, or the moron jokes—"The moron who went to the orphans' picnic," etc.—the healthy comedians who told good-natured religious jokes that found Pat and Abie and Rastus outside of St. Peter's gate all listening to those angels harping in stereotype.

Whatever happened to Joe E. Lewis? His contribution to comedy consisted of returning Bacchus to his godlike pose with an implicit social message: "If you're going to be a swinger and fun to be with, always have a glass of booze in your hand; even if you don't become part swinger, you're sure to end up with part liver."

Whatever happened to Henny Youngman? He involved himself with a nightly psychodrama named Sally, or sometimes Laura. She possessed features not sexually but economically stimulating. Mr. Youngman's Uglivac cross-filed and classified diabolic deformities definitively. "Her nose

was so big that every time she sneezed. . . ." "She was so
bowlegged that every time. . . ." "One leg was shorter than
the other . . ." and Mr. Youngman's mutant reaped financial
harvest for him. Other comedians followed suit with Cock-
eyed Jennies, et al., until the Ugly Girl routines became classics. I assume this fondness for atrophy gave the night-club
patron a sense of well-being.

And whatever happened to Jerry Lewis? His neorealistic
impression of the Japanese male captured all the subtleties
of the Japanese physiognomy. The buck-teeth malocclusion
was caricatured to surrealistic proportions until the teeth
matched the blades that extended from Ben-Hur's chariot.

Highlighting the absence of the iris with Coke-bottle-
thick lenses, this satire has added to the fanatical devotion
which Japanese students have for the United States. Just ask
Eisenhower.

Whatever happened to Milton Berle? He brought trans-
vestitism to championship bowling and upset a hard-core
culture of dykes that control the field. From *Charlie's Aunt*
to *Some Like It Hot* and Milton Berle, the pervert has been
taken out of Krafft-Ebing and made into a sometimes-fun
fag.

Berle never lost his sense of duty to the public, though.
Although he gave homosexuals a peek out of the damp cellar
of unfavorable public opinion, he didn't go all the way; he
left a stigma of menace on his fag—"I sweah I'w kiw you."

I was labeled a "sicknik" by *Time* magazine, whose editorial policy still finds humor in a person's physical short-

comings: "Shelly Berman has a face like a hastily sculptured hamburger." The healthy comic would never offend . . . unless you happen to be fat, bald, skinny, deaf or blind. The proxy vote from purgatory has not yet been counted.

Let's say I'm working at the Crescendo on the coast. There'll be Arlene Dahl with some New Wave writer from Algiers and on the whole it's a cooking kind of audience. But I'll finish a show, and some guy will come up to me and say, "I—I'm a club owner, and I'd like you to work for me. It's a beautiful club. You ever work in Milwaukee? Lots of people like you there, and you'll really do great. You'll kill 'em. You'll have a lot of fun. Do you bowl?"

The only thing is, I know that in those clubs, between Los Angeles and New York, the people in the audience are a little older than me. The most I can say to people over 50 or 55 is, "Thank you, I've had enough to eat."

I get to Milwaukee, and the first thing that frightens me to death is that they've got a 6:30 dinner show . . . 6:30 in the afternoon and people go to a night club! It's not even *dark* out yet. I don't wanna go in the house, it's not dark yet, man. If the dinner show is held up, it's only because the Jell-o's not hard.

The people look familiar, but I've never been to Milwaukee before. Then I realized—these are the Grayline Sightseeing Bus Tours before they leave—this is where they *live*. They're like 40-year-old chicks with prom gowns on.

They don't laugh, they don't heckle, they just stare at me

in disbelief. And there are walkouts, walkouts, every night, walkouts. The owner says to me, "Well, I never saw you do that religious bit . . . and those words you use!" The chef is confused—the desserts aren't moving.

I go to the men's room, and I see *kids* in there. Kids four years old, six years old. These kids are in awe of this men's room. It's the first time they've ever been in a place their mother isn't allowed in. Not even for a minute. Not even to get something, is she allowed in there. And the kids stay in there for hours.

"Come out of there!"

"No. Uh-uh."

"I'm going to come in and get you."

"No, you're not allowed in here, 'cause everybody's doing, making wet in here."

In between shows I'm a walker, and I'm getting nudgy and nervous. The owner decides to cushion me with his introduction: "Ladies and gentlemen, the star of our show, Lenny Bruce, who, incidentally, is an ex-GI and, uh, a hell of a good performer, folks, and a great kidder, know what I mean? It's all a bunch of silliness up here and he doesn't mean what he says. He kids about the Pope and about the Jewish religion, too, and the colored people and the white people—it's all a silly make-believe world. And he's a hell of a nice guy, folks. He was at the Veterans Hospital today doing a show for the boys. And here he is—his mom's out here tonight, too, she hasn't seen him in a couple of years— she lives here in town. . . . Now, a joke is a joke, right, folks?

What the hell. I wish that you'd try to cooperate. And whoever has been sticking ice picks in the tires outside, he's not
funny. Now Lenny may kid about narcotics, homosexuality,
and things like that . . ."

And *he* gets walkouts.

I get off the floor, and a waitress says to me, "Listen, there's
a couple, they want to meet you." It's a nice couple, about 50
years old. The guy asks me,

"You from New York?"

"Yes."

"I recognized that accent." And he's looking at me, with
a sort of searching hope in his eyes, and then he says, "Are
you Jewish?"

"Yes."

"What are you doing in a place like this?"

"I'm passing."

He says, "Listen, I know you show people eat all that crap
on the road. . . ." (Of course. What did you eat tonight? Crap
on the road.) And they invite me to have a nice dinner at their
house the next day. He writes out the address, you know,
with the ball-point pen on the wet cocktail napkin.

The next day I go to my hotel—I'm staying at the local
show-business hotel; the other show people consist of two
people, the guy who runs the movie projector and another
guy who sells Capezio shoes—and I read a little, write a little.
I finally get to sleep about seven o'clock in the morning.

The phone rings at nine o'clock.

"Hello, hello, hello, this is the Sheckners."

"The people from last night. We didn't wake you up, did we?"

"No, I always get up at nine in the morning. I like to get up about ten hours before work so I can brush my teeth and get some coffee. It's good you got me up. I probably would have overslept otherwise."

"Listen, why we called you, we want to find out what you want to eat."

"Oh, anything. I'm not a fussy eater, really."

I went over there that night, and I *do* eat anything—anything but what they had. Liver. And Brussels sprouts. That's really a double threat.

And the conversation was on the level of, "Is it true about Liberace?"

That's all I have to hear, then I really start to lay it on to them:

"Oh yeah, they're all queer out there in Hollywood. Rin Tin Tin's a junkie."

Then they take you on a tour around the house. They bring you into the bedroom with the dumb dolls on the bed. And what the hell can you tell people when they walk you around their house? "Yes, that's a very lovely closet; that's nice the way the towels are folded." They have a piano, with the big lace doily on top, and the bowl of wax fruit. The main function of these pianos is to hold an eight-by-ten picture of the son in the Army, saluting. "That's Morty, he lost a lot of weight."

The trouble is, in these towns — Milwaukee; Lima, Ohio — there's nothing else to do, except look at stars. In the daytime, you go to the park to see the cannon, and you've had it.

One other thing — you can hang out at the Socony Gas Station between shows and get gravel in your shoes. Those night attendants really swing.

"Lemme see the grease rack go up again," I say. "Can I try it?"

"No, you'll break it."

"Can I try on your black-leather bow tie?"

"No. Hey, Lenny, you wanna see a clean toilet? You been in a lot of service stations, right? Did you ever see one this immaculate?"

"It's beautiful."

"Now don't lie to me."

"Would I lie to you about something like that?"

"I thought you'd like it, because I know you've seen everything in your travels — "

"It's gorgeous. In fact, if anyone ever says to me, 'Where is there a clean toilet, I've been searching forever,' I'll say, 'Take 101 into 17 up through 50,' and I'll just send 'em right here."

"You could eat off the floor, right, Lenny?"

"Yon certainly could."

"Want a sandwich?"

"No, thanks."

Then I start fooling around with his condom-vending machine.

"You sell many of these here?"

"I don't know."

"You fill up the thing here?"

"No, a guy comes around."

"You wear condoms ever?"

"Yeah."

"Do you wear them all the time?"

"No."

"Do you have one on now?"

"Well, what do you do if you have to tell some chick, 'I'm going to put a condom on now'—it's going to kill every-thing."

I ask the gas-station attendant if I can put one on.

"Are you crazy or something?"

"No, I figure it's something to do. We'll both put con-doms on. We'll take a picture."

"Now, get the hell out of here, you nut, you."

I can't help it, though. Condoms are so dumb. They're sold for the prevention of love.

As far as chicks are concerned, these small towns are dead. The cab drivers ask *you* where to get laid. It's really a hang-up. Every chick I meet, the first thing they hit me with is, "Look, I don't know what kind of a girl you think I am, but I know you show people, you've got all those broads down in the dressing room and they're all ready for you and I'm not gonna..."

"That's a lie, there's nobody down there!"

"Never mind, I know you get all you want."

"I don't!"

That's what everybody thinks, but there's nobody in the dressing room. That's why Frank Sinatra never gets any. It's hip *not* to ball him. "Listen, now, they all ball him, I'm not gonna ball him." And the poor *schmuck* really sings *Only the Lonely* . . .

It's a real hang-up, being divorced when you're on the road. Suppose it's three o'clock in the morning, I've just done the last show, I meet a girl, and I like her, and suppose I have a record I'd like her to hear, or I just want to talk to her — there's no lust, no carnal image there — but because where I live is a dirty word, I can't say to her, "Would you come to my hotel?"

And every *healthy* comedian has given "motel" such a dirty connotation that I couldn't ask my *grandmother* to go to a motel, say I want to give her a Gutenberg Bible at three in the morning.

The next day at two in the afternoon, when the Kiwanis Club meets there, then "hotel" is clean. But at three o'clock in the morning, Jim. . . . Christ, where the hell can you live that's clean? You can't say hotel to a chick, so you try to think, what won't offend? What is a clean word to society? What is a clean word that won't offend any chick? . . .

Trailer. That's it, *trailer.*

"Will you come to my trailer?"

"All right, there's nothing dirty about trailers. Trailers are hunting and fishing and Salem cigarettes. Yes, of course, I'll come to your trailer. Where is it?"

"Inside my hotel room."

Why can't you just say, "I want to be with you, and hug and kiss you." No, it's "Come up while I change my shirt." Or coffee. "Let's have a cup of coffee."

In 50 years, coffee will be another dirty word.

[1963]

TOM WOLFE

＊

The Secret Vice

Real buttonholes. That's it! A man can take his thumb and forefinger and unbutton his sleeve at the wrist because this kind of suit has real buttonholes there. Tom, boy, it's terrible. Once you know about it, you start seeing it. All the time! There are just two classes of men in the world, men with suits whose buttons are just sewn onto the sleeve, just some kind of cheapie decoration, or — yes! — men who can unbutton the sleeve at the wrist because they have real buttonholes and the sleeve really buttons up. Fascinating! My friend Ross, a Good Guy, thirty-two years old, a lawyer Downtown with a good head of Scotch-Irish hair, the kind that grows right, unlike lower-class hair, is sitting in his corner on East 81st St., in his Thonet chair, with the Flemish brocade cushion on it, amid his books, sets of Thackeray, Hazlitt, Lamb, Walter Savage Landor, Cardinal Newman, and other studs of the rhetoric game, amid his prints, which are mostly Gavarni, since all the other young lawyers have Daumiers or these cute muvvas by

"Spy," or whatever it is, which everybody keeps laying on thatchy-haired young lawyers at Christmas—Ross is sitting among all these good tawny, smoke-cured props drinking the latest thing somebody put him onto, port, and beginning to talk about coats with real buttonholes at the sleeves. What a taboo smirk on his face!

It is the kind of look two eleven-year-old kids get when they are riding the Ferris wheel at the state fair, and every time they reach the top and start down they are staring right into an old midway banner in front of a sideshow, saying, "THE MYSTERIES OF SEX REVEALED! SIXTEEN NUDE GIRLS! THE BARE TRUTH! EXCITING! EDUCATIONAL!" In the sideshow they get to see 16 female fetuses in jars of alcohol, studiously arranged by age, but— that initial taboo smirk!

Ross, thirty-two years old, in New York City—the same taboo smirk.

"I want to tell you a funny thing," he says. "The first time I had any idea about this whole business of the buttonholes was a couple of Christmases ago, one Saturday, when I ran into Sturges at Dunhill's." Dunhill the tobacco shop. Sturges is a young partner in Ross's firm on Wall Street. Ross idealizes Sturges. Ross stopped carrying an attaché case, for example, because Sturges kept referring to attaché cases as leather lunch pails. Sturges is always saying something like, "You know who I saw yesterday? Stolz. There he was, walking along Exchange Place with his leather lunch pail, the poor bastard." Anyway, Ross says he ran into Sturges in Dunhill's.

"He was trying to get some girl a briar pipe for Christmas or some damn thing." That Sturges! "Anyway, I had just bought a cheviot tweed suit, land of Lovat-colored—you know, off the rack—actually it was a pretty good-looking suit. So Sturges comes over and he says, 'Well, old Ross has some new togs,' or something like that. Then he says, 'Let me see something,' and he takes the sleeve and starts monkeying around with the buttons. Then he says, 'Nice suit,' but he says it in a very half-hearted way. Then he goes off to talk to one of those scientific slenderellas he always has hanging around. So I went over to him and said, 'What was all that business with the buttons?' And he said, 'Well, I thought maybe you had it custom made.' He said it in a way like it was now pretty goddamned clear it wasn't custom made. Then he showed me his suit—it was a window-pane check, have you ever seen one of those?—he showed me his suit, the sleeve, and *his* suit had buttonholes on the sleeve. It was custom made. He showed me how he could unbutton it. Just like this. The girl wondered what the hell was going on. She stood there with one hip cocked, watching him undo a button on his sleeve. Then I looked at mine and the buttons were just sewn on. You know?" And you want to know something? That really got to old Ross. He practically couldn't *wear* that suit anymore. All right, it's ridiculous. He probably shouldn't even be confessing all this. It's embarrassing. And—the taboo smirk!

Yes! The lid was off, and poor old Ross was already hooked on the secret vice of the Big men in New York: custom

tailoring and the mania for the marginal differences that go
into it. Practically all the most powerful men in New York,
especially on Wall Street, the people in investment houses,
banks and law firms, the politicians, especially Brooklyn
Democrats, for some reason, outstanding dandies, those fellows, the blue-chip culturati, the major museum directors
and publishers, the kind who sit in offices with antique tex-
tile shades—practically all of these men are fanatical about
the marginal differences that go into custom tailoring. They
are almost like a secret club insignia for them. And yet it is
a taboo subject. They won't talk about it. They don't want
it known that they even care about it. But all the time they
have this fanatical eye, more fanatical than a woman's, about
the whole thing and even grade men by it. The worst jerks, as
far as they are concerned—and people can lose out on jobs,
promotions, the whole can of worms, because of this—are
men who have dumped a lot of money, time and care into
buying ready-made clothes from some Englishy dry goods
shop on Madison Avenue with the belief that they are really
"building fine wardrobes." Such men are considered to be
bush leaguers, turkeys and wet smacks, the kind of men who
tote the leather lunch pail home at night and look forward to
having a drink and playing with the baby.

God, it's painful to hear old Ross talk about all this. It's
taboo! Sex, well, all right, talk your head off. But this, these
men's clothes—a man must have to have beady eyes to even
see these things. But these are Big men! But—all right!

It's the secret vice! In Europe, all over England, in France, the mass ready-made suit industry is a new thing. All men, great and small, have had tailors make their suits for years, and they tend to talk a little more with each other about what they're getting. But in America it's the secret vice. At Yale and Harvard, boys think nothing of going over and picking up a copy of *Leer, Poke, Feel, Prod, Tickle, Hot Whips, Modern Mammaries*, and other such magazines, and reading them right out in the open. Sex is not taboo. But when the catalogue comes from Brooks Brothers or J. Press, that's something they whip out only in *private*. And they can hardly wait. They're in the old room there poring over all that tweedy, thatchy language about "Our Exclusive Shirtings," the "Finest Lairdsmoor Heather Hopsacking," "Clearspun Rocking Druid Worsteds," and searching like detectives for the marginal differences, the shirt with a flap over the breast pocket (J. Press), the shirt with no breast pocket (Brooks), the pants with military pockets, the polo coat with welted seams—and so on and on, through study and disastrous miscalculations, until they learn, at last, the business of marginal differentiations almost as perfectly as those teen-agers who make their mothers buy them button-down shirts and then make the poor old weepies sit up all night punching a buttonhole and sewing on a button in the back of the collar because they bought the wrong damn shirt; one of those hinkty ones without the button in the back.

And after four years of Daddy bleeding to pay the tabs, Yale, Harvard, and the rest of these schools turn out young gentlemen who are confident that they have at last mastered the secret vice, marginal differentiations, and they go right down to Wall Street or wherever and—blam!—they get it like old Ross, right between the eyes. A whole new universe to learn! Buttonholes! A whole new set of clothing firms to know about—places like Bernard Weatherill, probably the New York custom tailor with the biggest reputation, very English, Frank Brothers and Dunhill's, Dunhill's the tailor, which are slightly more—how can one say it?—flamboyant?—places like that, or the even more esoteric world of London tailors, Poole, Hicks, Wells, and God knows how many more, and people knock themselves out to get to London to get to these places, or else they order straight from the men these firms send through New York on regular circuits and put up in hotels, like the Biltmore, with big books of swatches, samples of cloths, piled up on the desk-table.

The secret vice! A whole new universe! Buttonholes! The manufacturers can't make ready-made suits with permanent buttonholes on the sleeves. The principle of ready-made clothes is that each suit on the rack can be made to fit about four different shapes of men. They make the sleeves long and then the store has a tailor, an unintelligible little man who does alterations, chop them off to fit men with shorter arms and move the buttons up.

And suddenly Ross found that as soon as you noticed this much, you started noticing the rest of it. Yes! The scyes, for example. The scyes! Imagine somebody like Ross knowing all this esoteric terminology. Ross is a good old boy, for godsake. The scyes! The scyes are the armholes in a coat. In ready-made clothes, they make the armholes about the size of the Holland Tunnel. Anybody can get in these coats. Jim Bradford, the former heavyweight weight-lifting champion, who has arms the size of a Chapman Valve fire hydrant, can put on the same coat as some poor bastard who is mooning away the afternoon at IBM shuffling memos and dreaming of going home and having a drink and playing with the baby. Naturally, for everybody but Jim Bradford, this coat is loose and looks sloppy, as you can imagine. That's why custom-made suits have high armholes; because they fit them to a man's own particular shoulder and arm. And then all these other little details. In Ross's league, Wall Street, practically all of these details follow the lead of English tailoring. The waist: the suits go in at the waist, they're fitted, instead of having a straight line, like the Ivy League look. This Ivy League look was great for the ready-made manufacturers. They just turned out simple bags and everybody was wearing them. The lapels: in the custom-made suits they're wider and have more "belly," meaning more of a curve or flared-out look along the outer edge. The collar: the collar of the coat fits close to the neck — half the time in ready-made suits it sits away from the neck, because it was made big to fit all kinds. The tailor-made suit fits closer and the collar itself will have a curve in it where it comes up to the notch. The sleeves: the sleeves are narrower and are slightly tapered down to the wrists. Usually, there are four buttons, sometimes three, and they really button and unbutton. The shoulders are padded to give the coat shape; "natural shoulders" are for turkeys and wet smacks. The vents: often the coat will have side vents or no vents, instead of center vents, and the vents will be deeper than in a ready-made suit. Well, hell, Ross could go on about all this—but there, you can already see what the whole thing is like.

Ross even knows what somebody is likely to say to this. You walk into a room and you can't tell whether somebody has real buttonholes on his sleeves or not. All of these marginal differences are like that. They're so small, they're practically invisible. All right! That's what's so maniacal about it. In women's clothes, whole styles change from year to year. They have new "silhouettes," waists and hems go up and down, collars go in and out, breasts blossom out and disappear; you can follow it. But in men's clothes there have been only two style changes in this century, and one of them was so esoteric, it's hard for a tailor to explain it without a diagram. It had to do with eliminating a breast seam and substituting something called a "dart." That happened about 1913. The other was the introduction of pleats in pants about 1922. Lapels and pants leg widths have been cut down some, but most of the flashy stuff in lapels and pants goes on in ready-made suits, because the manufacturers are naturally hustling to promote style changes and make a buck. In custom-made suits, at least among tailors in the English tradition, there have really been no changes for fifty years. The whole thing is in the marginal differences—things that show that you spent more money and had servitors in there cutting and sewing like madmen and working away just for you. Status! Yes!

Yes, and how can these so-called Big men really get obsessed with something like this? God only knows. Maybe these things happen the way they happened to Lyndon Johnson, Our President. Mr. Johnson was campaigning with John Kennedy in 1960, and he had to look at Kennedy's clothes and then look at his own clothes, and then he must have said to himself, in his winning, pastoral way, Great Hairy Ned on the mountaintop, my clothes look like Iron Boy overalls. Yus, muh cluths look luk Irun Bouy uvverulls. Now, this Kennedy, he had most of his clothes made by tailors in England. Anyway, however it came about, one day in December, 1960, after the election, if one need edit, Lyndon Johnson, the salt of the good earth of Austin, Texas, turned up on Savile Row in London, England, and walked into the firm of Carr, Son & Woor. He said he wanted six suits, and the instructions he gave were: "I want to look like a British diplomat." Lyndon Johnson! Like a British diplomat! You can look it up. Lyndon Johnson, President of the United States, Benefactor of the Po', Lion of NATO, Defender of the Faith of Our Fathers, Steward of Peace in Our Times, Falconer of Our Sly Asiatic Enemies, Leader of the Free World—is soft on real buttonholes! And I had wondered about Ross.

[1964]

JEAN SHEPHERD

✳

The Counterfeit Secret Circle Member Gets the Message, *or* The Asp Strikes Again

Every day when I was a kid I'd drop anything I was doing, no matter what it was—stealing wire, having a fistfight, siphoning gas—no matter what, and tear like a blue streak through the alleys, over fences, under porches, through secret shortcuts, to get home not a second too late for the magic time. My breath rattling in wheezy gasps, sweating profusely from my long cross-country run I'd sit glassy-eyed and expectant before our Crosley Notre Dame Cathedral model radio.

I was never disappointed. At exactly five-fifteen, just as dusk was gathering over the picturesque oil refineries and the faint glow of the muttering Open Hearths was beginning to show red against the gloom, the magic notes of an unforgettable theme song came rasping out of our Crosley:

"*Who's that little chatterbox...?*
The one with curly golden locks....

> *Who do I see . . . ?*
> *It's Little Orphan Annie."*

Ah, they don't write tunes like that any more. There was one particularly brilliant line that dealt with Sandy, Little Orphan Annie's airedale sidekick. Who can forget it?

> *Arf goes Sandy.*

I think it was Sandy more than anyone else that drew me to the Little Orphan Annie radio program. Dogs in our neighborhood never went "Arf." And they certainly were a lot of things, but never faithful.

Little Orphan Annie lived in this great place called Tompkins Corners. There were people called Joe Corntassle and Uncle. They never mentioned the poolroom. There were no stockyards or fistfights. Or drunks sleeping in doorways in good old Tompkins Corners. Orphan Annie and Sandy and Joe Corntassle were always out chasing pirates or trapping smugglers, neither of which we ever had in Indiana as far as I knew. We had plenty of hubcap stealers and once even a guy who stole a lawn. But no pirates. At least they didn't call them that.

She also had this friend named The Asp, who whenever she was really in a tight spot would just show up and cut everybody's head off. I figured that if there was anything a kid of seven needed it was somebody named The Asp. Especially in our neighborhood. He wore a towel around his head.

Immediately after the nightly adventure, which usually

took place near the headwaters of the dreaded Orinoco, on would come a guy named Pierre André, the *definitive* radio announcer.

"FELLAS AND GALS. GET SET FOR A MEETING OF THE LITTLE ORPHAN ANNIE SECRET CIRCLE!"

His voice boomed out of the Crosley like some monster, maniacal pipe organ played by the Devil himself. Vibrant, urgent, dynamic, commanding. Pierre André. I have long had a suspicion that an entire generation of Americans grew up feeling inferior to just the *names* of the guys on the radio, Pierre André. Harlow Wilcox. Vincent Pelletier. Truman Bradley. Westbrook Van Voorhees. André Baruch. Norman Brokenshire. There wasn't a Charlie Shmidlap in the lot. Poor little Charlie crouching next to his radio—a born Right Fielder. Playing right field all of his life, knee-deep in weeds, waiting for a flyball that never comes and more than half afraid that one day they *will* hit one in his direction.

"OKAY, KIDS. TIME TO GET OUT YOUR SECRET DECODER PIN. TIME FOR ANOTHER SECRET MESSAGE DIRECT FROM LITTLE ORPHAN ANNIE TO MEMBERS OF THE LITTLE ORPHAN ANNIE SECRET CIRCLE."

I got no pin. A member of an Out Group at the age of seven. And the worst kind of an Out Group. I am living in a non-Ovaltine-drinking neighborhood.

"ALL RIGHT. SET YOUR PINS TO B-7. SEVEN . . . TWENTY-TWO . . . NINETEEN . . . EIGHT . . . *FORTY-NINE* . . . SIX . . . THIRTEEN . . . *THREE!* . . . TWENTY-TWO . . . ONE . . . FOUR . . . NINETEEN."

Pierre André could get more out of just numbers than Orson Welles was able to squeeze out of *King Lear.*

"FOURTEEN . . . NINE . . . THIRTY-TWO. OKAY, FELLAS AND GALS, OVER AND OUT."

Then—silence. The show was over and you had a sinister feeling that out there in the darkness all over the country there were millions of kids—decoding. And all I could do was to go out into the kitchen where my mother was cooking supper and knock together a salami sandwich. And plot. Somewhere kids were getting the real truth from Orphan Annie. The message. And I had no pin. I lived in an Oatmeal-eating family and listened to an Ovaltine radio show. To get into the Little Orphan Annie Secret Circle you had to send in the silver inner seal from a can of what Pierre André called "that rich chocolate-flavored drink that all the kids love." I had never even *seen* an Ovaltine can in my life.

But as the old truism goes, every man has his chance, and when yours comes you had better grab it. They do not make appointments for the next day. One day while I am foraging my way home from school, coming down one of my favorite alleys, knee-deep in garbage and the thrown-out effluvia of kitchen life, there occurred an incident which forever changed my outlook on Existence itself, although of course at the time I was not aware of it, believing instead that I had struck the Jackpot and was at last on my way into the Big Time.

There was a standard game played solo by almost every male kid I ever heard of, at least in our neighborhood. It was simple, yet highly satisfying. There were no rules except those which the player improvised as he went along. The game had no name and is probably as old as creation itself. It consisted of kicking a tin can or tin cans all the way home. This game is not to be confused with a more formal athletic contest called Kick The Can, which *did* have rules and even teams. This kicking game was a solitary, dogged contest of kid against can, and is quite possibly the very earliest manifestation of the Golf Syndrome.

Anyway, I am kicking condensed milk cans, baked bean cans, sardine cans along the alley, occasionally changing cans at full gallop, when I suddenly found myself kicking a can of a totally unknown nature. I kicked it twice; good, solid, running belts, before I discovered that what I was kicking was an Ovaltine can, the first I had ever seen. Instantly I picked it up, astounded by the mere presence of an Ovaltine drinker in our neighborhood, and then discovered that they had not only thrown out the Ovaltine can but had left the silver inner seal inside. Some rich family had thrown it *all* away! Five minutes later I've got this inner seal in the mail and I start to wait. Every day I would rush home from school and ask:

"Is there any mail for me?"

Day after day, eon after eon. Waiting for three weeks for something to come in the mail to a kid is like being asked to build the Pyramids singlehanded, using the #3 Erector set, the one without the motor. We never did get much mail around our house anyway. Usually it was bad news when it *did* come. Once in a while a letter marked OCCUPANT arrived, offering my Old Man $300 on his signature only, no questions asked, "Even your employer will not be notified." They began with:

"Friend, are you in Money troubles?"

My Old Man could never figure out how they knew, especially since they only called him OCCUPANT. Day after day I watched our mailbox. On Saturdays when there was no school I would sit on the front porch waiting for the mailman and the sound of the yelping pack of dogs that chased him on his appointed rounds through our neighborhood, his muffled curses and thumping kicks mingling nicely with the steady uproar of snarling and yelping. One thing I knew. Trusty old Sandy never chased a mailman. And if he *had*, he would have caught him.

Everything comes to he who waits. I guess. At last, after at least 200 years of constant vigil, there was delivered to me a big, fat, lumpy letter. There are few things more thrilling in Life than lumpy letters. That rattle. Even to this day I feel a wild surge of exultation when I run my hands over an envelope that is thick, fat, and pregnant with mystery.

I ripped it open. And there it was! My simulated gold plastic Decoder pin. With knob. And my membership card.

It was an important moment. Here was a real milestone, and I knew it. I was taking my first step up that great ladder of becoming a real American. Nothing is as important to an American as a membership card with a seal. I know guys who have long strings of them, plastic-enclosed: credit cards, membership cards, identification cards, Blue Cross cards, driver's licenses, all strung together in a chain of Love. The longer the chain, the more they feel they belong. Here was my first card. I was on my way! And the best of all possible ways—I was making it as a Phony. A non-Ovaltine drinking Official Member.

BE IT KNOWN TO ALL AND SUNDRY THAT MR. RALPH WESLEY PARKER IS HEREBY APPOINTED A MEMBER OF THE LITTLE ORPHAN ANNIE SECRET CIRCLE AND IS ENTITLED TO ALL THE HONORS AND BENEFITS ACCRU-ING THERETO.

Signed: Little Orphan Annie. Countersigned: Pierre André. In ink.

Honors and benefits. Already, at the age of seven, I am *Mister* Parker. They hardly ever even called my Old Man that.

That night I can hardly wait until the adventure is over. I want to get to the real thing, the message. That's what counts. I had spent the entire day sharpening pencils, practicing twirling the knob on my plastic simulated gold Decoder pin. I had lined up plenty of paper and was already at the radio by three-thirty, sitting impatiently through the drone of the late afternoon Soap Operas and newscasts, waiting for my direct contact with Tompkins Corners, my first night as a full Member.

As five-fifteen neared, my excitement mounted. Running waves of goose pimples rippled up and down my spine as I hunched next to our hand-carved, seven-tube Cathedral in the living room. A pause, a station break. . . .

> *"Who's that little chatterbox. . . .*
> *The one with curly golden locks. . . .*
> *Who do I see . . . ?*
> *It's Little Orphan Annie."*

Let's get on with it! I don't need all this jazz about smugglers and pirates. I sat through Sandy's arfing and Little Orphan Annie's perils hardly hearing a word. On comes, at long last, old Pierre. He's one of *my* friends now. I am In. My first secret meeting.

"OKAY, FELLAS AND GALS. GET OUT YOUR DECODER PINS. TIME FOR THE SECRET MESSAGE FOR ALL THE REGULAR PALS OF LITTLE ORPHAN ANNIE, MEMBERS OF THE LITTLE ORPHAN ANNIE SECRET CIRCLE. ALL SET? HERE WE GO. SET YOUR PINS AT B-12."

My eyes narrowed to mere slits, my steely claws working with precision, I set my simulated gold plastic Decoder pin to B-12.

"ALL READY? PENCILS SET?"

Old Pierre was in great voice tonight. I could tell that tonight's message was really important.

"SEVEN . . . TWENTY-TWO . . . THIRTEEN . . . NINETEEN . . . *EIGHT!*"

I struggled furiously to keep up with his booming voice dripping with tension and excitement. Finally:

"OKAY, KIDS. THAT'S TONIGHT'S SECRET MESSAGE. LISTEN AGAIN TOMORROW NIGHT, WHEN YOU HEAR. . . ."

> *"Who's that little chatterbox. . . .*
> *The one with curly golden locks. . . ."*

Ninety seconds later I am in the only room in the house where a boy of seven could sit in privacy and decode. My pin is on one knee, my Indian Chief tablet on the other. I'm starting to decode.

7....

I spun the dial, poring over the plastic scale of letters. Aha! B. I carefully wrote down my first decoded number. I went to the next.

22....

Again I spun the dial. E...

The first word is B-E.

13...S...

It was coming easier now.

19...U.

From somewhere out in the house I could hear my kid brother whimpering, his wail gathering steam, then the faint shriek of my mother:

"Hurry up! Randy's gotta go!"

Now what!

"I'LL BE RIGHT OUT, MA! GEE WHIZ!"

I shouted hoarsely, sweat dripping off my nose.

S...U...15...R...E. BE SURE! A message was coming through!

Excitement gripped my gut: I was getting The Word. BE SURE...

14...8...T...O...BE SURE TO what? What was Little Orphan Annie trying to say?

17...9...DR...16...12...I...9...N...K...32... OVA..19..LT...

I sat for a long moment in that steamy room, staring down at my Indian Chief notebook. A crummy commercial! Again a high, rising note from my kid brother.

"I'LL BE RIGHT OUT, MA! FOR CRYING OUT LOUD."

I pulled up my corduroy knickers and went out to face the meat loaf and the red cabbage. The Asp had decapitated another victim.

[1966]

HUNTER S. THOMPSON

✳

The Kentucky Derby Is
Decadent and Depraved

I got off the plane around midnight and no one spoke as I crossed the dark runway to the terminal. The air was thick and hot, like wandering into a steam bath. Inside, people hugged each other and shook hands . . . big grins and a whoop here and there: "By God! You old *bastard*! *Good* to see you, boy! *Damn* good . . . and I *mean* it!"

In the air-conditioned lounge I met a man from Houston who said his name was something or other—"but just call me Jimbo"—and he was here to get it on. "I'm ready for *anything*, by God! Anything at all. Yeah, what are you drinkin?" I ordered a Margarita with ice, but he wouldn't hear of it: "Naw, naw . . . what the hell kind of drink is that for Kentucky Derby time? What's *wrong* with you, boy?" He grinned and winked at the bartender. "Goddam, we gotta educate this boy. Get him some good *whiskey* . . ."

I shrugged. "Okay, a double Old Fitz on ice." Jimbo nodded his approval.

"Look." He tapped me on the arm to make sure I was listening. "If know this Derby crowd, I come here every year, and let me tell you one thing I've learned—this is no town to be giving people the impression you're some kind of faggot. Not in public, anyway. Shit, they'll roll you in a minute, knock you in the head and take every goddam cent you have."

I thanked him and fitted a Marlboro into my cigarette holder. "Say," he said, "you look like you might be in the horse business . . . am I right?"

"No," I said. "I'm a photographer."

"Oh yeah?" He eyed my ragged leather bag with new interest. "Is that what you got there—cameras? Who you work for?"

"*Playboy*," I said.

He laughed. "Well, goddam! What are you gonna take pictures of—nekkid horses? Haw! I guess you'll be workin' pretty hard when they run the Kentucky Oaks. That's a race just for fillies." He was laughing wildly. "Hell yes! And they'll all be nekkid too!"

I shook my head and said nothing; just stared at him for a moment, trying to look grim. "There's going to be trouble," I said. "My assignment is to take pictures of the riot."

"What riot?"

I hesitated, twirling the ice in my drink. "At the track. On Derby Day. The Black Panthers." I stared at him again. "Don't you read the newspapers?"

The grin on his face had collapsed. "What the *hell* are you talkin about?"

"Well . . . maybe I shouldn't be telling you . . ." I shrugged. "But hell, everybody else seems to know. The cops and the National Guard have been getting ready for six weeks. They have 20,000 troops on alert at Fort Knox. They've warned us—all the press and photographers—to wear helmets and special vests like flak jackets. We were told to expect shooting. . . ."

"No!" he shouted; his hands flew up and hovered momentarily between us, as if to ward off the words he was hearing. Then he whacked his fist on the bar. "Those sons of bitches! God Almighty! The Kentucky Derby!" He kept shaking his head. "No! *Jesus!* That's almost too bad to believe!" Now he seemed to be sagging on the stool, and when he looked up his eyes were misty. "Why? Why *here*? Don't they respect *anything*?"

I shrugged again. "It's not just the Panthers. The FBI says busloads of white crazies are coming in from all over the country—to mix with the crowd and attack all at once, from every direction. They'll be dressed like everybody else. You know—coats and ties and all that. But when the trouble starts . . . well, that's why the cops are so worried."

He sat for a moment, looking hurt and confused and not quite able to digest all this terrible news. Then he cried out: "Oh . . . Jesus! What in the name of God is happening in this country? Where can you get *away* from it?"

"Not here," I said, picking up my bag. "Thanks for the drink . . . and good luck."

He grabbed my arm, urging me to have another, but I said I was overdue at the Press Club and hustled off to get my act together for the awful spectacle. At the airport newsstand I picked up a *Courier-Journal* and scanned the front page headlines: "Nixon Sends GI's into Cambodia to Hit Reds" . . . "B-52's Raid, then 2,000 GI's Advance 20 Miles" . . . "4,000 U.S. Troops Deployed Near Yale as Tension Grows Over Panther Protest." At the bottom of the page was a photo of Diane Crump, soon to become the first woman jockey ever to ride in the Kentucky Derby. The photographer had snapped her "stopping in the barn area to fondle her mount, Fathom." The rest of the paper was spotted with ugly war news and stories of "student unrest." There was no mention of any trouble brewing at a university in Ohio called Kent State.

I went to the Hertz desk to pick up my car, but the moon-faced young swinger in charge said they didn't have any. "You can't rent one anywhere," he assured me. "Our Derby reservations have been booked for six weeks." I explained that my agent had confirmed a white Chrysler convertible for me that very afternoon but he shook his head. "Maybe we'll have a cancellation. Where are you staying?"

I shrugged. "Where's the Texas crowd staying? I want to be with my people."

He sighed. "My friend, you're in trouble. This town is *full*. Always is, for the Derby."

I leaned closer to him, half-whispering: "Look, I'm from *Playboy*. How would you like a job?"

He backed off quickly. "What? Come on, now. What kind of a job?"

"Never mind," I said. "You just blew it." I swept my bag
off the counter and went to find a cab. The bag is a valuable
prop in this kind of work; mine has a lot of baggage tags on
it—SF, LA, NY, Lima, Rome, Bangkok, that sort of thing—
and the most prominent tag of all is a very official, plastic-
coated thing that says "Photog. Playboy Mag." I bought it
from a pimp in Vail, Colorado, and he told me how to use
it. "Never mention *Playboy* until you're sure they've seen
this thing first," he said. "Then, when you see them notice it,
that's the time to strike. They'll go belly up every time. This
thing is magic, I tell you. Pure magic."

Well . . . maybe so. I'd used it on the poor geek in the
bar, and now, humming along in a Yellow Cab toward town,
I felt a little guilty about jangling the poor bugger's brains
with that evil fantasy. But what the hell? Anybody who wan-
ders around the world saying, "Hell yes, I'm from Texas,"
deserves whatever happens to him. And he had, after all,
come here once again to make a nineteenth-century ass of
himself in the midst of some jaded, atavistic freakout with
nothing to recommend it except a very saleable "tradition."
Early in our chat, Jimbo had told me that he hasn't missed
a Derby since 1954. "The little lady won't come anymore,"
he said. "She just grits her teeth and turns me loose for this
one. And when I say 'loose' I do mean *loose!* I toss ten-dollar
bills around like they were goin' outa style! Horses, whiskey, women . . . shit, there's women in this town that'll do
anything for money."

Why not? Money is a good thing to have in these twisted

times. Even Richard Nixon is hungry for it. Only a few days before the Derby he said, "If I had any money I'd invest it in the stock market." And the market, meanwhile, continued its grim slide.

The next day was heavy. With only thirty hours until post time I had no press credentials and—according to the sports editor of the Louisville *Courier-Journal*—no hope at all of getting any. Worse, I needed *two* sets; one for myself and another for Ralph Steadman, the English illustrator who was coming from London to do some Derby drawings. All I knew about him was that this was his first visit to the United States. And the more I pondered that fact, the more it gave me the fear. How would he bear up under the heinous culture shock of being lifted out of London and plunged into a drunken mob scene at the Kentucky Derby? There was no way of knowing. Hopefully, he would arrive at least a day or so ahead, and give himself time to get acclimated. Maybe a few hours of peaceful sightseeing in the Bluegrass country around Lexington. My plan was to pick him up at the airport in the huge Pontiac Ballbuster I'd rented from a used-car salesman named Colonel Quick, then whisk him off to some peaceful setting that might remind him of England.

Colonel Quick had solved the car problem, and money (four times the normal rate) had bought two rooms in a scumbox on the outskirts of town. The only other kink was the task of convincing the moguls at Churchill Downs that *Scanlan's* was such a prestigious sporting journal that common sense compelled them to give us two sets of the best press pickets. This was not easily done. My first call to the publicity office resulted in total failure. The press handler was shocked at the idea that anyone would be stupid enough to apply for press credentials two days before the Derby. "Hell, you can't be serious," he said. "The deadline was two months ago. The press box is full; there's no more room . . . and what the hell is *Scanlan's Monthly* anyway?"

I uttered a painful groan. "Didn't the London office call you? They're flying an artist over to do the paintings. Steadman. He's Irish, I think. Very famous over there. Yes. I just got in from the Coast. The San Francisco office told me we were all set."

He seemed interested, and even sympathetic, but there was nothing he could do. I flattered him with more gibberish, and finally he offered a compromise: he could get us two passes to the clubhouse grounds but the clubhouse itself and especially the press box were out of the question.

"That sounds a little weird," I said. "It's unacceptable. We *must* have access to everything. *All* of it. The spectacle, the people, the pageantry and certainly the race. You don't think we came all this way to watch the damn thing on television, do you? One way or another we'll get inside. Maybe we'll have to bribe a guard—or even Mace somebody." (I had picked up a spray can of Mace in a downtown drugstore for $5.98 and suddenly, in the midst of that phone talk, I was struck by the hideous possibilities of using it out at the track. Macing ushers at the narrow gates to the clubhouse inner sanctum, then slipping quickly inside, firing a huge load of Mace into the governor's box, just as the race starts. Or Macing helpless drunks in the clubhouse restroom, for their own good ...)

By noon on Friday I was still without credentials and still unable to locate Steadman. For all I knew he'd changed his mind and gone back to London. Finally, after giving up on Steadman and trying unsuccessfully to reach my man in the press office, I decided my only hope for credentials was to go out to the track and confront the man in person, with no warning—demanding only one pass now, instead of two, and talking very fast with a strange lilt in my voice, like a man trying hard to control some inner frenzy. On the way out, I stopped at the motel desk to cash a check. Then, as a useless afterthought, I asked if by any wild chance a Mr. Steadman had checked in.

The lady on the desk was about fifty years old and very peculiar-looking; when I mentioned Steadman's name she nodded, without looking up from whatever she was writing, and said in a low voice, "You bet he did." Then she favored me with a big smile. "Yes, indeed. Mr. Steadman just left for the racetrack. Is he a friend of yours?"

I shook my head. "I'm supposed to be working with him, but I don't even know what he looks like. Now, goddammit, I'll have to find him in that mob at the track."

She chuckled. "You won't have any trouble finding him. You could pick *that* man out of any crowd."

"Why?" I asked. "What's wrong with him? What does he look like?"

"Well ..." she said, still grinning, "he's the funniest looking thing I've seen in a long time. He has this . . . ah . . . this *growth* all over his face. As a matter of fact it's all over his *head*." She nodded. "You'll know him when you see him; don't worry about that."

Creeping Jesus, I thought. That screws the press credentials. I had a vision of some nerve-rattling geek all covered with matted hair and string-warts showing up in the press office and demanding *Scanlan's* press packet. Well . . . what the hell? We could always load up on acid and spend the day roaming around the clubhouse grounds with big sketch pads, laughing hysterically at the natives and swilling mint juleps so the cops wouldn't think we're abnormal. Perhaps even make the act pay: set up an easel with a big sign saying, "Let a Foreign Artist Paint Your Portrait, $10 Each. Do It NOW!"

I took the expressway out to the track, driving very fast and jumping the monster car back and forth between lanes, driving with a beer in one hand and my mind so muddled that I almost crushed a Volkswagen full of nuns when I swerved to catch the right exit. There was a slim chance, I thought, that I might be able to catch the ugly Britisher before he checked in.

But Steadman was already in the press box when I got there, a bearded young Englishman wearing a tweed coat and RAF sunglasses. There was nothing particularly odd about him. No facial veins or clumps of bristly warts. I told him about the motel woman's description and he seemed puzzled.

"Don't let it bother you," I said. "Just keep in mind for the next few days that we're in Louisville, Kentucky. Not London. Not even New York. This is a weird place. You're lucky that mental defective at the motel didn't jerk a pistol out of the cash register and blow a big hole in you." I laughed, but he looked worried.

"Just pretend you're visiting a huge outdoor loony bin," I said. "If the inmates get out of control we'll soak them down with Mace." I showed him the can of "Chemical Billy," resisting the urge to fire it across the room at a rat-faced man typing diligently in the Associated Press section. We were standing at the bar, sipping the management's Scotch and congratulating each other on our sudden, unexplained luck in picking up two sets of fine press credentials. The lady at the desk had been very friendly to him, he said. "I just told her my name and she gave me the whole works."

By midafternoon we had everything under control. We had seats looking down on the finish line, color TV and a free bar in the press room, and a selection of passes that would take us anywhere from the clubhouse to the jockey room. The only thing we lacked was unlimited access to the clubhouse inner sanctum in sections "F&G" . . . and I felt we needed that, to see the whiskey gentry in action. The governor, a swinish neo-Nazi hack named Louie Nunn, would be in "G," along with Barry Goldwater and Colonel Sanders. I felt we'd be legal in a box in "G" where we could rest and sip juleps, soak up a bit of atmosphere and the Derby's special vibrations.

The bars and dining rooms are also in "F&G," and the clubhouse bars on Derby Day are a very special kind of scene. Along with the politicians, society belles and local captains of commerce, every half-mad dingbat who ever had any pretensions to anything at all within five hundred miles of Louisville will show up there to get strutting drunk and slap a lot of backs and generally make himself obvious. The Paddock bar is probably the best place in the track to sit and watch faces. Nobody minds being stared at; that's what they're in there for. Some people spend most of their time in the Paddock; they can hunker down at one of the many wooden tables, lean back in a comfortable chair and watch the ever-changing odds flash up and down on the big tote board outside the window. Black waiters in white serving jackets move through the crowd with trays of drinks, while the experts ponder their racing forms and the hunch bettors pick lucky numbers or scan the lineup for right-sounding names. There is a constant flow of traffic to and from the pari-mutuel windows outside in the wooden corridors. Then, as post time nears, the crowd thins out as people go back to their boxes.

Clearly, we were going to have to figure out some way to spend more time in the clubhouse tomorrow. But the "walkaround" press passes to F&G were only good for thirty minutes at a time, presumably to allow the newspaper types to rush in and out for photos or quick interviews, but to prevent drifters like Steadman and me from spending all day in the clubhouse, harassing the gentry and rifling the odd handbag or two while cruising around the boxes. Or Macing the governor. The time limit was no problem on Friday, but on Derby Day the walkaround passes would be in heavy demand. And since it took about ten minutes to get from the press box to the Paddock, and ten more minutes to get back, that didn't leave much time for serious people-watching. And unlike most of the others in the press box, we didn't give a hoot in hell what was happening on the track. We had come there to watch the *real* beasts perform.

Later Friday afternoon, we went out on the balcony of the press box and I tried to describe the difference between what we were seeing today and what would be happening tomorrow. This was the first time I'd been to a Derby in ten years, but before that, when I lived in Louisville, I used to go every year. Now, looking down from the press box, I pointed to the huge grassy meadow enclosed by the track. "That whole thing," I said, "will be jammed with people; fifty thousand or so, and most of them staggering drunk. It's a fantastic scene— thousands of people fainting, crying, copulating, trampling each other and fighting with broken whiskey bottles. We'll have to spend some time out there, but it's hard to move around, too many bodies."

"Is it safe out there? Will we *ever* come back?"

"Sure," I said. "We'll just have to be careful not to step on anybody's stomach and start a fight." I shrugged. "Hell, this clubhouse scene right below us will be almost as bad as the infield. Thousands of raving, stumbling drunks, getting angrier and angrier as they lose more and more money. By midafternoon they'll be guzzling mint juleps with both hands and vomiting on each other between races. The whole place will be jammed with bodies, shoulder to shoulder. It's hard to move around. The aisles will be slick with vomit; people falling down and grabbing at your legs to keep from being stomped. Drunks pissing on themselves in the betting lines. Dropping handfuls of money and fighting to stoop over and pick it up."

He looked so nervous that I laughed. "I'm just kidding," I said. "Don't worry. At the first hint of trouble I'll start pumping this 'Chemical Billy' into the crowd."

He had done a few good sketches, but so far we hadn't seen that special kind of face that I felt we would need for the lead drawing. It was a face I'd seen a thousand times at every Derby I'd ever been to. I saw it, in my head, as the mask of the whiskey gentry—a pretentious mix of booze, failed dreams and a terminal identity crisis; the inevitable result of too much inbreeding in a closed and ignorant culture. One of the key genetic rules in breeding dogs, horses or any other kind of thoroughbred is that close inbreeding tends to magnify the weak points in a bloodline as well as the strong points. In horse breeding, for instance, there is a definite risk in breeding two fast horses who are both a little crazy. The offspring will likely be very fast and also very crazy. So the trick in breeding thoroughbreds is to retain the good traits and filter out the bad. But the breeding of humans is not so wisely supervised, particularly in a narrow Southern society where the closest kind of inbreeding is not only stylish and acceptable, but far more convenient—to the parents—than setting their offspring free to find their own mates, for their own reasons and in their own ways. ("Goddam, did you hear about Smitty's daughter? She went crazy in Boston last week and married a nigger!")

So the face I was trying to find in Churchill Downs that weekend was a symbol, in my own mind, of the whole doomed atavistic culture that makes the Kentucky Derby what it is.

On our way back to the motel after Friday's races I warned Steadman about some of the other problems we'd have to cope with. Neither of us had brought any strange illegal drugs, so we would have to get by on booze. "You should keep in mind," I said, "that almost everybody you talk to from now on will be drunk. People who seem very pleasant at first might suddenly swing at you for no reason at all." He nodded, staring straight ahead. He seemed to be getting a little numb and I tried to cheer him up by inviting him to dinner that night, with my brother.

Back at the motel we talked for a while about America, the South, England—just relaxing a bit before dinner. There was no way either of us could have known, at the time, that it would be the last normal conversation we would have. From that point on, the weekend became a vicious, drunken nightmare. We both went completely to pieces. The main problem was my prior attachment to Louisville, which naturally led to meetings with old friends, relatives, etc., many of whom were in the process of falling apart, going mad, plotting divorces, cracking up under the strain of terrible debts or recovering from bad accidents. Right in the middle of the whole frenzied Derby action, a member of my own family had to be institutionalized. This added a certain amount of strain to the situation, and since poor Steadman had no choice but to take whatever came his way, he was subjected to shock after shock.

Another problem was his habit of sketching people he met in the various social situations I dragged him into—then giving them the sketches. The results were always unfortunate. I warned him several times about letting the subjects see his foul renderings, but for some perverse reason he kept doing it. Consequently, he was regarded with fear and loathing by nearly everyone who'd seen or even heard about his work. He couldn't understand it. "It's sort of a joke," he kept saying. "Why, in England it's quite normal. People don't take offense. They understand that I'm just putting them on a bit."

"Fuck England," I said. "This is Middle America. These people regard what you're doing to them as a brutal, bilious insult. Look what happened last night. I thought my brother was going to tear your head off."

Steadman shook his head sadly. "But I liked him. He struck me as a very decent, straightforward sort."

"Look, Ralph," I said. "Let's not kid ourselves. That was a very horrible drawing you gave him. It was the face of a monster. It got on his nerves very badly." I shrugged. "Why in hell do you think we left the restaurant so fast?"

"I thought it was because of the Mace," he said.

"What Mace?"

He grinned. "When you shot it at the headwaiter, don't you remember?"

"Hell, that was nothing," I said. "I missed him . . . and we were leaving, anyway."

"But it got all over us," he said. "The room was full of that damn gas. Your brother was sneezing and his wife was crying. My eyes hurt for two hours. I couldn't see to draw when we got back to the motel."

"That's right," I said. "The stuff got on her leg, didn't it?"

"She was angry," he said.

"Yeah . . . well, okay . . . Let's just figure we fucked up about equally on that one," I said. "But from now on let's try to be careful when we're around people I know. You won't sketch them and I won't Mace them. We'll just try to relax and get drunk."

"Right," he said. "We'll go native."

It was Saturday morning, the day of the Big Race, and we were having breakfast in a plastic hamburger palace called the Fish-Meat Village. Our rooms were just across the road in the Brown Suburban Hotel. They had a dining room, but the food was so bad that we couldn't handle it anymore. The waitresses seemed to be suffering from shin splints; they moved around very slowly, moaning and cursing the "darkies" in the kitchen.

Steadman liked the Fish-Meat place because it had fish and chips. I preferred the "French toast," which was really pancake batter, fried to the proper thickness and then chopped out with a sort of cookie cutter to resemble pieces of toast.

Beyond drink and lack of sleep, our only real problem at that point was the question of access to the clubhouse. Finally we decided to go ahead and steal two passes, if necessary, rather than miss that part of the action. This was the last coherent decision we were able to make for the next forty-eight hours. From that point on—almost from the very moment we started out to the track—we lost all control of events and spent the rest of the weekend churning around in a sea of drunken horrors. My notes and recollections from Derby Day are somewhat scrambled.

But now, looking at the big red notebook I carried all through that scene, I see more or less what happened. The book itself is somewhat mangled and bent; some of the pages are torn, others are shriveled and stained by what appears to be whiskey, but taken as a whole, with sporadic memory flashes, the notes seem to tell the story. To wit:

Rain all nite until dawn. No sleep. Christ, here we go, a nightmare of mud and madness . . . But no. By noon the sun burns through—perfect day, not even humid.

Steadman is now worried about fire. Somebody told him about the clubhouse catching on fire two years ago. Could it happen again? Horrible. Trapped in the press box. Holocaust. A hundred thousand people fighting to get out.

Drunks screaming in the flames and the mud, crazed horses running wild. Blind in the smoke. Grandstand collapsing into the flames with us on the roof. Poor Ralph is about to crack. Drinking heavily, into the Haig & Haig.

Out to the track in a cab, avoid that terrible parking in people's front yards, $25 each, toothless old men on the street with big signs: PARK HERE, flagging cars in the yard. "That's fine, boy, never mind the tulips." Wild hair on his head, straight up like a clump of reeds.

Sidewalks full of people all moving in the same direction, towards Churchill Downs. Kids hauling coolers and blankets, teenyboppers in tight pink shorts, many blacks ... black dudes in white felt hats with leopard-skin bands, cops waving traffic along.

The mob was thick for many blocks around the track; very slow going in the crowd, very hot. On the way to the press box elevator, just inside the clubhouse, we came on a row of soldiers all carrying long white riot sticks. About two platoons, with helmets. A man walking next to us said they were waiting for the governor and his party. Steadman eyed them nervously. "Why do they have those clubs?"

"Black Panthers," I said. Then I remembered good old "Jimbo" at the airport and I wondered what he was thinking right now. Probably very nervous; the place was teeming with cops and soldiers. We pressed on through the crowd, through many gates, past the paddock where the jockeys bring the horses out and parade around for a while before each race so the bettors can get a good look. Five million dollars will be bet today. Many winners, more losers. What the hell. The press gate was jammed up with people trying to get in, shouting at the guards, waving strange press badges: Chicago Sporting Times, Pittsburgh Police Athletic League ... they were all turned away. "Move on, fella, make way for the working press." We shoved through the crowd and into the elevator, then quickly up to the free bar. Why not? Get it on. Very hot today, not feeling well, must be this rotten climate. The press box was cool and airy, plenty of room to walk around and balcony seats for watching the race or looking down at the crowd. We got a betting sheet and went outside.

Pink faces with a stylish Southern sag, old Ivy styles, seersucker coats and buttondown collars. "Mayblossom Senility" (Steadman's phrase) ... burnt out early or maybe just not much to burn in the first place. Not much energy in these faces, not much *curiosity*. Suffering in silence, nowhere to go after thirty in this life, just hang on and humor the children. Let the young enjoy themselves while they can. Why not?

The grim reaper comes early in this league ... banshees on the lawn at night, screaming out there beside that little iron nigger in jockey clothes. Maybe he's the one who's screaming. Bad DT's and too many snarls at the bridge club. Going down with the stock market. Oh Jesus, the kid has wrecked the new car, wrapped it around the big stone pillar at the bottom of the driveway. Broken leg? Twisted eye? Send him off to Yale, they can cure anything up there.

Yale? Did you see today's paper? New Haven is under siege. Yale is swarming with Black Panthers. . . . I tell you, Colonel, the world has gone mad, stone mad. Why, they tell me a goddam woman jockey might ride in the Derby today.

I left Steadman sketching in the Paddock bar and went off to place our bets on the fourth race. When I came back he was staring intently at a group of young men around a table not far away. "Jesus, look at the corruption in that face!" he whispered. "Look at the madness, the fear, the greed!" I looked, then quickly turned my back on the table he was sketching. The face he'd picked out to draw was the face of an old friend of mine, a prep school football star in the good old days with a sleek red Chevy convertible and a very quick hand, it was said, with the snaps of a 32 B brassiere. They called him "Cat Man."

"But now, a dozen years later, I wouldn't have recognized him anywhere but here, where I should have expected to find him, in the Paddock bar on Derby Day . . . fat slanted eyes and a pimp's smile, blue silk suit and his friends looking like crooked bank tellers on a binge . . .

Steadman wanted to see some Kentucky Colonels, but he wasn't sure what they looked like. I told him to go back to the clubhouse men's rooms and look for men in white linen suits vomiting in the urinals. "They'll usually have large brown whiskey stains on the fronts of their suits," I said. "But watch the shoes, that's the tip-off. Most of them manage to avoid vomiting on their own clothes, but they never miss their shoes."

In a box not far from ours was Colonel Anna Friedman Goldman, *Chairman and Keeper of the Great Seal of the Honorable Order of Kentucky Colonels*. Not all the 76 million or so Kentucky Colonels could make it to the Derby this year, but many had kept the faith, and several days prior to the Derby they gathered for their annual dinner at the Seelbach Hotel.

The Derby, the actual race, was scheduled for late afternoon, and as the magic hour approached I suggested to Steadman that we should probably spend some time in the infield, that boiling sea of people across the track from the clubhouse. He seemed a little nervous about it, but since none of the awful things I'd warned him about had happened so far—no race riots, firestorms or savage drunken attacks— he shrugged and said, "Right, let's do it."

To get there we had to pass through many gates, each one a step down in status, then through a tunnel under the track. Emerging from the tunnel was such a culture shock that it took us a while to adjust. "God almighty!" Steadman muttered. "This is a . . . Jesus!" He plunged ahead with his tiny camera, stepping over bodies, and I followed, trying to take notes.

Total chaos, no way to see the race, not even the track . . . nobody cares. Big lines at the outdoor betting windows, then stand back to watch winning numbers flash on the big board, like a giant bingo game.

Old blacks arguing about bets; "Hold on there, I'll handle

this" (waving pint of whiskey, fistful of dollar bills); girl riding piggyback, T-shirt says, "Stolen from Fort Lauderdale Jail." Thousands of teen-agers, group singing "Let the Sun Shine In," ten soldiers guarding the American flag and a huge fat drunk wearing a blue football jersey (No. 80) reeling around with quart of beer in hand.

No booze sold out here, too dangerous . . . no bathrooms either. Muscle Beach . . . Woodstock . . . many cops with riot sticks, but no sign of a riot. Far across the track the clubhouse looks like a postcard from the Kentucky Derby.

We went back to the clubhouse to watch the big race. When the crowd stood to face the flag and sing "My Old Kentucky Home," Steadman faced the crowd and sketched frantically. Somewhere up in the boxes a voice screeched, "Turn around, you hairy freak!" The race itself was only two minutes long, and even from our super-status seats and using 12-power glasses, there was no way to see what was really happening. Later, watching a TV rerun in the press box, we saw what happened to our horses. Holy Land, Ralph's choice, stumbled and lost his jockey in the final turn. Mine, Silent Screen, had the lead coming into the stretch, but faded to fifth at the finish. The winner was a 16–1 shot named Dust Commander.

Moments after the race was over, the crowd surged wildly for the exits, rushing for cabs and buses. The next day's *Courier* told of violence in the parking lot; people were punched and trampled, pockets were picked, children lost, bottles hurled. But we missed all this, having retired to the press box for a bit of post-race drinking. By this time we were both half-crazy from too much whiskey, sun fatigue, culture shock, lack of sleep and general dissolution. We hung around the press box long enough to watch a mass interview with the winning owner, a dapper little man named Lehmann who said he had just flown into Louisville that morning from Nepal, where he'd "bagged a record tiger." The sportswriters murmured their admiration and a waiter filled Lehmann's glass with Chivas Regal. He had just won $127,000 with a horse that cost him $6,500 two years ago. His occupation, he said, was "retired contractor." And then he added, with a big grin, "I just retired."

The rest of that day blurs into madness. The rest of that night too. And all the next day and night. Such horrible things occurred that I can't bring myself even to think about them now, much less put them down in print. Steadman was lucky to get out of Louisville without serious injuries, and I was lucky to get out at all. One of my clearest memories of that vicious time is Ralph being attacked by one of my old friends in the billiard room of the Pendennis Club in downtown Louisville on Saturday night. The man had ripped his own shirt open to the waist before deciding that Ralph was after his wife. No blows were struck, but the emotional effects were massive. Then, as a sort of final horror, Steadman put his fiendish pen to work and tried to patch things up by doing a little sketch of the girl he'd been accused of hustling. That finished us in the Pendennis.

———

Sometime around ten-thirty Monday morning I was awakened by a scratching sound at my door. I leaned out of bed and pulled the curtain back just far enough to see Steadman outside. "What the fuck do you want?" I shouted.

"What about having breakfast?" he said.

I lunged out of bed and tried to open the door, but it caught on the night-chain and banged shut again. I couldn't cope with the chain! The thing wouldn't come out of the track—so I ripped it out of the wall with a vicious jerk on the door. Ralph didn't blink. "Bad luck," he muttered.

I could barely see him. My eyes were swollen almost shut and the sudden burst of sunlight through the door left me stunned and helpless like a sick mole. Steadman was mumbling about sickness and terrible heat; I fell back on the bed and tried to focus on him as he moved around the room in a very distracted way for a few moments, then suddenly darted over to the beer bucket and seized a Colt .45. "Christ," I said. "You're getting out of control."

He nodded and ripped the cap off, taking a long drink. "You know, this is really awful," he said finally. "I *must* get out of this place . . ." he shook his head nervously. "The plane leaves at three-thirty, but I don't know if I'll make it."

I barely heard him. My eyes had finally opened enough for me to focus on the mirror across the room and I was stunned at the shock of recognition. For a confused instant I thought that Ralph had brought somebody with him—a model for that one special face we'd been looking for. There he was, by God—a puffy, drink-ravaged, disease-ridden caricature . . . like an awful cartoon version of an old snapshot in some once-proud mother's family photo album. It was the face we'd been looking for—and it was, of course, my own. Horrible, horrible. . . .

"Maybe I should sleep a while longer," I said. "Why don't you go on over to the Fish-Meat place and eat some of those rotten fish and chips? Then come back and get me around noon. I feel too near death to hit the streets at this hour."

He shook his head. "No . . . no . . . I think I'll go back upstairs and work on those drawings for a while." He leaned down to fetch two more cans out of the beer bucket. "I tried to work earlier," he said, "but my hands keep trembling . . . It's teddible, teddible."

"You've got to stop this drinking," I said.

He nodded. "I know. This is no good, no good at all. But for some reason it makes me feel better . . ."

"Not for long," I said. "You'll probably collapse into some kind of hysterical DT's tonight—probably just about the time you get off the plane at Kennedy. They'll zip you up in a straitjacket and drag you down to the Tombs, then beat you on the kidneys with big sticks until you straighten out."

He shrugged and wandered out, pulling the door shut behind him. I went back to bed for another hour or so, and later—after the daily grapefruit juice run to the Nite Owl Food Mart—we had our last meal at Fish-Meat Village: a fine lunch of dough and butcher's offal, fried in heavy grease.

By this time Ralph wouldn't even order coffee; he kept asking for more water. "It's the only thing they have that's fit for human consumption," he explained. Then, with an hour or so to kill before he had to catch the plane, we spread his drawings out on the table and pondered them for a while, wondering if he'd caught the proper spirit of the thing . . . but we couldn't make up our minds. His hands were shaking so badly that he had trouble holding the paper, and my vision was so blurred that I could barely see what he'd drawn. "Shit," I said. "We both look worse than anything you've drawn here."

He smiled. "You know — I've been thinking about that," he said. "We came down here to see this teddible scene: people all pissed out of their minds and vomiting on themselves and all that . . . and now, you know what? It's us. . . ."

Huge Pontiac Ballbuster blowing through traffic on the expressway.

A radio news bulletin says the National Guard is massacring students at Kent State and Nixon is still bombing Cambodia. The journalist is driving, ignoring his passenger who is now nearly naked after taking off most of his clothing, which he holds out the window, trying to wind-wash the Mace out of it. His eyes are bright red and his face and chest are soaked with the beer he's been using to rinse the awful chemical off his flesh. The front of his woolen trousers is soaked with vomit; his body is racked with fits of coughing and wild choking sobs. The journalist rams the big car through traffic and into a spot in front of the terminal, then he reaches over to open the door on the passenger's side and shoves the Englishman out, snarling: "Bug off, you worthless faggot! You twisted pigfucker! [Crazed laughter.] If I weren't sick I'd kick your ass all the way to Bowling Green—you scumsucking foreign geek. Mace is too good for you ... We can do without your kind in Kentucky."

[1970]

WOODY ALLEN

✳

A Look at Organized Crime

It is no secret that organized crime in America takes in over forty billion dollars a year. This is quite a profitable sum, especially when one considers that the Mafia spends very little for office supplies. Reliable sources indicate that the Cosa Nostra laid out no more than six thousand dollars last year for personalized stationery, and even less for staples. Furthermore, they have one secretary who does all the typing, and only three small rooms for headquarters, which they share with the Fred Persky Dance Studio.

Last year, organized crime was directly responsible for more than one hundred murders, and *mafiosi* participated indirectly in several hundred more, either by lending the killers carfare or by holding their coats. Other illicit activities engaged in by Cosa Nostra members included gambling, narcotics, prostitution, hijacking, loansharking, and the transportation of a large whitefish across the state line for immoral purposes. The tentacles of this corrupt empire even reach into the government itself. Only a few months ago, two gang lords under federal indictment spent the night at the White House and the President slept on the sofa.

HISTORY OF ORGANIZED CRIME
IN THE UNITED STATES

In 1921, Thomas (The Butcher) Covello and Ciro (The Tailor) Santucci attempted to organize disparate ethnic groups of the underworld and thus take over Chicago. This was foiled when Albert (The Logical Positivist) Corillo assassinated Kid Lipsky by locking him in a closet and sucking all the air out through a straw. Lipsky's brother Mendy (alias Mendy Lewis, alias Mendy Larsen, alias Mendy Alias) avenged Lipsky's murder by abducting Santucci's brother Gaetano (also known as Little Tony, or Rabbi Henry Sharpstein) and returning him several weeks later in twenty-seven separate mason jars. This signalled the beginning of a bloodbath.

Dominick (The Herpetologist) Mione shot Lucky Lorenzo (so nicknamed when a bomb that went off in his hat failed to kill him) outside a bar in Chicago. In return, Corilo and his men traced Mione to Newark and made his head into a wind instrument. At this point, the Vitale gang, run by Giuseppe Vitale (real name Quincy Baedeker), made their move to take over all bootlegging in Harlem from Irish Larry Doyle—a racketeer so suspicious that he refused to let anybody in New York ever get behind him, and walked down the street constantly pirouetting and spinning around.

Doyle was killed when the Squillante Construction Company decided to erect their new offices on the bridge of his nose. Doyle's lieutenant, Little Petey (Big Petey) Ross, now took command; he resisted the Vitale takeover and lured Vitale to an empty midtown garage on the pretext that a costume party was being held there. Unsuspecting, Vitale walked into the garage dressed as a giant mouse, and was instantly riddled with machine-gun bullets. Out of loyalty to their slain chief, Vitale's men immediately defected to Ross. So did Vitale's fiancée, Bea Moretti, a showgirl and star of the hit Broadway musical *Say Kaddish*, who wound up marrying Ross, although she later sued him for divorce, charging that he once spread an unpleasant ointment on her.

Fearing federal intervention, Vincent Columbraro, the Buttered Toast King, called for a truce. (Columbraro has such tight control over all buttered toast moving in and out of New Jersey that one word from him could ruin breakfast for two-thirds of the nation.) All members of the underworld were summoned to a diner in Perth Amboy, where Columbraro told them that internal warfare must stop and that from then on they had to dress decently and stop slinking around. Letters formerly signed with a black hand would in the future be signed "Best Wishes," and all territory would be divided equally, with New Jersey going to Columbraro's mother. Thus the Mafia, or Cosa Nostra (literally, "my toothpaste" or "our toothpaste"), was born. Two days later, Columbraro got into a nice hot tub to take a bath and has been missing for the past forty-six years.

Mob Structure

The Cosa Nostra is structured like any government or large corporation—or group of gangsters, for that matter. At the top is the *capo di tutti capi*, or boss of all bosses. Meetings are held at his house, and he is responsible for supplying all cold cuts and ice cubes. Failure to do so means instant death. (Death, incidentally, is one of the worst things that can happen to a Cosa Nostra member, and many prefer simply to pay a fine.) Under the boss of bosses are his lieutenants, each of whom runs one section of town with his "family." Mafia families do not consist of a wife and children who always go to places like the circus or on picnics. They are actually groups of rather serious men, whose main joy in life comes from seeing how long certain people can stay under the East River before they start gurgling.

Initiation into the Mafia is quite complicated. A proposed member is blindfolded and led into a dark room. Pieces of Cranshaw melon are placed in his pockets, and he is required to hop around on one foot and cry out, "Toodles! Toodles!" Next, his lower lip is pulled out and snapped back by all the members of the board, or *commissione*; some may even wish to do it twice. Following this, some oats are put on his head. If he complains, he is disqualified. If, however, he says, "Good, I like oats on my head," he is welcomed into the brotherhood. This is done by kissing him on the cheek and shaking his hand. From that moment on, he is not permitted to eat chutney, to amuse his friends by imitating a hen, or to kill anybody named Vito.

CONCLUSIONS

Organized crime is a blight on our nation. While many young Americans are lured into a career of crime by its promise of an easy life, most criminals actually must work long hours, frequently in buildings without air-conditioning. Identifying criminals is up to each of us. Usually they can be recognized by their large cufflinks and their failure to stop eating when the man sitting next to them is hit by a falling anvil. The best methods of combatting organized crime are:

1. Telling the criminals you are not at home.

2. Calling the police whenever an unusual number of men from the Sicilian Laundry Company begin singing in your foyer.

3. Wiretapping.

Wiretapping cannot be employed indiscriminately, but its effectiveness is illustrated by this transcript of a conversation between two gang bosses in the New York area whose phones had been tapped by the F.B.I.

Anthony: Hello? Rico?
Rico: Hello?
Anthony: Rico?
Rico: Hello.
Anthony: Rico?
Rico: I can't hear you.
Anthony: Is that you, Rico? I can't hear you.
Rico: What?
Anthony: Can you hear me?
Rico: Hello?

Anthony: Rico?
Rico: We have a bad connection.
Anthony: Can you hear me?
Rico: Hello?
Anthony: Rico?
Rico: Hello?
Anthony: Operator, we have a bad connection.
Operator: Hang up and dial again, sir.
Rico: Hello?

Because of this evidence, Anthony (The Fish) Rotunno and Rico Panzini were convicted and are currently serving fifteen years in Sing Sing for illegal possession of Bensonhurst.

[1970]

BRUCE JAY FRIEDMAN

*

The Tax Man

Locked in combat with the government over back taxes, Ullman won some points, lost a few, but could not get the revenue service to accept his plush East Side apartment as a "working office."

"What do they think I use it for?" Ullman asked his accountant.

"They don't know," said Tisch. "They just sense it isn't for work."

"Then let them come up and see it," said Ullman. "I've got nothing to hide."

"I wouldn't do that," said the cautious Tisch. "I'd settle."

"No way," said Ullman. "I'm entitled to have whatever kind of office I like. Send 'em up."

In truth, Ullman worked a little in the apartment and played a lot. But what business was that of the government's? For all they knew, he slaved away in the place from dawn till midnight and never had any fun there. The plush decor? He needed it to put him in the mood for hard work. Howard Hughes probably had twenty such places, all over the globe, each of them a clean tax deduction. Why not one for Ullman?

On the day before the agent arrived, Ullman ran around and tried to give the place more of an office-type look. He wheeled the bar into a closet, put away his erotic statuary and scattered paperclips, rubber bands and file cards on the end tables. Here and there he set up tired piles of manuscripts.

The agent's name was Gowran, a fellow who kept his teeth gnashed together as though he were in severe abdominal pain.

"Would you like a drink?" Ullman asked him. "I don't know the protocol."

"Not just now," said Gowran, running his finger along the edge of a handsomely designed leather couch. "So this is the so-called office."

"Not so-called," said Ullman. "Just the office."

"Some place," said Gowran. "Must have cost you a bundle to furnish it."

"Not really," said Ullman. "You use tricks. Decorator short-cuts that make a little go a long way. Look, let's not fool around. This is my office. I work here. I happen to like nice surroundings. What's the government saying? That I have to work in a drab little place?"

"The government is saying take it easy," said Gowran, easing himself into a white futuristic armchair and practically disappearing in the cushions. "What about the bedroom? You work back there, too?" Ullman had hoped he wouldn't get around to that. He had devoted most of his money and effort to that room, paneling all four walls with mirrors, and the ceiling as well. He had bought the thickest rug made and put in a heavily gadgeted bed—in the great man-about-town tradition. Just his luck, the revenue agent had taken a peek at the set-up on the way into the living room. "I take naps back there," said Ullman. "Half a dozen a day. That's my style of working. Work a little, take a nap, then work some more. You want me to stop that and not take any naps, is that it?"

"Let me see your calendar," said Gowran. Ullman could not tell if he was winning or losing with this fellow, who kept his teeth gnashed together but otherwise had a neutral expression. He was prepared to go along with Gowran until the fellow stepped out of line, at which point he would ask that his case be turned over to higher-ups. Tisch had told him he could do that. But it was difficult to tell if Gowran was stepping out of line. He probably wasn't. So Ullman handed over his daily record book. He had worked on it for two weeks to make it look completely legitimate.

"You certainly take a lot of cabs," said Gowran, flipping through the diary. "No, the government isn't saying you should walk. The government is merely making an observation."

"The government is cute," said Ullman. Gowran snickered, a gray civil service exhalation of breath, and then plowed on. "Who's this guy Berger?" he asked, still studying the diary. "You've had him to lunch six times and I'm still in January. You both must be very hungry guys."

Actually, this was a break for Ullman. Most of the Berger lunches were legitimate, and in addition, he had called Berger, a public relations man, and put him on alert that the government might be in touch. And to please back him up all the way. He was in great shape on Berger, not so good on Hellwig, Danziger and Ferris, all of whom were down for fake lunches and might not come through if Gowran checked them out. "Why don't you call Phil Berger and ask him if we talked business all those times or not," said Ullman. "Here, I'll give you his number."

"That's all right," said Gowran, making a few notations in his record book and then putting it away. "Let's take a break. I know about these calendars. Everybody bullshits their way through them. You probably just got finished padding yours the second I got here. How about that drink you mentioned before?" Gowran loosened his collar, kicked out his legs and made himself comfortable. Ullman winced at the thought of this fellow with his two-bit civil service suit getting comfortable on his fine furniture, but he rushed to mix a drink all the same. If it ever got down to a pitched battle, he could say that Gowran drank on the job.

"You go to a lot of restaurants," said Gowran. "Try a place called Andy's. Terrific parmigiana and you get unlimited pasta and fruit for the same price. You get out of there, you feel like you're gonna bust."

Ullman could just about imagine what kind of place Andy's was. With its all-you-can-eat policy on pasta and fruit. He almost threw up at the thought of it, but he made believe he was jotting down the name and address for future reference.

"I don't care how many restaurants you know," he said, joining Gowran in a drink. "You can always use another one."

"Must be nice work you do," said Gowran. "Going to all those lunches and then sitting around in a place like this to do your work. With this view."

"I really do work up here," said Ullman, still defensive. "I just happen to like nice surroundings. I've worked in flophouses and now I figure I deserve this."

"Hey," said Gowran, waggling a finger. "We're taking a break, right?"

"Right," said Ullman, relaxing slightly.

"You must meet a lot of nice people," said Gowran, "a lot of good-looking chicks."

"That's right," said Ullman. "They do sort of drift into the theater if they're good-looking."

"What do you do," said Gowran, "you get these thoughts and then you sort of write them down on paper?"

"Something like that," said Ullman.

"That's nice work," said Gowran. "Hey," he said, looking at his watch and springing to his feet. "I'm supposed to meet my new girl. Can I use your phone?"

"Sure," said Ullman. "If it would make it more convenient, she can pick you up here." The drink had evidently made him feel a bit more convivial than he realized.

"That'd be terrific," said Gowran. "She'd love to see a place like this."

Gowran gave the girl the address over the phone, Ullman

wondering how he could speak through those gnashed and battered teeth. He called the girl "little one," and Ullman figured this was internal revenue style. Romantic internal revenue style. He could just about imagine the girl.

Actually, she wasn't that bad. For one thing she probably should have been called "big one." She was a heavy-set girl, probably German, with languid, somewhat dazed eyes and an attractively slow-rolling style of movement. From the moment she showed up, she slowed everything in the room down. It took a few beats for Ullman to realize how attractive she was and when he did he was a little annoyed. For one thing, it had to change his view of Gowran. He had put the fellow into some kind of cramped and petty second-rate internal revenue slot. If that was his proper category, what was he doing with Ingrid? Also, it made Ullman look bad. He worked in the theater. He was supposed to be the one with Ingrids.

"The thing about this girl," said Gowran, who suddenly looked a bit dashing, "is that she'll do anything."

"Nothing bothers me," said Ingrid.

"Do something crazy," said Gowran, with a heavy-handed wink at Ullman.

Slowly, lazily, the girl stood on her hands, using Ullman's expensive bookshelves to balance herself. Her skirt poured over her head, Ullman dazzled by the erotically chunky spectacle. "It means nothing to me," said Ingrid, lightly regaining her feet after just the right amount of time and with a single movement getting her blonde hair to fall back over her shoulders. The doorbell rang and Ullman braced himself. More Ingrids? It was the dry cleaner, after Ullman's dirty suits. Ullman had them ready in a bundle and tossed it to the fellow. As the cleaner sorted it out, Gowran said, "Let's have some fun," and motioned to Ingrid. She took off her blouse, undid her bra and thrust a heavy breast against the startled dry cleaner's face. "Say," he said, "what kind of party is this?" Ingrid allowed him to enjoy it a moment and then dismissed him with a light kiss on the forehead. "She something?" said Gowran, with a chuckle. "Whatever you like," said Ingrid, with an almost bored snap of her fingers, "I do it."

"Yet I feel sorry for the kid," said Gowran, when the puzzled dry cleaner had left. "They're going to send her back to Germany." He spoke almost as though Ingrid were not in the room.

"You said you'd get me girls," said Ingrid, removing her bra entirely now, as though it were an annoyance.

"I'm working on it," said Gowran.

"I like it with girls."

"Listen," said Gowran, "how's the grass situation up here?" The question put Ullman right on the spot. He had some, but what if he produced a few joints and Gowran slipped the cuffs on him, booking him not only on tax evasion but also on a drug rap. Maybe that's what Ingrid's presence was all about. On a simpler level—if he brought out grass it would be clear-cut evidence that the apartment was more than just an office. Still, a certain inevitability began to surround the evening. He went and got some. From the second Ingrid had walked in, he had felt a little stoned anyway. Gowran seized his joint and began to suck on it elaborately in the style of the suburban experimenter; more predictably, Ingrid declined, saying, "I don't need this. It is a waste of time. Come. What do you want to do?" She took a seat between them on the couch, cradling both Ullman's and the tax collector's head against her giant bosom and saying, "Poor babies." Ullman wasn't sure if it was the grass or a certain drugged aroma that came from the girl's flesh, but there was a jump in time, some minutes or perhaps a large part of an hour that fell out of the evening, like a skipped piece of film, and the next thing he knew the three were standing on his Swedish rug, arms around each other, none of them wearing clothes. "A little music," the tax collector whispered to Ullman. Gowran's voice, in a whisper, had none of the reedy internal revenue style to it. It was surprisingly continental. As Ullman made the adjustments on his stereo set, he became aware of a sharply attractive fragrance which he took to be Ingrid's Germanic cologne. Then, too, there was the possibility that it might be Gowran's aftershave, a subtle concoction which Ullman would never have dreamed was favored by federal tax agents. Selecting an album somewhere between hard rock and the big band sound of the forties, Ullman turned and for a panicky moment saw that the couple was gone. But then he tracked them into the bedroom and found them on his heart-shaped bed, a hundred versions of them reflected in his craftily arranged wall-and-ceiling mirrors.

Ullman slipped in beside the couple, who had begun, tentatively, without him, and soon caught their rhythm, he and the tax collector wandering across the girl's heavy-duned body, Ingrid, not bored, but somewhere beyond them, as though she were a huge piece of experiential statuary stretching herself voluptuously in the sunlight. The unspoken rules were that Ullman and the tax man were to make love to her, but that both were to occupy separate zones and never to make contact with one another. Until one moment, deep in the night, when Ullman heard the revenue man whisper "over this way" and it seemed natural to alter the rules somewhat and finally, to abandon them altogether. And then, in an even deeper chamber of the night, the girl was gone and Ullman could recall no effort on either his or Gowran's part to keep her there.

In the morning, Ullman awoke with an awareness that he had not slept very long. At the same time, he felt none of the staleness that generally went with lack of sleep. A moment later, Gowran, fully dressed except for the thin civil service necktie, stood above him with an open can of condensed milk, wanting to know if it was fresh enough to use with his coffee. "I think it's okay," said Ullman. He brushed his teeth then, put in his contact lenses and showered, deliberately keeping his thoughts vague in the stream of hot water and preferring not to confront just yet the central new fact of his existence: that no matter how he sliced it, he had spent half the night in a tax collector's arms. After changing the sheets and making the bed, he dressed, making sure that everything he wore was spotlessly new and clean—and then he appeared in the breakfast alcove.

"Get some sleep?" asked Gowran, sipping his coffee and riffling through Ullman's daily record book, making a note or two.

"Not bad," said Ullman. "What happened to your girl friend?"

"Nice kid, huh?" said Gowran. "She had an appointment. You want to start now or get some breakfast first? I've got some questions about April 1968. Your figures don't add up."

"All right, hold it right there," said Ullman, pouring some juice and then slamming down the container. "I don't think you quite realize what's happened. You know, I just don't do this. This is a very big thing to me. I've never done this in my life. I won't kid you, I've had the thought a few times and maybe I even knew that some day I'd get around to it and give it a try. But I've never actually done it before. Never even come near it. This is a very strong new thing for me. I haven't even begun to assess the effect of it yet. I may not even be able to function normally when it hits me. My whole personality could be out the window. For Christ's sakes, I haven't done anything like this since Roger Lacey in Bunk Nine at Camp Deerfleet and that was nothing compared to last night. That was just a harmless little cupcake. For all I know this may turn out to be the single most shattering thing I've ever done in my thirties. I may get a goddamned nervous breakdown over last night and you want to casually jump in and review calendar notes for April '68."

"That's right," said Gowran, munching on a toasted English muffin and turning the pages of Ullman's diary until he came to the page he wanted. "Now who's this fellow Benziger and what do you fellows find to talk about three times a week at expensive French restaurants?"

"Bitch," said Ullman and was shocked by the unmistakably female hiss that accompanied the outburst.

[1971]

PHILIP ROTH

✳

Letters to Einstein

Dear Mr. Einstein:

I am writing you with a wonderful suggestion that I know would bring about gigantic changes in the world and improve the lot of Jews everywhere. Mr. Einstein, I am a fellow Jew, and proud of it. Your name is sacred to me as to people of our faith around the globe. That the Nazis chased you from Germany is our gain and their loss a million times over, if they even know what a loss is, and I only hope and pray that you are happy here in "the land of the free."

Here is my suggestion. Why don't you go on the radio every week with your own show? If you would agree I would like to manage you, so that your famous mind would not have to be cluttered up with business and so on. I am ashamed to say this in the same breath with your name, but probably you are aware of "The Answer Man" program which is on every night from seven to seven-fifteen. If you're not, just listen for a minute some night. Children all over

America think this fake is "an Einstein" probably, when the real Einstein is something they would faint to hear in person. I would like them to know THE GENIUS OF ALL TIME IS A JEW! This is something the world must know, and soon.

Respectfully yours,
M. Lippman,
Talent Agent

P.S. You will probably want to know what right I have even to suggest myself as a manager to the great Einstein. And all I can say is that if I had a list of the greatest names in the entertainment industry as my clientele, I would be as ashamed of my credentials as I am right now where you are concerned, The Great Albert Einstein. I feel it is even a sin to write out your whole name, that it is too holy for me to utter. But if I didn't write it out, how would you even get this letter? So forgive me. Until now, I have to tell you, I have not had a famous list of acts. Mostly I represent colored. I probably have the best tap dancing talent in the state under contract to me at this very moment, and am helping some of these young men—for instance, the famous Famous Brothers (Buck and Wing)—to raise themselves into a respectable life. With my new talent discoveries since Buck and Wing, I am changing their old names to names of famous American presidents, only backwards. This way I think they still sound colored, which they should as tap dancers, and yet have a little class. Also I attend an average of two or three *bar mitzvah* parties of a single Saturday, in my endless search for young Jewish talent in singing, bandleading, etcetera.

I hope I will be hearing from you soon, and favorably, about "The Albert Einstein Show."

Again respectfully,
M. Lippman

Dear Mr. Einstein:

I can understand how busy you must be thinking, and appreciate that you did not answer my letter suggesting that I try to get you on a radio program that would make "The Answer Man" look like the joke it is. Will you reconsider, if the silence means no? I realize that one of the reasons you don't wear a tie or even bother to comb your hair is because you are as busy as you are, thinking new things. Well, don't think that you would have to change your ways once you became a radio personality. Your hair is a great gimmick, and I wouldn't change it for a second. It's a great trademark. Without disrespect, it sticks in your mind the way Harpo Marx's does. Which is excellent. (Now I wonder if you even have the time to know who The Marx Brothers are? They are four zany Jewish brothers, and you happen to look a little like one of them. You might get a kick out of catching one of their movies. Probably they don't even show movies in Princeton, but maybe you could get somebody to drive you out of town. You can get the entire plot in about a minute, but the resemblance between you and Harpo, and his hair and yours, might reassure you that you are a fine personality in terms of show business just as you are.)

The kind of program I have in mind is something I would certainly have to talk with you about before embarking upon making the right contacts. For instance, should we follow "The Answer Man" format with questions sent in? Should we have a theme song? Would you object to another personality asking the questions? Something strikes me right about the idea of you being interviewed by Tony Martin, the singer. He has a beautiful speaking voice and makes a wonderful impression in a dinner jacket, and is also (contrary to the belief that he is of Italian extraction) a Jewish boy with whom you would feel completely at home. Easygoing is his whole style, *but with respect*. Whether I can get him is another story. I don't want to make promises I can't deliver so as to entice the famous Einstein. I wouldn't dare. But what I'm saying is the sky is the limit once I get an okay from you. I am tempted to spell that with a capital letter. You. But in the middle of the sentence.

Perhaps I should have told You that my fee is ten per cent. But truly and honestly I am not in this business for money. I want to help people. I have taken colored off the streets, shoeshine kit and all, and turned them into headline tap dancers at roadhouses and nightclubs overnight. And my satisfaction comes not from the money, which in all honesty is not so much, but in seeing those boys getting dressed up in dinner jackets and learning to face an audience of people out for a nice time. Dignity far more than money is my business.

With you, Mr. Einstein, I think I could really break through into something of worldwide importance in terms of doing good. Who better than you knows the persecution the Jews have taken around the globe? It will only stop when they look up to us and recognize that when it comes to smart, we are the tops. It will only stop when our own little Jewish boys and girls realize that there is an Einstein in the world who is a Jew just like them, and is a million times smarter than some *goy* radio announcer with a stuffy voice who they also give the answers to anyway. Do we want our children to grow up admiring such fakes? I have a little boy of my own, and I know what it would mean to me if I could sit with him at night once a week and listen to the Famous Albert Einstein talking around a fireside with someone of the caliber of a Tony Martin.

If you are too busy to write and discuss these matters, how about if I came to see you some Sunday? It would be a thrill if I could bring my son along.

> Respectfully yours,
> M. Lippman, Agent to
>   The Famous Brothers,
>   Roosevelt Franklin,
>   Jefferson Thomas,
>   Cleveland Grover, &
>   Monroe James

Dear *Dr.* Einstein:
No word, but I understand. I hope and pray you were not offended that I have been addressing you all along as Mister. I cannot express all my admiration for you, and it breaks my

heart if you think any disrespect was intended. I am not an educated person, though I try to make up for it in hard work and quick thinking what I don't know from books. Every day, and this is no exaggeration, I have a hundred wonderful ideas that could improve the world. My idea to encourage you to go on the air on a regular basis is only one, Doctor.

I am sure that you are naturally nervous about me and the millions of others who probably write to you looking for "an easy buck." I have to assure you, *the money is secondary.* Uppermost is getting you on the radio and showing those *goyim* what smart really means. Why hide under a barrel something that could change the life of *every Jew alive and their children to come?* This is how strongly I believe in the power of radio. I think sometimes that the Bible stories of God talking from above to the people down below is just what they had in those days instead of radio. People, whether then or now, like to hear "the real thing." Hearing is believ ing! (Maybe that could be our motto for the show—if you approve. For a theme song I have been thinking along robust lines, but still meaningful—something like "The Whole World is Singing My Song.") Today we don't *hear* God as they did in the Bible—and what is the result? It is impossible for some people to believe He is there. There. The same holds true with you, Doctor Einstein, I'm sorry to say. To the gen-eral public, who is Einstein? A name who doesn't comb his hair (not that I have any objection) and is *supposed* to be the smartest person alive. A lot of good that does the Jews, if you understand what I'm saying. At this stage of the game, I'm

afraid that if an election were held tonight between you and
The Answer Man, more people would vote for him than for
you. I have to be honest with you.

Here is my proposal. I will drive to Princeton next Sunday,
arriving around two P.M. If you are not home, fine. If you
are, and you happen to be at the window, and you happen to
feel only like waving and that's all, well let me tell you, that
would be a wonderful experience in itself. But if you want to
ask a question or two about my suggestion, even through the
window if that's all you have the time for, fine with me, I'll
do that too, from the lawn. I will leave my wife and child in
the car so that they don't bother you, though if you should
want to wave at the boy, I would be most appreciative. And
he of course would remember it for life.

To make a joke, don't put on a tie for my account, Doctor.

                    Your fellow Jew and humble admirer,
                    M. Lippman

                                              [1971]

NORA EPHRON

✳

A Few Words about Breasts

I have to begin with a few words about androgyny. In grammar school, in the fifth and sixth grades, we were all tyrannized by a rigid set of rules that supposedly determined whether we were boys or girls. The episode in *Huckleberry Finn* where Huck is disguised as a girl and gives himself away by the way he threads a needle and catches a ball—that kind of thing. We learned that the way you sat, crossed your legs, held a cigarette, and looked at your nails—the way you did these things instinctively was absolute proof of your sex. Now obviously most children did not take this literally, but I did. I thought that just one slip, just one incorrect cross of my legs or flick of an imaginary cigarette ash would turn me from whatever I was into the other thing; that would be all it took, really. Even though I was outwardly a girl and had many of the trappings generally associated with girldom—a girl's name, for example, and dresses, my own telephone, an autograph book—I spent the early years of my adolescence absolutely certain that I might at any point gum it up. I did not feel at all like a girl. I was boyish. I was athletic, ambitious, outspoken, competitive, noisy, rambunctious. I had scabs on my knees and my socks slid into my loafers and I could throw a football. I wanted desperately not to be that way, not to be a mixture of both things, but instead just one, a girl, a definite indisputable girl. As soft and as pink as a nursery. And nothing would do that for me, I felt, but breasts.

I was about six months younger than everyone else in my class, and so for about six months after it began, for six months after my friends had begun to develop (that was the word we used, develop), I was not particularly worried. I would sit in the bathtub and look down at my breasts and know that any day now, any second now, they would start growing like everyone else's. They didn't. "I want to buy a bra," I said to my mother one night. "What for?" she said. My mother was really hateful about bras, and by the time my third sister had gotten to the point where she was ready to want one, my mother had worked the whole business into a comedy routine. "Why not use a Band-Aid instead?" she would say. It was a source of great pride to my mother that she had never even had to wear a brassiere until she had her fourth child, and then only because her gynecologist made her. It was incomprehensible to me that anyone could ever be proud of something like that. It was the 1950s, for God's sake. Jane Russell. Cashmere sweaters. Couldn't my mother see that? *I am too old to wear an undershirt.* Screaming.

Weeping. Shouting. "Then don't wear an undershirt," said my mother. "But I want to buy a bra." "What for?"

I suppose for most girls, breasts, brassieres, that entire thing, has more trauma, more to do with the coming of adolescence, with becoming a woman, than anything else. Certainly more than getting your period, although that, too, was traumatic, symbolic. But you could see breasts; they were there; they were visible. Whereas a girl could claim to have her period for months before she actually got it and nobody would ever know the difference. Which is exactly what I did. All you had to do was make a great fuss over having enough nickels for the Kotex machine and walk around clutching your stomach and moaning for three to five days a month about The Curse and you could convince anybody. There is a school of thought somewhere in the women's lib/women's mag/gynecology establishment that claims that menstrual cramps are purely psychological, and I lean toward it. Not that I didn't have them finally. Agonizing cramps, heating-pad cramps, go-down-to-the-school-nurse-and-lie-on-the-cot cramps. But, unlike any pain I had ever suffered, I adored the pain of cramps, welcomed it, wallowed in it, bragged about it. "I can't go. I have cramps." "I can't do that. I have cramps." And most of all, gigglingly, blushingly: "I can't swim. I have cramps." Nobody ever used the hard-core word. Menstruation. God, what an awful word. Never that. "I have cramps."

The morning I first got my period, I went into my mother's bedroom to tell her. And my mother, my utterly-hateful-about-bras mother, burst into tears. It was really a lovely moment, and I remember it so clearly not just because it was one of the two times I ever saw my mother cry on my account (the other was when I was caught being a six-year-old kleptomaniac), but also because the incident did not mean to me what it meant to her. Her little girl, her firstborn, had finally become a woman. That was what she was crying about. My reaction to the event, however, was that I might well be a woman in some scientific, textbook sense (and could at least stop faking every month and stop wasting all those nickels). But in another sense—in a visible sense—I was as androgynous and as liable to tip over into boyhood as ever.

I started with a 28 AA bra. I don't think they made them any smaller in those days, although I gather that now you can buy bras for five-year-olds that don't have any cups whatsoever in them; trainer bras they are called. My first brassiere came from Robinson's Department Store in Beverly Hills. I went there alone, shaking, positive they would look me over and smile and tell me to come back next year. An actual fitter took me into the dressing room and stood over me while I took off my blouse and tried the first one on. The little puffs stood out on my chest. "Lean over," said the fitter. (To this day I am not sure what fitters in bra departments do except to tell you to lean over.) I leaned over, with the fleeting hope that my breasts would miraculously fall out of my body and into the puffs. Nothing.

"Don't worry about it," said my friend Libby some

months later, when things had not improved. "You'll get them after you're married."

"What are you talking about?" I said.

"When you get married," Libby explained, "your husband will touch your breasts and rub them and kiss them and they'll grow."

That was the killer. Necking I could deal with. Intercourse I could deal with. But it had never crossed my mind that a man was going to touch my breasts, that breasts had something to do with all that, petting, my God, they never mentioned petting in my little sex manual about the fertilization of the ovum. I became dizzy. For I knew instantly—as naïve as I had been only a moment before—that only part of what she was saying was true: the touching, rubbing, kissing part, not the growing part. And I knew that no one would ever want to marry me. I had no breasts. I would never have breasts.

My best friend in school was Diana Raskob. She lived a block from me in a house full of wonders. English muffins, for instance. The Raskobs were the first people in Beverly Hills to have English muffins for breakfast. They also had an apricot tree in the back, and a badminton court, and a subscription to *Seventeen* magazine, and hundreds of games, like Sorry and Parcheesi and Treasure Hunt and Anagrams. Diana and I spent three or four afternoons a week in their den reading and playing and eating. Diana's mother's kitchen was full of the most colossal assortment of junk food I have ever been exposed to. My house was full of apples and peaches and milk and homemade chocolate-chip cookies—which were nice, and good for you, but-not-right-before-dinner-or-you'll-spoil-your-appetite. Diana's house had nothing in it that was good for you, and what's more, you could stuff it in right up until dinner and nobody cared. Bar-B-Q potato chips (they were the first in them, too), giant bottles of ginger ale, fresh popcorn with melted butter, hot fudge sauce on Baskin-Robbins jamoca ice cream, powdered-sugar doughnuts from Van de Kamp's. Diana and I had been best friends since we were seven; we were about equally popular in school (which is to say, not particularly), we had about the same success with boys (extremely intermittent), and we looked much the same. Dark. Tall. Gangly.

It is September, just before school begins. I am eleven years old, about to enter the seventh grade, and Diana and I have not seen each other all summer. I have been to camp and she has been somewhere like Banff with her parents. We are meeting, as we often do, on the street midway between our two houses, and we will walk back to Diana's and eat junk and talk about what has happened to each of us that summer. I am walking down Walden Drive in my jeans and my father's shirt hanging out and my old red loafers with the socks falling into them and coming toward me is . . . I take a deep breath . . . a young woman. Diana. Her hair is curled and she has a waist and hips and a bust and she is wearing a straight skirt, an article of clothing that I have been repeatedly told I will be unable to wear until I have the hips to hold it up. My jaw drops, and suddenly I am crying, crying hysterically, can't catch my breath sobbing. My best friend has betrayed me. She has gone ahead without me and done it. She has shaped up.

Here are some things I did to help:

Bought a Mark Eden Bust Developer.

Slept on my back for four years.

Splashed cold water on them every night because some French actress said in *Life* magazine that that was what *she* did for her perfect bustline.

Ultimately, I resigned myself to a bad toss and began to wear padded bras. I think about them now, think about all those years in high school I went around in them, my three padded bras, every single one of them with different-sized breasts. Each time I changed bras I changed sizes: one week nice perky but not too obtrusive breasts, the next medium-sized slightly pointy ones, the next week knockers, true knockers; all the time, whatever size I was, carrying around this rubberized appendage on my chest that occasionally crashed into a wall and was poked inward and had to be poked outward—I think about all that and wonder how anyone kept a straight face through it. My parents, who normally had no restraints about needling me—why did they say nothing as they watched my chest go up and down? My friends, who would periodically inspect my breasts for signs of growth and reassure me—why didn't they at least counsel consistency?

And the bathing suits. I die when I think about the bathing suits. That was the era when you could lay an uninhabited bathing suit on the beach and someone would make a pass at it. I would put one on, an absurd swimsuit with its enormous bust built into it, the bones from the suit stabbing me in the rib cage and leaving little red welts on my body, and there I would be, my chest plunging straight downward absolutely vertically from my collarbone to the top of my suit and then suddenly, wham, out came all that padding and material and wiring absolutely horizontally.

Buster Klepper was the first boy who ever touched them. He was my boyfriend my senior year of high school. There is a picture of him in my high-school yearbook that makes him look quite attractive in a Jewish, horn-rimmed-glasses sort of way, but the picture does not show the pimples, which were air-brushed out, or the dumbness. Well, that isn't really fair. He wasn't dumb. He just wasn't terribly bright. His mother refused to accept it, refused to accept the relentlessly average report cards, refused to deal with her son's inevitable destiny in some junior college or other. "He was tested," she would say to me, apropos of nothing, "and it came out a hundred and forty-five. That's near-genius." Had the word "underachiever" been coined, she probably would have lobbed that one at me, too. Anyway, Buster was really very sweet—which is, I know, damning with faint praise, but there it is. I was the editor of the front page of the high-school newspaper and he was editor of the back page; we had to work together, side by side, in the print shop, and that was how it started. On our first date, we went to see *April Love*, starring Pat Boone. Then we started going together. Buster had a green coupe, a 1950 Ford with an engine he had hand-chromed until it shone, dazzled, reflected the image of anyone who looked into it, anyone usually being Buster polishing it or the gas-station attendants he constantly asked to check the oil in order for them to be overwhelmed by the sparkle on the valves. The car also had a boot stretched over the back seat for reasons I never understood; hanging from the rearview mirror was a pair of angora dice. A previous girlfriend named Solange, who was famous throughout Beverly Hills High School for having no pigment in her right eyebrow, had knitted them for him. Buster and I would ride around town, the two of us seated to the left of the steering wheel. I would shift gears. It was nice.

There was necking. Terrific necking. First in the car, overlooking Los Angeles from what is now the Trousdale Estates. Then on the bed of his parents' cabana at Ocean House. Incredibly wonderful, frustrating necking, I loved it, really, but no further than necking, please don't, please, because there I was absolutely terrified of the general implications of going-a-step-further with a near-dummy and also terrified of his finding out there was next to nothing there (which he knew, of course; he wasn't that dumb).

I broke up with him at one point. I think we were apart for about two weeks. At the end of that time, I drove down to see a friend at a boarding school in Palos Verdes Estates and a disc jockey played "April Love" on the radio four times during the trip. I took it as a sign. I drove straight back to

Griffith Park to a golf tournament Buster was playing in (he
was the sixth-seeded teen-age golf player in southern California) and presented myself back to him on the green of the
18th hole. It was all very dramatic. That night we went to a
drive-in and I let him get his hand under my protuberances
and onto my breasts. He really didn't seem to mind at all.

"Do you want to marry my son?" the woman asked me.

"Yes," I said.

*I was nineteen years old, a virgin, going with this woman's
son, this big strange woman who was married to a Lutheran
minister in New Hampshire and pretended she was gentile
and had this son, by her first husband, this total fool of a son
who ran the hero-sandwich concession at Harvard Business
School and whom for one moment one December in New
Hampshire I said—as much out of politeness as anything
else—that I wanted to marry.*

*"Fine," she said. "Now, here's what you do. Always make
sure you're on top of him so you won't seem so small. My bust
is very large, you see, so I always lie on my back to make it
look smaller, but you'll have to be on top most of the time."*

I nodded. "Thank you," I said.

*"I have a book for you to read," she went on. "Take it with
you when you leave. Keep it." She went to the bookshelf,
found it, and gave it to me. It was a book on frigidity.*

"Thank you," I said.

That is a true story. Everything in this article is a true story,
but I feel I have to point out that that story in particular is

true. It happened on December 30, 1960. I think about it often. When it first happened, I naturally assumed that the woman's son, my boyfriend, was responsible. I invented a scenario where he had had a little heart-to-heart with his mother and had confessed that his only objection to me was that my breasts were small; his mother then took it upon herself to help out. Now I think I was wrong about the incident. The mother was acting on her own, I think: that was her way of being cruel and competitive under the guise of being helpful and maternal. You have small breasts, she was saying; therefore you will never make him as happy as I have. Or you have small breasts; therefore you will doubtless have sexual problems. Or you have small breasts; therefore you are less woman than I am. She was, as it happens, only the first of what seems to me to be a never-ending string of women who have made competitive remarks to me about breast size. "I would love to wear a dress like that," my friend Emily says to me, "but my bust is too big." Like that. Why do women say these things to me? Do I attract these remarks the way other women attract married men or alcoholics or homosexuals? This summer, for example, I am at a party in East Hampton and I am introduced to a woman from Washington. She is a minor celebrity, very pretty and Southern and blond and outspoken, and I am flattered because she has read something I have written. We are talking animatedly, we have been talking no more than five minutes, when a man comes up to join us. "Look at the two of us," the woman says to the man, indicating me and her. "The two of us together couldn't fill an A cup." Why does she say that? It isn't even true, dammit, so why? Is she even more addled than I am on this subject? Does she honestly believe there is something wrong with her size breasts, which, it seems to me, now that I look hard at them, are just right? Do I unconsciously bring out competitiveness in women? In that form? What did I do to deserve it?

As for men.

There were men who minded and let me know that they minded. There were men who did not mind. In any case, *I* always minded.

And even now, now that I have been countlessly reassured that my figure is a good one, now that I am grown-up enough to understand that most of my feelings have very little to do with the reality of my shape, I am nonetheless obsessed by breasts. I cannot help it. I grew up in the terrible fifties—with rigid stereotypical sex roles, the insistence that men be men and dress like men and women be women and dress like women, the intolerance of androgyny—and I cannot shake it, cannot shake my feelings of inadequacy. Well, that time is gone, right? All those exaggerated examples of breast worship are gone, right? Those women were freaks, right? I know all that. And yet here I am, stuck with the psychological remains of it all, stuck with my own peculiar version of breast worship. You probably think I am crazy to go on like this: here I have set out to write a confession that is meant to hit you with the shock of recognition, and instead you are sitting there thinking I am thoroughly warped. Well, what can I tell you? If I had had them, I would have been a completely different person. I honestly believe that.

After I went into therapy, a process that made it possible for me to tell total strangers at cocktail parties that breasts were the hang-up of my life, I was often told that I was insane to have been bothered by my condition. I was also frequently told, by close friends, that I was extremely boring on the subject. And my girl friends, the ones with nice big breasts, would go on endlessly about how their lives had been far more miserable than mine. Their bra straps were snapped in class. They couldn't sleep on their stomachs. They were stared at whenever the word "mountain" cropped up in geography. And *Evangeline*, good God what they went through every time someone had to stand up and recite the Prologue to Longfellow's *Evangeline*: "... stand like druids of eld ... / With beards that rest on their bosoms." It was much worse for them, they tell me. They had a terrible time of it, they assure me. I don't know how lucky I was, they say.

I have thought about their remarks, tried to put myself in their place, considered their point of view. I think they are full of shit.

[1972]

HENRY BEARD, MICHAEL O'DONOGHUE, AND GEORGE W. S. TROW

*

Our White Heritage

WHITE MYTHS AND STEREOTYPES

Although White people have been in America for over four hundred years, there still exists an enormous amount of misunderstanding about Whites, some of it willfully malicious, but most of it the result of a lack of proper education or just plain ignorance. Millions of otherwise good citizens regularly contribute to the atmosphere of fear, confusion, and mistrust in which Whites have to work and play by repeating racial slurs they have heard to their children or to their friends, never stopping to think of the damage they might be causing. You can do your part to dispel a lot of the misinformation that surrounds uncolored people by "debunking" these common myths whenever and wherever you hear them voiced, or by protesting strongly whenever the media

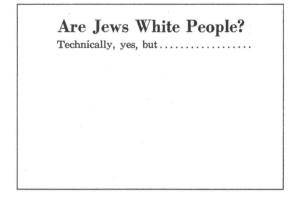

Are Jews White People?
Technically, yes, but.................

or anyone in public life resorts to one of these demeaning stereotypes to describe or portray persons of Anglo-American ancestry:

Whites have "natural reason," or extra lobes in their brains, which makes them good aesthetes.

They are adult-like, brooding, and worry a great deal.

They spend all their money on stocks and bonds.

They smell good, talk too softly, and can't dance.

When they move into a neighborhood, they tear down all the bars and pool halls and put up historical societies and Christian Science Reading Rooms, and send real-estate prices sky-high.

They are sexually frigid, or "hung like hamsters."

They won't accept welfare.

They eat nothing but cantaloupe and caviar and lie around "white linening," that is, drinking vintage wine out of bottles wrapped in napkins.

They all look like Commander Whitehead or the Arrow
   Shirt Man, and they go around reflectively rubbing
   their chins and saying, "Slide rule do your stuff," or
   "Brain don't fail me now."
They are clean, chaste, and prudish.

You should also discourage racist humor, of which the
countless series of "Standard & Poor" jokes is by far the
most common example. One sample of these demeaning and
racially insulting jokes should be a sufficient illustration of
their tastelessness:

STANDARD: Say, Mr. Poor, I'm so rich, I just bought my dog
a little boy.
POOR: That's nothing, Mr. Standard. Why, I'm so rich, I don't
have my Bentleys air-conditioned. I just keep a dozen cold
ones in the freezer.

WHITES IN AMERICA

The first White person to hold elective office in America was William Bradford, who served as governor of Plymouth Colony from 1621 to 1632.

————

A mere few years later, in 1634, the first White Studies program was inaugurated at the College of William & Mary in Williamsburg, Va. The curriculum consisted of a number of courses in White culture, including mathematics, geography, geometry, rhetoric, political economy, the sciences, Latin, Greek, theology, oratory, composition, medicine, and law.

————

With the ratification of the Articles of Confederation in 1781, Whites gained their basic rights.

————

Among the many all-White military units that distinguished themselves in battle in the course of the Civil War were the Army of the Potomac and the Army of Northern Virginia.

————

Throughout the Civil War thousands of White people fled north on the Overground Railroad thanks to the courage and selfless dedication of countless engineers, conductors, and brakemen of, among others, the Chesapeake & Ohio, the Norfolk & Western, and the Alabama & Northern railroads.

————

Although many came to America in the seventeenth and eighteenth centuries, the largest influx of uncolored people occurred in the latter part of the nineteenth and early twentieth centuries, when hundreds of thousands of whites traveled to these shores in giant steamships, often undergoing a considerable amount of unpleasantness along the way, while shipping-line owners made a tidy sum on their "human cargo." Packed in groups of two and even three, in stuffy cabins with difficult-to-open portholes or, for the unlucky passengers with inside cabins, no portholes at all, these White people suffered from seasickness, nasty tumbles on the promenade deck, boring table companions, rude stewards, inconveniently timed lifeboat drills, and poor deck-chair assignments, to name just a few of the many hardships.

In the 1930s noted author and literary figure Ernest Hemingway led a back-to-Europe movement, which at its height saw thousands of White persons return to the continent of their origin to renew their ties with the peoples whose

Ernest Hemingway

racial ancestry they shared. But in all too many cases, after a century or more of separation, the gap proved too great to bridge, and after finding difficulties adjusting to new languages, different money, and a foreign measurement system, or disgusted by the lack of central heating, telephone service, and indoor plumbing, most came back to America.

———

Ralph Bunche, the first American citizen to hold high office at the United Nations, had "a touch of the old whitewash."

CLOTHES MAKE "THE MAN" (AND "THE WOMAN")!

Mr. and Mrs. Ronald Sveinbjörn of Dover, Delaware, proudly don native White dress as part of recent White Awareness Millennium festivities. He sports full Viking regalia while she wears the colorful peasant garb of Holland, complete with wooden shoes, the traditional teased and feathered Anglo hairdo, and a fetching wrist corsage.

OUR WHITE CULTURAL HERITAGE

Archaeologists have long believed that Whites had developed a rich, flourishing civilization in the Mediterranean

Basin area, possibly as early as 2500 B.C., and from time to time over the last several centuries a number of important artifacts that tend to support this theory have come to light in Greece, Italy, Egypt, Crete, Southern France, Spain, and North Africa. It is now generally accepted that by the time of the birth of Christ (who was, Himself, technically a White man) Whites did in fact possess at least the rudiments of a culture, and ethnic historians who hold this view point to such varied artistic accomplishments of that era as the *Iliad*, Plato's *Republic*, the plays of Sophocles, the poems of Horace, the Venus de Milo, and Euclidean geometry as further proof of their hypothesis.

The Acropolis, considered by many to be strong evidence of the existence of a White civilization in Europe in ancient times.

PORTRAITS IN WHITE

Throughout history, Whites have played an important, even deciding, role in the events that have shaped mankind. The list of White achievers is a lengthy and distinguished one, and "calling the roll" of these giants of the uncolored world would take a long time indeed (according to Dr. Livingston Wingate of the White Studies department at Tulane, if twenty persons each read the name of one White achiever every three seconds, twenty-four hours a day, it would take 114 years!), so here is just a sample to give some feeling of the depth and diversity of the White experience:

> All of the participants in the Thirty Years' War were Whites.
>
> Emperor Charles IX of Sweden was a White man.
>
> Cardinal Lanfranc was uncolored.

General Meade   *Baruch Spinoza*   *Charles IX*

Gouverneur Morris   Downtown Bruges   Xenophon

The population of Bruges, noted center of Flemish culture, was in former times, and remains today, entirely White.

The famous composer and organist Dietrich Buxtehude was a White man.

Gouverneur Morris, one of the original signers of the Constitution, was of Anglo-American ancestry.

Emile Durkheim was a White man.

Both of the pretenders to the Hapsburg throne in the War of the Spanish Succession were White men.

Lake Meade is named after Gen. George Meade, a White man.

Xenophon was White, as were all of his Ten Thousand.

Spinoza was, technically speaking, a White man.

TALKING WHITE

A number of White expressions have become a part of our language—in fact, the noted semanticists and ethnologists

Merriam, Webster, and Roget collected more than 140,000 such usages! Here is just one that illustrates the extent to which White words have enriched our daily speech:

I am	We are
You are	You are
He, she, it is	They are

Some of the many White terms that have become household words:

"some"	"that"
"of"	"have"
"the"	"become"
"many"	"household"
"White"	"words"
"terms"	

In addition, a wealth of White slang has found its way into our native tongue. Some instances of this trend:

Angstrom—a measurement of light-wave length equal to one ten-thousandth of a micron

Tort—any wrongful act involving a breach of contract for which a civil action will lie

Debenture—any of various instruments, either secured or unsecured, issued by a corporation as an evidence of debt

Erg—a unit of energy expressing the work done by one dyne acting through a distance of one centimeter

Oxymoron—a combination for epigrammatic effect of contradictory or incongruous words

Metope—the space between two triglyphs of the Doric frieze

Chiasmatypy—the supposed spiral twisting of homologus chromosomes about each other during parasynapsis

Appoggiatura—an accessory tone preceding an essential tone as an embellishment of melody

Teleost—a fish of the group Teleostei, the bony fishes, as distinguished from the ganoids, dipnoans, and elasmobranchs

Futtock—one of the crooked timbers scarfed together to form part of the compound rib of a vessel

Syzygy—the point in its orbit at which a planet is in conjunction or opposition

Spotlight on White Music

"Although it takes both white keys and black keys to play a tune on the piano, the vast majority of tunes are played, for the most part, on the white keys."

Centuries ago, one had to frequent remote concert halls to hear White Music, but today one can't step into an elevator or wait in an air terminal without sampling a White Music medley that usually includes at least one of the following: "Thumbelina," "The Petticoats of Portugal," "The Naughty Lady of Shady Lane," "Holiday for Strings," or "The Pizzicato Polka." This "pop" music originated in the prep schools of Connecticut and came down the Merrill Parkway to Tin Pan Alley, where, quick to grasp its potential, such capable performers as Fred Waring and the Pennsylvanians and "The Singing Rage," Miss Patti Page, soon had Caucasians all over the country two- (or "box") stepping to these memorable melodies. Of course, much of the credit for the advancement of White Music must go to Arthur Fiedler, who, in any given concert, spans the White Musical experience by performing both light classics (i.e., "The Typewriter Song") and serious works (i.e., "The Grand Canyon Suite") alike.

Arthur Fiedler receives polite applause from enthralled Australian concert-goers.

WHITE DANCING

No one is more interested in "cutting a rug" than the Anglo-American, as evidenced by the disproportionately high number of Whites among those who take dance lessons. Here, under qualified instructors, they learn everything from the waltz to the bunny hop, including the most popular of all the White-oriented dances, the two- (or "box") step.

Tripping the White Fantastic: The Two- (or "Box") Step

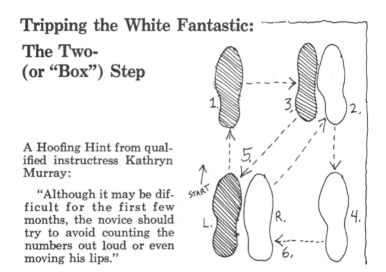

A Hoofing Hint from qualified instructress Kathryn Murray:

"Although it may be difficult for the first few months, the novice should try to avoid counting the numbers out loud or even moving his lips."

FOCUS ON THE FIRST WORLD

In an effort to achieve greater White Solidarity, representatives of the First World countries meet regularly in a number of forums, including the International Monetary Fund, NATO, and the Council of Ten, to give voice to the legitimate needs and aspirations of the Australian, North American, and European peoples and to gain international support for these basic First World demands:

Protection of overseas investments from illegal seizure without just compensation

Speedy repayment of development loans

Allotment of votes in the United Nations based on member states' contributions to the U.N. budget

Recognition of the use of force as the primary means of settling disputes between nations

Noninterference with military interventions in First World spheres of influence

An end to exorbitant "blackmailing" of First World countries in the sale of oil and the use of territory for air and naval bases

Unhindered access to worldwide natural resources for responsible consortiums

Acknowledgment of the fundamental right to rule for white minorities

Acceptance of the First World nuclear-weapons hegemony as the soundest basis for a stable world order

Immediate payment of reparations for the religions, moral codes, and languages; the educational, legal, and governmental systems; the traditions of hard work and fair play; and the centuries of efficient rule provided to former colonial possessions for free by First World countries

Universal adherence to the principle of narrow self-interest in the conduct of international affairs

CONCEPTS IN WHITE

cardigan sweaters
drop-leaf tables
marmalade
the National Guard
tax loss
rug pads
salad plates
Ilka Chase
rondos
penicillin
Seattle
between-meal snacks
parallel parking
Chartres
The Bell Telephone Hour
sculling
curling
footnotes
quality control
percale

penology
Martin Chuzzlewit
wine-tasting parties
Manifest Destiny
matched luggage
the Doublemint Twins
melody
Forbes magazine
polite applause
scientific method
Danskware
Wedgwood
conference calls
William Rose Benét
Wyoming
Velveeta
dermatology
explorers
well-balanced meals
Swedish Tanning Secret

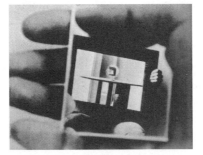

WHITE PRIDE

What you can do to further the cause of White Pride in your community:

Join with other uncolored people in planning and participating in activities as part of the Fifth White Awareness Millennium (A.D. 1000–2000).

Observe such White holidays as Arbor Day, Independence Day, and George Washington's birthday.

Insist on the display of White symbols, such as the American flag; busts of Shakespeare, Descartes, and Plato; and quotes from Ralph Waldo Emerson in schools and other public buildings.

See to it that your local school provides your younger children with reading texts that contain depictions of farm animals, pastures, suburban life, and other scenes they can relate to, and make sure that American History courses stress important events in White history like the discovery of the New World, the American Revolution, the Louisiana Purchase, and World War I.

Plan a White meal for your family. (Places specializing in White foods are easy to find: just look in the Yellow Pages under "Supermarkets" or, if you prefer to eat out, under "Restaurants.")

Arrange a neighborhood Scrabble tournament.

The White Handshake

1. Reach forward and grasp the proffered hand.
2. Apply pressure in a "manly" fashion. (Note: Although less pressure is required of women, the handshake should never be limp or "cold fish.")
3. Move the joined hands firmly up and down.
4. Release the hand.

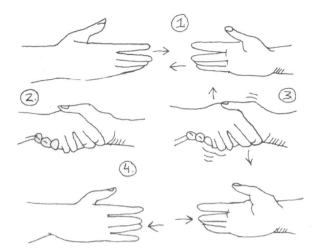

WHITE LINE . . . . . CARL GRIFFITH OF RAHWAY, N.J., A WHITE MAN, HAS BEEN PROMOTED TO THE POSITION OF ASSISTANT MANAGER IN CHARGE OF QUALITY CONTROL FOR THE BRUNSWICK CORPORATION, A WHITE-OWNED COMPANY. THE THIRTY-SEVEN-YEAR-OLD MR. GRIFFITH WAS FORMERLY A MARKET FEASIBILITY RESEARCHER.

CONCEPTS IN WHITE

overhead	written language
Fabian Bachrach	Thorstein Veblen
Early American furniture	storm windows
Scotchguard	philosophy
duck presses	Boston lettuce
file cards	Margaret Whiting
summa cum laude	tulips
city managers	Shaker Heights
the use of perspective in painting	heraldry

WHITE PRIDE

A number of organizations, foundations, and other groups are dedicated to the advancement and betterment of uncolored people. This is only a partial list:

   The Standing Committee of the General Agreement on
       Trades and Tariffs (GATT)
   The Republican Party
   The Knights of Columbus
   The State of Louisiana
   The Fraternal Order of Moose
   The AFL-CIO
   The Church of Jesus Christ of Latter-day Saints
   The United States Navy
   The American Medical Association
   The Supreme Court of the United States (since 1972)
   The construction industry
   Australia

Did you know that both the Dewey Decimal System *and* the Cutter Classification System were developed by White people?

WHITE CAPITALISM

If you, as an Involved White Person (IWP), wish to support White-owned businesses, here are the names of a few:

General Motors	Eastman Kodak
Standard Oil of New Jersey	Monsanto Chemical
U.S. Steel	National Biscuit
Crown Zellerbach	IBM
Borden	Kennecott Copper
Union Carbide	B. F. Goodrich
RCA	Continental Can
General Electric	Du Pont
Procter & Gamble	

For the names of other White-owned (and often, operated!) businesses in your community, contact your local chamber of commerce or write the National Association of Manufacturers, 277 Park Avenue, New York, N.Y.

Did you know that, although George Washington Carver discovered many uses for the peanut, White people own *all* of the major peanut-butter companies?

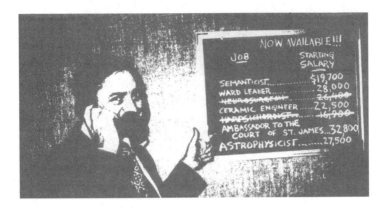

THE WHITE JOB CORPS

Corps head Clifford Baumann warns applicants, "Just because you're White, don't expect to walk in here and start pulling down fifty thou a year. Be prepared to tighten your purse strings for two or three years and squeak along on a meager twenty or thirty grand per until you move up to a comfortable income."

Did you know that the first white man in organized baseball was Abner Doubleday?

WHITE MARTIAL ARTS

Whites are no "slouches" when it comes to the Martial Arts, and as far as many forms of combat are concerned, Whites "wrote the book." Among these are: enfilade, defilade, and search-and-traverse machine-gun-firing techniques; saturation bombing; toxic-gas deployment; armored assault tactics;

amphibious landings; naval battle formations and submarine warfare; and atomic war.

A pair of Whites go through a "simulated countdown" exercise, one of the complex, almost ballet-like moves involved in achieving a state of "readiness" for the launching of an ICBM, an integral part of the White art of thermonuclear warfare.

THE WONDERFUL WIDE WORLD OF WHITE SPORTS

Stamina, a sense of determination, and intellectual agility are a must in this no-holds-barred Scrabble contest. Here, North, playing off an existing *o* and *y*, forms the word *oxymorons*, scoring, with a Double Letter square and a Double Word square, 38 points plus an additional 50-point premium for playing all seven of his tiles, for a total of 88 points.

The White Arts

Whites have nothing to be ashamed of when it comes to the Arts. They have made significant contributions in just about every area of artistic endeavor, including, in the field of literature: the epic, lyric poetry, tragedy, comedy, the essay, and the novel; in the field of music: the symphony, the concerto, the fugue, rondos, operas, masses, quartets, motets, counterpoint, orchestration, and melody; in the field of architecture:

Souvenir de Mortefontaine *by Jean Baptiste Camille Corot, the renowned White post-Romantic painter*

the arch, the flying buttress, the cantilever, geodesics, and the Gothic, Romanesque, Baroque, Palladian, and Bauhaus styles; in the field of painting: chiaroscuro, perspective, composition, tempera, portraiture, and the fresco; in the field of photography: photography; and in the field of movies: movies.

In addition, there are a number of White folk arts of which uncolored people may feel justly proud. Among the better-known products of this tradition are Chippendale furniture, Gobelin tapestries, Meissen porcelain, Georgian silver, Delft faience, stained glass, and illuminated manuscripts.

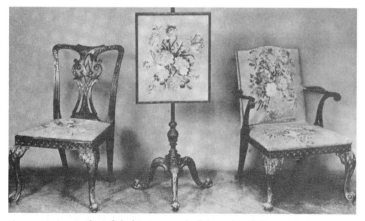

An attractive and useful object typical of the White folk-art tradition

WHITE LINE..... AN ALL-WHITE PRODUCTION OF AN-
DROCLES AND THE LION WAS RECENTLY STAGED AT
HOBART COLLEGE.

Did you know that Alexandre Dumas, author of the adventure classic *The Three Musketeers*, was part White?

Angry White Poet Alexander Pope in Praise of Anarchy:

"Lo! thy dread empire Chaos! is restor'd:
Light dies before thy uncreating word;
Thy hand, great Anarch! lets the curtain fall,
And universal darkness buries all."
            —The *Dunciad*

ACCENT ON THE INVOLVED WHITE WOMAN

Says Involved White Woman Happy Rockefeller, "Nothing more perfectly complements a meal of Cheez Whiz, Roast 'n

Boast, Cool Whip, Diet Cola, and Hawaiian Skillet than these taste-tempting *Marshmallow Treats*! Why not whip up a batch tonight? Your family will love you for it!

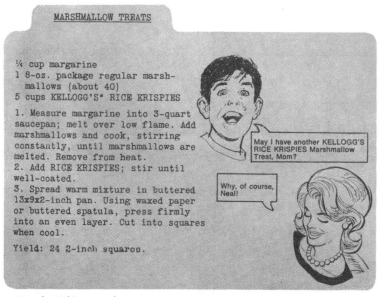

MARSHMALLOW TREATS

¼ cup margarine
1 8-oz. package regular marshmallows (about 40)
5 cups KELLOGG'S* RICE KRISPIES

1. Measure margarine into 3-quart saucepan; melt over low flame. Add marshmallows and cook, stirring constantly, until marshmallows are melted. Remove from heat.
2. Add RICE KRISPIES; stir until well-coated.
3. Spread warm mixture in buttered 13x9x2-inch pan. Using waxed paper or buttered spatula, press firmly into an even layer. Cut into squares when cool.

Yield: 24 2-inch squares.

May I have another KELLOGG'S RICE KRISPIES Marshmallow Treat, Mom?

Why, of course, Neal!

*Another White-owned company!

[1972]

FRAN LEBOWITZ

✳

Better Read Than Dead: A Revised Opinion

My attendance at grammar school coincided rather unappealingly with the height of the cold war. This resulted in my spending a portion of each day sitting cross-legged, head in lap, either alone under my desk or, more sociably, against the wall in the corridor. When not so occupied I could be found sitting in class reading avidly about the horrors of life under Communism. I was not a slow child, but I believed passionately that Communists were a race of horned men who divided their time equally between the burning of Nancy Drew books and the devising of a plan of nuclear attack that would land the largest and most lethal bomb squarely upon the third-grade class of Thomas Jefferson School in Morristown, New Jersey. This was a belief widely held among my classmates and it was reinforced daily by teachers and those parents who were of the Republican persuasion.

Among the many devices used to keep this belief alive was a detailed chart that appeared yearly in our social studies book. This chart pointed out the severe economic hardships of Communist life. The reading aloud of the chart was accompanied by a running commentary from the teacher and went something like this:

"This chart shows how long a man must work in Russia in order to purchase the following goods. We then compare this to the length of time it takes a man in the United States to earn enough money to purchase the same goods."

RUSSIA	U.S.A.
A PAIR OF SHOES — 38 HOURS	A PAIR OF SHOES — 2 HOURS
"And they only have brown oxfords in Russia, so that nobody ever gets to wear shoes without straps even for dress-up. Also they have never even heard of Capezios, and if they did, no one would be allowed to wear them because they all have to work on farms whenever they are not busy making atom bombs."	"And we have all kinds of shoes, even Pappagallos."
A LOAF OF BREAD — 2½ HOURS	A LOAF OF BREAD — 5 MINUTES
"They do not have peanut butter in Russia, or Marshmallow Fluff, and their bread has a lot of crust on it, which they force all the children to eat."	We have cinnamon raisin bread and english muffins and we can put whatever we like on it because we have democracy."

A POUND OF NAILS — 6 HOURS
"And they need a lot of nails in Russia because everyone has to work very hard all the time building things — even mothers."

A POUND OF NAILS — 8 MINUTES
"Even though we don't need that many nails because we have Scotch tape and staples."

A STATION WAGON — 9 YEARS
"If they were even permitted to own them, which they are not, so everyone has to walk everywhere even though they are very tired from building so many things like atom bombs."

A STATION WAGON — 4 MONTHS
"And we have so many varieties to choose from — some painted to look like wood on the sides and some that are two different colors. We also have lots of other cars, such as convertible sports cars."

A PAIR OF OVERALLS — 11 HOURS
"And everyone has to wear overalls all the time and they're all the same color so nobody gets to wear straight skirts even if they're in high school."

A PAIR OF OVERALLS — 1 HOUR
"But since we can choose what we want to wear in a democracy, mostly farmers wear overalls and they like to wear them."

A DOZEN EGGS — 7 HOURS
"But they hardly ever get to eat them because eggs are a luxury in Russia and there are no luxuries under Communism."

A DOZEN EGGS — 9 MINUTES
"We have lots of eggs here and that is why we can have eggnog, egg salad, even Easter eggs, except for the Jewish children in the class, who I'm sure have something just as nice on their holiday, which is called Hanukkah."

A TELEVISION SET — 2 YEARS
"But they don't have them.
That's right, they do not have
TV in Russia because they know
that if the people in Russia were
allowed to watch *Leave It to
Beaver* they would all want to
move to the United States, and
probably most of them would
want to come to Morristown."

A TELEVISION SET — 2 WEEKS
"And many people have two
television sets and some people
like Dougie Bershey have color
TV so that he can tell everyone
in class what color everything
was on *Walt Disney*."

All of this was duly noted by both myself and my classmates, and the vast majority of us were rather right-wing all
through grammar school. Upon reaching adolescence, however, a number of us rebelled and I must admit to distinctly
leftist leanings during my teen years. Little by little, though,
I have been coming around to my former way of thinking
and, while I am not all that enamored of our local form of
government, I have reacquired a marked distaste for Theirs.

My political position is based largely on my aversion to
large groups, and if there's one thing I know about Communism it's that large groups are definitely in the picture. I do
not work well with others and I do not wish to learn to do so.
I do not even dance well with others if there are too many of
them, and I have no doubt but that Communist discotheques
are hideously overcrowded. "From each according to his
ability, to each according to his needs" is not a decision I care
to leave to politicians, for I do not believe that an ability to
remark humorously on the passing scene would carry much
weight with one's comrades or that one could convince them

of the need for a really reliable answering service. The common good is not my cup of tea—it is the uncommon good in which I am interested, and I do not deceive myself that such statements are much admired by the members of farming collectives. Communists all seem to wear small caps, a look I consider better suited to tubes of toothpaste than to people. We number, of course, among us our own cap wearers, but I assure you they are easily avoided. It is my understanding that Communism requires of its adherents that they arise early and participate in a strenuous round of calisthenics. To someone who wishes that cigarettes came already lit the thought of such exertion at any hour when decent people are just nodding off is thoroughly abhorrent. I have been further advised that in the Communist world an aptitude for speaking or writing in an amusing fashion doesn't count for spit. I therefore have every intention of doing my best to keep the Iron Curtain from being drawn across Fifty-seventh Street. It is to this end that I have prepared a little chart of my own for the edification of my fellow New Yorkers.

The following chart compares the amount of time it takes a Communist to earn enough to purchase the following goods against the amount of time it takes a New Yorker to do the same.

COMMUNIST	NEW YORKER
A CO-OP APARTMENT IN THE EAST SEVENTIES ON THE PARK—4,000 YEARS. And even	A CO-OP APARTMENT IN THE EAST SEVENTIES ON THE PARK— No time at all if you were lucky

then you have to share it with the rest of the collective. There is not a co-op in the city with that many bathrooms.

A SUBSCRIPTION TO *The New Yorker*—3 WEEKS. And even then it is doubtful that you'd understand the cartoons.

A FIRST-CLASS AIRPLANE TICKET TO PARIS—6 MONTHS. Paris, Comrade? Not so fast.

A FERNANDO SANCHEZ NIGHT-GOWN—3 MONTHS. With the cap? Very attractive.

DINNER AT A FINE RESTAURANT—2 YEARS to earn the money; 27 years for the collective to decide on a restaurant.

in the parent department. If you have not been so blessed it could take as long as twenty years, but at least you'd have your own bathroom.

A SUBSCRIPTION TO *The New Yorker*—1 HOUR, maybe less, because in a democracy one frequently receives such things as gifts.

A FIRST-CLASS AIRPLANE TICKET TO PARIS—Varies widely, but any smart girl can acquire such a ticket with ease if she plays her cards right.

A FERNANDO SANCHEZ NIGHT-GOWN—1 WEEK, less if you know someone in the business, and need I point out that your chances of being so connected are far greater in a democracy such as ours than they are in Peking.

DINNER AT A FINE RESTAURANT—No problem if one has chosen one's friends wisely.

[1976]

CHARLES PORTIS

*

Your Action Line

(YOUR ACTION LINE SOLVES PROBLEMS,
ANSWERS QUESTIONS, CUTS RED TAPE,
STANDS UP FOR RIGHTS. YOUR ACTION LINE
WANTS TO HELP!)

Q—I have a 1966 Roosevelt dime that has turned brown. A guy in the office told me it was worth $750 and I now have it hidden in a pretty good place. Where can I sell it?

A—Benny Mann of Benny's Stamp and Coin Nook informs Action Line that the "1966 Brown" is not as valuable as many people seem to think. In fact, he tells us that some shops and restaurants will not even accept it at face value. But if you take your dime by the Coin Nook, in the Lark Avenue Arcade, Benny will be glad to examine it under his Numismascope and give you a free appraisal.

———

Q—Last May I ordered a four-record album called "Boogie Hits of the Sixties" from Birtco Sales in Nome, N.J. They cashed my check fast enough, but I got no records. I tried to call the place and the operator said the phone had been disconnected. I wrote and threatened legal action and they finally sent me a one-record album of Hawaiian music. Now they won't even answer my letters.

A—Your boogie tunes are on the way. Action Line tracked down the president of Birtco, Al Birt, to Grand Bahama Island, where he moved after the settlement of the Birtco bankruptcy case (the company's inventory and good will are going to Zodiac Studios, of Nash, N.J.), and Mr. Birt explained that your misorder was probably attributable to an "anarchy" condition in the shipping room. Zodiac has knocked the bugs out of the system, he assures Action Line, and all orders will be processed within seven months or he'll "know the reason why!"

———

Q—We have just moved into the Scales Estates. The house is O.K., but we can't get a television picture at all, and we can't pick up anything on our radio except for American Legion baseball games and rodeo news. We can't even tell where these broadcasts are coming from, what town or what state, because the announcers never say.

A—Developer Zane Scales tells Action Line that part of the Scales Estates lies on top of the old Gumbo No. 2 mercury mine. This cinnabar deposit, in combination with the

30-story, all-aluminum Zane Scales Building, makes for a "bimetallic wave-inversion squeeze," he says, and that sometimes causes freakish reception. Scales hastens to add that the condition is nothing to worry about, and that only about 400 houses are affected.

————

Q—There is a beer joint called Hester's Red Door Lounge in the 9300 block of Lark Avenue. It doesn't look like much from the outside, but I have heard some very curious and interesting discussions there at the bar. I am told that you can send off somewhere and get transcripts of what is said there and who said it. I can't stop at the lounge every day, you see, and even when I do I forget most of the stuff as soon as I leave.

A—Only weekly summaries of the conversation at the Red Door Lounge are available at this time. Send one dollar and a stamped, self-addressed envelope to Box 202, Five Points Station, and ask for Hester's White Letter. Hester Willis tells Action Line that complete daily transcripts (Hester's Red Letter) have been discontinued because of soaring stenographic and printing costs. Many subscribers actually prefer the summary, she says, particularly during football season, when there is necessarily a lot of repetitive matter. Hester hastened to assure Action Line that all the major points of all the discussions are included in the White Letter, as well as many of the humorous sallies. Sorry, no names. The speaking parties cannot be identified beyond such tags as "fat lawyer," "the old guy from Texarkana," and "retired nurse."

———

Q—Can you put me in touch with a Japanese napkin-folding club?

A—Not with a club as such, but you might try calling Meg Sparks at 696-2440. Meg holds a brown belt in the sushi school of folding, and she takes a few students along as her time permits. Beginner napkin kits ($15.95) are available at the International House of Napkins, on Victory Street, across from Barling Park.

———

Q—What happened with the Salute to Youth thing this year? I drove out there Saturday night and the place was dark. If they are going to cancel these things at the last minute, the least they can do is let somebody know about it. We had a busload of very disappointed kids, some of them crying.

A—Drove out where? The Salute to Youth rally was held Saturday night at Five Points Stadium, where it has always been held. The program lasted seven hours and the stadium lights could be seen for thirteen miles. There were eighty-one marching bands in attendance, and when they played the finale the ground shook and windows were broken almost a mile away in the Town and Country Shopping Center.

———

Q—I joined the Apollo Health Spa on June 21st, signing a thirty-year contract. It was their "Let's Get Acquainted" deal. I have attended four sessions at the place and I am not satisfied with either their beef-up program or their weight-loss program, which seem to be identical, by the way. The equipment is mostly just elastic straps that you pull. No matter how early you get there, the lead shoes are always in use. I want out, but they say they will have to "spank" me if I don't meet all the terms of the contract. Those people are not from around here and I don't know what they mean exactly, whether it is just their way of talking or what. That's all they will say.

A—Action Line will say it once again: Never sign any document until you have read it carefully! Don't be pushed! So much for the scolding. You will be interested to learn that the Attorney General's office is currently investigating a number of spanking threats alleged to have been made by the sales staff at Apollo. Ron Rambo, the Apollo Spa's proxy and a former Mr. Arizona, tells Action Line that he, too, is looking into the matter and that he has his eye on "one or two bad apples." As for their equipment, he says your cut-rate membership plan does not entitle you to the use of the Hell Boots, the Rambo Bars, the Olympic Tubs, or the Squirrel Cage except by appointment.

———

Q—Help! I live on Railroad Street and I have been driving to work for many years by way of Lark Avenue. Now they have put up a "NO LEFT TURN" sign at the intersection of Railroad and Lark and I have to turn right and go all the way to the airport before I can make a U-turn and double back. This means I have to get up in the dark every morning to allow for the long drive.

A—You don't say where you work. If it's downtown, then

why not forget Lark and stay on Railroad until you reach Gully, which has a protected left turn. You may not know it, but Gully is now one-way going east all the way to Five Points, where you can take the dogleg around Barling Park (watch for slowpokes in the old people's crossing) and onto Victory. Bear right over the viaduct to twenty-seventh and then hang a left at the second stoplight and go four blocks to the dead end at Lagrange. Take Lagrange as far as the zoo (stay in the right lane), and from there it's a straight shot to the Hopper Expressway and the Rotifer Bridge.

———

Q—My science teacher told me to write a paper on the "detective ants" of Ceylon, and I can't find out anything about these ants. Don't tell me to go to the library, because I've already been there.

A—There are no ants in Ceylon. Your teacher may be thinking of the "journalist ants" of central Burma. These bright-red insects grow to a maximum length of one-quarter inch, and they are tireless workers, scurrying about on the forest floor and gathering tiny facts, which they store in their abdominal sacs. When the sacs are filled, they coat these facts with a kind of nacreous glaze and exchange them for bits of yellow wax manufactured by the smaller and slower "wax ants." The journalist ants burrow extensive tunnels and galleries beneath Burmese villages, and the villagers, reclining at night on their straw mats, can often hear a steady hum from the earth. This hum is believed to be the ants sifting fine particles of information with their feelers in the dark. Diminu-

tive grunts can sometimes be heard, but these are thought
to come not from the journalist ants but from their albino
slaves, the "butting dwarf ants," who spend their entire lives
tamping wax into tiny storage chambers with their heads.

[1977]

DONALD BARTHELME

✳

In the Morning Post

In the morning post I received what I regard as a rather astonishing communication from the magazine *Writer's Digest*. The magazine, addressing me by name, disclosed that it was planning, for yearly publication, a cover story "on the link that some people see between writing and drinking" and that it would like to include me "in a roundup piece summarizing the drinking habits of the top writers in America today."

After noting that I had been promoted to Top Writer (gratifying indeed after so many years of corporalship), my second, scandalized reaction was, *"How did they find out?"* I mean, I do take a drink now and again. In fact my doctor, who is the soul of tact, once characterized my consumption as "slightly imprudent." But how the devil did *Writer's Digest* discover this? Does the *whole city* know?

Zizzled with horror, as you may well imagine, I turned next to the magazine's questions, my answers to which they proposed to print (along with a recent photo and a listing of my vodka-soaked work to date). Such is the power of the questionnaire *qua* mechanism that, helplessly, I began penciling in answers, as follows:

1. "How would you describe your own drinking habits? —— Light —— Medium —— Heavy —— Other?"

Medium. Light is sissy and Heavy doesn't go down so well with Deans, Loan Officers and Publishers, and who in the world would want to be Other?

2. "When you feel like having a few drinks, what do you usually have?"

Zip-Strip on the rocks. Too easy, let us proceed to—

3. "Any favorite hangouts for drinking?"

Yes, Godot's, but I can't give you the address because you know the place is and I mean we want to keep it that way even though the toppest writers in America "hang out" as you put it there and goodness gracious Elaine's is what we *don't*—Also, in bed, sobbing lightly.

4. "Favorite drinking companions?"

Joe Conrad, Steverino Crane, Pete Hamill and Tom Aquinas.

5. "Heaviest drinkers/writers that you know—or *have* known—of?"

Oh, this is a mean one, WD. I could do a lot of I-didn't-know-what-I-was-doing-my-God-I-didn't-think-they'd-actually-*print*-the-Goddamn-thing damage here, couldn't I? Because I know for a fact that ************* is even more slightly imprudent than I, and that ****** von ******, thought to be sober as white bread, takes a little bang at ten o'clock in the morning, to get himself started. Off the record, I'll tell you nothing.

6. "Do you see any affinity between hard drinking and the writing life? Explain."

Well, climb up on my knees here, WD. When you've been staring at this Billy-by-damn keyboard all your life, decade after decade, you get a little thirsty. The thing is, *the keys don't move*. The "e" is in the same place, every day. The "h" is in the same place, decade in, decade out. The "g" is fixed, eternally. It makes you, like, *thirsty*. Any piano tuner would understand, I think.

[1978]

VERONICA GENG

✳

Curb Carter Policy Discord Effort Threat

WASHINGTON, OCT. 11 — In a surprise move, a major spokesman announced yesterday that a flurry of moves has forestalled deferment of the Administration's controversial hundred-pronged strategy. The nine-page indictment provides a minimum of new details about the alleged sharp apprehensions now being voiced in key areas. As holiday traffic flowed into and out of the nation's cities, President Carter acknowledged in a telephone interview that there is "cause for some optimism." But Senate conferees quickly vowed to urge the challenging of this view as over-optimistic.

In a shocking about-face, it was confirmed that the package will serve as the basis for mounting pressures. However, no target date has been set for the fueling of speculations.

In an unexpected development, it is expected that fresh pleas will be issued for a brightened outlook. "Sharply higher deficits will rise in the long run," said a senior expert. Token collection of heavy weapons has been reported near the austerity programs, where a newly minted spirit of fairness has caused anticipated losses.

The focal point of this change of focus is the Administration's broad-gauge diplomatic push. According to officials in the vogue for docu-dramas, these figures indicate that a shrinking supply of farmland, swept by strong emotional tides and waves of public resentment, is considering another round of direct contacts with the globe's expanding circle of treelessness. However, flagrant lobbying, emerging violations, and tenacious complicating factors have now knocked the expected bloodbath into an increasingly powerful cocked hat, say sources. Meanwhile, cracks in the alliance have erupted, linking harsh inroads with a lagging industrial base.

Last week, the coalition warned that 152 recommendations would be submitted, cutting deeply into the support for renewed wrangling. But such policies have long irked the delegates, and the fear now is that they will sound a death knell to the Constitution by muting their quarrels or adding that there are still elements to be ironed out.

Embattled leaders have long lengthened the rift by using such strategies as sidedown, slowmate, staletracking, and stiffening. Now aides predict a downgrading and stymying of routine foreign cutoffs, unless the nuclear family can be bailed out of this legal vacuum. Dr. Bourne reasserted his innocence of any wrongdoing.

The transitional Government will close for defusing next week, without having resolved core conflicts or posed the uneasy questions that might assuage local hardliners. However, an authorized biography is likely to continue for months, possibly even years, to come. Not all styles in all sizes.

Continued on Page D6, Column 1

[1978]

JOHN HUGHES

*

Vacation '58

If Dad hadn't shot Walt Disney in the leg, it would have been our best vacation ever. We were going to Disneyland. It was a dream come true. The rides! The thrills! The Mouseketeers! I was so excited that I spent the whole month of May feeling like I had to go to the bathroom. When school finally let out on a Tuesday, I sprinted home as fast as I could, even though we weren't leaving until Friday.

Dad picked up our brand-new 1958 Plymouth Sport Suburban Six station wagon on Thursday morning. The speedometer had only six and three-tenths miles on it. Dad said that it would be a pleasure to travel for six days in a car that smelled as good as our new Plymouth. It was nice to see Dad excited about our trip. For months Mom had to act moody and beg to get him to drive out to California. "What good will it do the kids to see their country from an airplane seat? she wanted to know. Finally, Dad gave in and said we would get a station wagon and drive the 2,448 miles from 74 Rivard

259

Boulevard, Grosse Pointe, Michigan, to 1313 Harbor Boulevard, Anaheim, California.

It took almost all day Friday to pack the car. Dad loaded
and unloaded it again and again to save a square foot here, a
square inch there. Then he simonized the car and hung litter
bags in the front and back seats, attached a compass to the
dashboard, and put a first aid kit in the glove compartment.
Then he called everyone outside to take one item apiece out
of the car so he could close the back.

After dinner, Dad ran the Plymouth up to Richie's Mara-
thon Service to gas up and have Richie check under the hood
and see if everything was A-O.K. When Dad backed out of
the driveway the car scraped bottom. Not a little scrape but
a *sccccccrrrrraaaaaape*!

Dad got back at 8:00. We heard the *scccrrrraaaaape*! and
knew it was him. Richie had said that everything was beautiful under the hood. The car was gassed up, there was plenty
of oil, the tire pressure was perfect, the AAA maps were
organized in the glove compartment, and the speedometer
read exactly 20.00 miles.

"Okay, all you Indians! Time for bed!" Mom said.

"But it's only 8:30!" I protested.

"We have to get up at 4:00 in the morning! I want to make
Chicago by lunch!" Dad said, shooing us upstairs.

The telephone rang at 9:45 the next morning. It was
Grandpa Pete calling to see why we hadn't gone yet. We had all
overslept—even the baby. Dad was furious. I could hear him
screaming and pounding his fists on the bathroom sink.

"We're five hours behind schedule!" he yelled. "And we haven't even left the goddamn house!"

"*I* wasn't the one who sat up all night rearranging the suitcases!" Mom yelled back.

Everyone hurried downstairs, dressed and ready to go.

"We don't need breakfast, Mom," I said.

"I'm still full from last night," Patty said, grinning in a way that she hoped would calm Dad. He was even angrier after he had tried to shave real fast.

Mom insisted that we all sit down and have a good breakfast, and Dad argued that no one ever died from skipping *one* breakfast. We gobbled down our pancakes and bacon, and chugged our juice. Dad sat outside in the car revving the engine. By the time we were ready to leave, the car had stopped, and Dad couldn't get it going again.

"Goddamn Plymouth Motors! I should have gone with a Ford—they know how to make an ignition! These damn Plymouths!"

"Just calm down, Clark!" Mom snarled. "You're making the whole neighborhood smell of gasoline!"

After we sat for five minutes quietly listening to Dad breathe in and out of his nose, the car started and we backed out of the driveway. Mr. McMillan came running up to the car.

"Hey! You folks left your sprinkler on!"

Not only did we leave the sprinkler on, but when we got to the Edsel Ford Expressway, Mom said she thought she left the oven on, and we had to turn around and go all the way back home only to find that she hadn't left it on. While Mom was inside the house checking the oven, the phone rang. It was my Aunt Catherine calling to say that Great Aunt Edythe needed a ride to her son's house in Tucson, Arizona, and would we mind taking her since we were going in that general direction anyway.

It looked like we were finally on our way when Mom said that it was almost lunchtime and we could save some money by having lunch at home.

She had thrown out all the milk so that it wouldn't sour and smell up the refrigerator, so Dad had to go up to Kroger's and get a fresh quart. That took almost an hour because Dad locked the keys in the car by accident and had to wreck the vent window to get in.

Dad was so exhausted from being mad all morning that when he got home he said we would leave the next day.

"But I told Catherine that we would be there on Sunday, and if we lose today and tonight we won't make it," Mom said.

"Call her back and tell her we'll see her on Monday instead."

"Well," Mom said cautiously, "Auntie Edythe wants to be in Tucson by Wednesday."

"What?"

"I told Catherine that we would drive Auntie Edythe to Normie's in Tucson. It's on our way, and she's such a sweet thing."

Dad didn't say a word until we reached Battle Creek

and then all he said was, "Shut up back there!" He made up a rule about no eating in the car, and he wouldn't let us listen to the radio or roll down the windows. All through Michigan he went over the speed limit, except when we went under bridges and past clumps of trees where a State Police car might be hiding. I wanted desperately to belt Patty for not sharing the Jujubees she was sneaking. She had brought along a whole bunch of stuff she'd bought with baby-sitting money, and she wouldn't share any of it with me. There was absolutely nothing to do but stare out the window at the moonlit fields of corn.

Mom pleaded with Dad to stop at a motel when we got to Springfield, Illinois. Several times he crossed completely over the median lines and drove in the opposite lane. Once, while going through a little town, Dad drove up on the sidewalk and ran over a bike and some toys. Mom accused him of being asleep at the wheel, but he said he was just unfamiliar with Illinois traffic signs.

He took off his shoes, rolled, down the window, turned the radio way up, and made us all sing the Michigan State fight song. But after a few minutes we were all sound asleep, our new station wagon racing down U.S. 55 like a bedroom on wheels. I don't know how far we traveled like that. Fortunately, there wasn't much traffic at that hour so we didn't hit anything. We finally woke up when Missy asked Dad to get her a drink of water and Dad said, "Go ask Mommy, Daddy's sleeping." I heard that and so did Mom, and she screamed and Dad slammed on the brakes, and the luggage tumbled forward onto the back seat and Dad's golf clubs scattered all over the highway.

We slept beside the road for the rest of the night. When we woke we all felt miserable. Our teeth were coated with night slime, our necks were stiff, and we all had to go to the bathroom. We hadn't eaten dinner, so we were all hungry. Dad was even crabbier because he hadn't had any coffee yet.

After we washed our faces and brushed our teeth at a gas station and ate breakfast, we felt a little better. Even Dad managed a smile, and when we pulled back out on the highway, he suggested a game of Auto Bingo.

We rolled into Aunt Catherine's driveway about 10:00 P.M. She lived in Wichita, Kansas, in a farmhouse that was not on a farm but in town. She and Uncle Stan had two kids: Dale, who was my age, and Vicki, who was a year younger than Patty. I hated the two of them like I hated the flu. I was glad we were only staying the night.

I had to sleep in Dale's room on a bed that was lumpy and smelled funny. Patty and Vicki slept together and got along fine, but I think it was just because Patty was trying to act big in front of Vicki, who was a hick. The baby and Missy slept with Mom and Dad in Aunt Catherine's room. Uncle Stan was a baby about having to sleep on the couch in the family room. "I work tomorrow, you know," he said.

I didn't remember Aunt Edythe because the last time I had seen her I was practically a baby. I tried to be polite and not register my horror when I saw her. She looked like the Mummy with a wig on. She smelled like a combination of mothballs and vitamin pills. I couldn't believe that I had to ride next to her.

"Put her by the window," Dad whispered to Mom as Uncle Stan helped Aunt Edythe into the car. "I don't want her to upchuck on the seats."

"She can't sit by the window!" Mom snapped. "She might fall out."

We were ready to go when Dale came around the side of the house with a beagle on a leash.

"Here he is, Uncle Clark," he said. "All walked and everything!"

"Who is he?" Dad asked.

"Auntie Edythe's dog. His name is Dinkie," Dale said. "He's neato. He watches 'Ed Sullivan.'"

We had to rearrange the seating so that the dog would be way in the back. Mom didn't want him near the baby. She was afraid the dog might bite his face or lick his breath away. So we ended up with the baby in the front, the dog in the back, Patty next to the window, Missy beside her, then Aunt Edythe, and then me by the other window. Aunt Edythe was pressed right up against me so tight I could feel her nose breath on my arm.

At Mullinville we jogged northwest about twenty miles across the Arkansas River, which wasn't as much a river as a gash filled with water the color of beef broth. I tried to spit in it as we crossed, but succeeded only in "frogging" my cheek.

"You don't want to take Highway 50," Aunt Edythe said to Dad. "You want to stay on U.S. 54."

"We're going to Dodge City," Dad shouted so that Aunt Edythe could hear.

"Why in heavens would you want to go to that filthy, dirty tourist trap?"

Unfortunately, Aunt Edythe was right about Dodge City. It wasn't the authentic frontier town I had dreamed it would be. It was sort of like St. Claire Shores, Michigan, only dustier and minus a lake. There were used car lots named after Wyatt Earp and Doc Holliday and trailer homes right in town. The Long Branch Saloon smelled like popcorn and toilet ice. Dad refused to pay seventy-five cents for a beer so we left.

"If you really want to see something," Aunt Edythe said in an "I-told-you-so" voice, "you get back on U.S. 54 like I told you before and go down to Liberal and see the House of Mud. It's entirely made out of mud and it's really something to see!"

There was no House of Mud. At one time, a gas station attendant told us, there was a House of Mud, but just after World War I it caved in, killing the curator and his family.

"If you want to see something special," he said, "go back to Mullinville and take Highway 50 up to Dodge City."

At first glance, Oklahoma looked the same as Kansas. At second and third glance, it also looked like Kansas. Even after Dad pointed out that the portion of Oklahoma that we were traveling through was one of the nation's top producers of fossils and dinosaur bones, it still looked like Kansas. As a matter of fact, it looked like Kansas deep into Texas, where we stopped for the night.

The Ranger Inn was like my friend Earl Denkinger's attic bedroom in his stepfather's house. It had a rug made out of rags, cowboy beds, a horseshoe on the door, a bathtub with feet, a chipped mirror, and only half a roll of toilet paper. The rooms were so small that Dad had to get three. Aunt Edythe and her dog had one room; Mom, Dad, and Mark had another; and Missy, Patty, and I had the other. Although it was sort of scary being alone in a strange room, it gave me an opportunity to bash Patty for being so stingy with her Milk Duds.

Everyone except Aunt Edythe was real cheerful when we got in the car the next day. Her arthritis was flaring up and she claimed that it would kill her before we got to Tucson.

"Beans, baloney, and horseflies!" Dad said under his breath to Mom. "No one ever died from stiff fingers."

"Don't be so sure, Mr. Know-It-All," Aunt Edythe barked. She swatted Dad with her *Reader's Digest*.

Dad's face turned as red as the flashing Highway Patrol lights behind us. That's the way it is with old people; claiming they are hard of hearing, they make you shout, but as soon as you say something about them, they can hear 100 percent. Later on Dad told me that Aunt Edythe could hear an ant fart, but set an H-Bomb off in her drawers and she wouldn't hear a thing.

That flashing red light got closer and closer. Dad edged over to let the patrolman pass, but he didn't want to pass. He wanted Dad to pull over.

"I haven't gone over seventy miles per hour," Dad said.

"Well, he's not stopping you to chat," Mom said in her voice that sounds pleasant to children, but nasty to adults.

Dad pulled over and reached for his wallet. The cop came to the window. "What's the problem, officer?" Dad asked, offering his driver's license.

"You better step out of the car for a moment, sir."

Dad got out of the car and walked around behind it. His mouth dropped open and his eyes showed white. I jumped into the back and looked out the rear window. It was the most sickening thing I'd ever seen in my life. Aunt Edythe's dog was laying on the ground behind the car. He was flat on his belly with his legs out to the sides and his neck stretched out, so that he looked a beagle version of a bear rug. There was a wide red trail leading up to his body.

"We have anti-cruelty laws in this state," the cop told Dad.

"My God, you can't think I'd do a thing like that on purpose!" Dad protested, looking away from the carcass. "I tied the dog to the bumper while I put my wife's aunt in the car. It takes so long to get her in and out, I guess I forgot about him."

The cop bought Dad's explanation. He kneeled down and tenderly examined the dog.

"I had one of these when I was a boy," he said with a sad smile. "From the looks of his foot pads I'd say this little guy kept up with you for half a mile or so."

After the cop pulled away, Dad untied the leash from the

bumper and got back in the car. He just drove away telling everyone that we had a loose license plate and the cop was helping fix it. He must have figured Aunt Edythe wouldn't miss the dog now if she hadn't missed him all day.

On Wednesday we got off to a good, early start. Dad had consented to a side trip to Carlsbad Caverns. Carlsbad, Mom explained, was the largest cave in the world and New Mexico's only national park.

Mom took out all the maps and spread them across the front seat. Mark got ahold of one corner of the map and sucked it soft from Kermit, Texas, to Artesia, New Mexico, including Carlsbad. His tongue was spotted black with trip planner's ink, which Mom was afraid might be poisonous. Dad pointed out that thousands of kids suck on maps and that the government wouldn't let the auto club use poison ink. It didn't make much difference whether or not the map was wrecked because no map showed the road we were on. We had gotten on it by mistake after missing a couple of detour-this-way signs. After a few miles, we drove off a cliff.

It wasn't a big cliff. It was only about four feet high. But it was enough to blow out the front tire, knock off the back bumper, break Dad's glasses, make Aunt Edythe spit out her false teeth, spill a jug of Kool-Aid, bump Missy's head, spread the Auto Bingo pieces all over, and make Mark do number two.

We sat there stunned, rubbing our banged-up arms and shins. Aunt Edythe howled about her internal organs getting the shock of their lives. Mom was in a panic because she thought a flying orange had hit Mark's soft spot. Dad just sat gripping the steering wheel and clicking his tongue. Personally, I enjoyed the accident and was particularly impressed with the distance Dad had gotten out of a heavy, loaded-up station wagon.

Dad cut all the adhesive strips of the Band-Aids and taped his glasses together. He stood on the roof of the car and studied the landscape to determine the best route back to civilization.

"Where's my little dog?" Aunt Edythe suddenly screamed. "Has he gotten loose in the desert? Where is he? I have to find him!" She tried to get out of the car.

"Stay in the car," Mom said sternly. "It's hot and dangerous out there."

"Don't you tell me what to do!" Aunt Edythe shot back. "I'll do what I want. I should never have come on this trip! I should have taken the airplane!"

She pointed a finger at Dad. "He can't even drive," she shouted.

Dad drew back his fist to deck her, but Mom got to her first, grabbing her arm and firmly pressing her back into her seat. "You move and I'll split your lip!" Mom yelled.

A glorious desert sunset bathed the tow truck in orange light as it hauled our car back to the dirt detour road.

"I never seen nothin' so mother bless'ed dumb," the toothless tow driver said to Dad. "You musta got shit fer brains!"

Dad would have punched the guy in the mouth, but he knew there probably wasn't another tow truck in Loco Hills, New Mexico. He didn't even complain when all the men at the gas station laughed when he asked how much the tow and tire repair was.

"Well, how much? Five bucks? Ten bucks? What?" Dad inquired. The men laughed. Dad sort of laughed along with them.

"How much you got?" the avocado-shaped station owner asked.

"I'm asking how much the charge is," Dad said.

"Why on earth do you need to know how much money I have to tell me how much it costs to tow my car?"

"'Cause I'm a-gonna charge you all the money you got."

It cost us 588 dollars. They even took the money out of Aunt Edythe's shoe. The owner of the station made it a point to explain to Dad that what he was doing wasn't robbery. "I should know," he laughed. "I'm the sheriff."

We spent the night in Alamagordo, New Mexico. Since the only money we had was Patty's twenty-nine dollars from baby-sitting, Dad had to rob the motel in the morning when he went to check out. He didn't actually rob it; he just reached into the cash register and took a handful of money. The manager came out of the back room, where he had been checking on our breakfast charges and saw Dad. He was pretty old and he didn't move too fast, so we got away clean.

About five miles outside of Lordsburg, Patty and I were

singing "One Hundred Bottles of Beer on the Wall." All of a sudden Dad shouted, "Hold your hats!" He gunned the engine and we lunged forward. I could hear sirens wailing. I looked out the back. A highway patrol car was chasing us.

"Pull over, Clark!" Mom shouted. "Pull over!"

"Not on your life!" Dad growled. He pounded his fist on the steering wheel. "Come on, you gas-eating bastard, *go!*"

The cop was gaining on us. His Ford was light and tuned-up. Our Plymouth was heavy and loaded-down, and it shimmied and vibrated from driving off the cliff. The cop jerked his car into the passing lane. A truck coming in the opposite direction forced him back. He came up almost to our bumper. "Throw out the ice chest!" Dad shouted to me. "Throw it out the back window!"

I crawled back and lowered the window, and the rush of air and the change in pressure sucked a baby sheet and a Wichita newspaper out of our car and onto the windshield of the cop car. The cop swerved and ripped into the dirt shoulder, sending up a rooster tail of dirt and gravel. Dad laughed.

"What are you doing?" Mom screamed. She didn't know about the robbery. I knew, but Dad made me promise not to tell Mom.

"I'm running from the law!"

"What? Are you crazy?"

"I robbed the Roadrunner Motel!" he shouted. "To get money!"

The cop was back on our tail. A second car was coming from behind him.

"This is *so* cool!" I yelled out the back window.

"I have to go tinkle!" Missy cried.

Suddenly Dad slammed on the brakes. The Plymouth fishtailed to a screeching, rubber-stink stop. The cops locked up their brakes and dove to the sides of the road. Dad put the hammer down and we took off. One of the cops was stuck in the ditch. The other was in pursuit after a moment. That's when I threw out the ice chest. It hit the front of the cop car on the first bounce. The cop lost momentary control of his car and sideswiped a convertible in the other lane.

"It pays to watch 'Dragnet'!" Dad laughed.

Mom was in a trance, shaking her head. Tears were collecting in her eyes. Missy had wet her dress and was crying. Patty was saying her prayers, Mark was sleeping, and Aunt Edythe was looking sort of sick. I was having a great time planning what I would throw out the back trap next if some cop got brave enough to try and run in *my* Dad.

"Uh-oh!" Dad said.

I looked out the front and saw a flickering mass of lights.

"Roadblock," Dad said. He leaned forward and tried to coax a little more speed out of the Plymouth. "We'll run it!"

We split a row of sawhorses as if they weren't even there, and then plowed into two cop cars joined at the front bumpers, opening them up like supermarket doors. We smacked them so hard, they spun around until they met at the rear bumpers.

Dad kept it to the floorboards until we came to San Simon Creek, Arizona. He slowed down and cut off the main highway onto a dirt service road. That road ran into a larger road and then we were back on pavement. Dad calmed down and breathed a sigh of relief. He even let us stop at a place called the Horrors of Mexico, which was a barn that had a dead person in a bottle and some wads of hair mounted in cases. There was also a chicken with five legs.

An hour later we arrived in Bisbee. Dad wanted to show us the largest open-pit copper mine in the country. "It says in the guidebook that this mine would hold nearly one billion pillows!"

As we examined the mine, Dad switched license plates with a car belonging to an elderly couple from Michigan. Then Dad called us back into the car and we got onto Highway 80 and headed north to Tucson to drop off Aunt Edythe, who, by now, didn't look very good at all.

"Leave her alone," Dad said to Mom. "She's sleeping. If you wake her, we'll just have to listen to her guff."

"I wonder if she's hungry," Mom replied. "We didn't wake her for lunch."

"Old people sleep a lot. She's fine."

Only she wasn't fine.

"Mom?" Patty said about an hour later. "Mom!"

"What is it!" Mom said angrily. She had just gotten Mark to stop screaming.

"Aunt Edythe is leaning on me and she won't get off. And I can't wake her up."

"Pull over, Clark," Mom said.

"We'll be in Tucson in another twenty minutes. She'll be fine."

"Pull over! She's not fine!"

Dad pulled over to the side of the road. Mom hurried out and opened the back door. Patty jumped out and Aunt Edythe slowly fell over, sort of like a tree being cut down. She stayed in a sitting position, even though she was on her side.

"She's dead!"

Patty shrieked and rubbed the spot on her arm where Aunt Edythe's head had rested. Dad pounded the steering wheel.

"Well, goddamn it anyway!" he yelled.

We figured that she must have died back around Deming, New Mexico. That's the last time anyone could remember her saying anything. She told us to roll the windows up because she was freezing cold. She was dead about ten hours and missed out on the cop chase.

"What are we going to do, Clark?" Mom asked, choking back tears.

"We could leave her here and call Normie and you could tell him to come and ..."

"We can't do that!"

"Well, hell, then let's take her to Tucson. I just don't want to get caught up in questioning and funerals and all that baloney."

"How can you be so cold and insensitive?" Mom asked.

"I'm not being insensitive, I'm being practical. We have only three days at Disneyland at the tops—three days. It was your idea to take a car vacation to Disneyland, not mine. I didn't rob a motel, ruin my car, and kill a dog to spend my vacation at a funeral for a crusty old bag."

Mom could hardly argue with that so we continued on to Tucson with Aunt Edythe on the roof covered with Dad's raincoat. She was real light and Dad was able to get her up there by himself, which was good because no one else would touch her.

"Come on, let's play I Spy," Dad said, trying to cheer us up and make us forget that there was an eighty-four-year-old dead woman on our roof. "I spy something . . . green!"

When we got to Tucson, we had to stop at a gas station and get a fill-up. Mom looked up Normie's address in the phone book. He lived over near the University of Arizona. The gas station attendant helped us with directions, and we found the house with no trouble at all. The only problem was, Normie wasn't home. His neighbor said he went up to Flagstaff for the week.

"I hope he don't get this rain," the man said as he hurried inside his house. He shouted from the porch, "First rain in eleven weeks!"

"It's a damn good thing it's night," Dad said as he carried Aunt Edythe into Normie's backyard and sat her down in a patio chair.

"You can't leave her here," Mom said. "It's raining."

"Is she going to catch a cold and die?"

"No, but have some respect!"

"Up your ass with a red hot poker!" Dad finally lost his temper. He stormed back to the car and lit up a cigarette.

Mom found her umbrella in the back and opened it up. She fixed it so it rested in Aunt Edythe's hand and protected her from the rain. Then she wrote a note and stuck it between Aunt Edythe's knees. The note said, "Sorry, Normie. Will talk later. Love, Ruth and Clark and the kids."

The vacation sort of went downhill after that. Mom continued to feel badly about how we just dumped Aunt Edythe on the porch and how upset Normie would be to find his Mom all wet and dead. Dad tried to be cheerful from time to time, but it wasn't sincere. He couldn't cheer anyone up, not the way he felt.

We ran into a little excitement the next day at the Yuma Proving Grounds, near the Arizona/California border. Dad thought that we might enjoy a brief trip to the Imperial Dam. At Roll, Arizona, we took a little dirt road that both Mom and Dad thought would go through to the reservoir and dam. Instead, it went through the proving grounds, and on that particular day they were proving missiles.

We were just driving along trying to ignore the bumps and chuckholes, when all of a sudden a missile cleared the top of the car by a foot and exploded about a half mile away. The force of the explosion rocked the car and woke up the baby.

Another missile zinged past and blew up.

"Holy Christ! Someone's shooting at us!"

Dad hit the gas and we all dove on the floor and covered our heads. Gimme your walkie-talkie!" Dad shouted to me. I fumbled around on the floor and found my Kaptain Kismet walkie-talkie set.

"Come on, you idiot! Hand it over!"

I gave it to Dad and he pressed the button. "*Weeeeeeeee-ooooooooowop!*" Dad screamed into the little plastic walkie-talkie.

I looked up and saw a missile explode in front of us.

"See, son? Missiles are radio controlled. I just interfered with its signal and changed its course!"

"But Dad . . ."

"Here comes another! *Weeeeeeeeeooooooooowop!*"

"But Dad!"

"*Look out!*"

That was it! *Blam!* The force of the exploding shell knocked the car over on its side. We all fell against the passenger-side doors. Dad's glasses broke again. Patty chipped her two-thousand-dollar front teeth. Mom just started to whimper and coo and tap her foot on the floor.

"Dad," I finally said, "there isn't any batteries in it."

"*Aren't* any batteries," Mom said softly.

Dad and I were able to get the car back on its wheels. No missile came by until we were on our way again. At first, Dad didn't do anything but drive. It was as though we were going down Woodward Avenue in Detroit and the explod-ing missiles were pigeon poops. Then one came pretty close and Dad jumped on the accelerator and we took off again. Dad dodged and swerved, stopped, sped up, spun around. He got so good at avoiding missiles that I felt a little dis-appointed when we reached the north entrance to the range.

A pair of startled guards approached the car. Dad rolled

down the window and grinned. "You better hope to God that the Russians aren't flying Plymouth station wagons, 'cause they're invincible!"

We drove off and had a good laugh. As a matter of fact, we laughed nonstop until the Indian attack.

We crossed the Colorado River, stopping to admire its muddy brown majesty. Then we continued, driving through the Yuma Indian reservation. Highway 80 cut through the southwest corner of the reservation, which was littered with beat-up trailers, tin sheds, garbage, pick-up trucks, and semi-naked kids. It smelled of sewage.

As we passed a driveway, a truck pulled out and followed us. Every driveway had a pick-up truck and every pick-up truck pulled out and followed us. The lead truck pulled out and passed us. He slowed to a crawl as the other trucks came alongside.

"Lock your doors!" Mom ordered.

Dad honked the horn and waved for the Indians to let us pass. They responded with a shower of beer cans and liquor bottles.

"Indian attack!" I shouted.

"But they're Yuma Indians. The guidebook says that they are primarily agrarian people with no tradition of warfare!" Mom said.

"Look out!" Dad shouted. "A rifle!"

Five rifles poked out from the truck windows. Dad coasted to a stop, steering with his knees so he could keep his hands up in the air. One of the Indians got out of his truck. He knocked on the window with his rifle. Dad rolled it down a crack.

"Yes? May I help you?" Dad said with a smile.

"Give me your money," the Indian mumbled. He was drunk.

Dad counted out the last of the stolen money. He slipped a twenty, a five, and three ones out the window.

"Open the hood of your car."

"Why?"

The Indian trained his rifle on Dad. He reached down and pulled the hood latch. A couple of the other Indians began robbing the engine of parts. The rest of the Yumas surrounded the car and made lewd remarks and gestures at Patty and Mom.

"Hey, look here!" Dad said. "If you take too much off my engine, we won't be able to drive away."

We let the Indians fleece us. They took everything, even Dad's Pall Malls. They took our hubcaps, headlights, chrome strips, radio, antenna, and air filter. Then one of the Indians asked for our tires. He said he would trade his tires for ours. Three Indians helped jack-up the front and got the front tires off, while two other Indians jacked-up the back and took off those tires. Another truck came by loaded with screaming Indians waving bottles in paper bags.

"Let's fergit this," the leader said, and they left us with one tire on and three off. The three that were off were snow tires and slightly larger than the original tire that remained.

At about sun-up we passed through Joshua Tree National

Monument. Dad slammed on the brakes and made us all get out of the car. "See," he said. "That's a Joshua tree." Then he made us get back in and we sped off. It was sort of scary.

We hit Riverside, California, around breakfast, but no one dared suggest we stop. At Ontario it began to rain. Dad turned on the wipers. They started up and then stopped. Dad had to slow down because the rain formed an opaque film on the glass and he couldn't see. When he slowed down, the wipers went on. As he accelerated, they slowed and stopped. That's when he started to cry. We all started to cry. There we were, crawling down U.S. 10, bawling like babies.

We idled into Pomona. The rain cleared and Dad punched it, and we roared south to Anaheim.

"We're getting close," I shouted as I spotted a Disneyland sign. "We're going to make it!"

Our odyssey was nearing an end, and even though we had less than a day to spend in the fabled fun capital of America, it didn't matter. Our tears were now for joy. I patted Dad on the back and said in a choked voice, "Thanks, Dad. I love you." Mom gave him a kiss and so did Patty, and Missy grabbed him around his neck and squeezed.

"*There it is! I see it! I see it!*" I screamed when I saw the turrets of Cinderella's castle.

"Oh, my God! It's Disneyland!" Mom cried. She thanked God and made us give thanks, which we gladly did.

We pulled into the massive parking lot. It was empty.

"We have the place to ourselves!" Dad announced with

a smile that quickly turned to a drooling idiot's frown as he read a sign that said Closed for Repairs and Cleaning.

"There is no god!" Mom shouted. "No god would treat us like this!"

"Don't say that, Mom," Patty pleaded.

"We are in the hands of the devil! We have sinned, we bathed in sin, and the devil stole our souls!" Mom grabbed out at us. We started to cry.

"Closed for repairs and cleaning," Dad fumed. "You son-of-a-bitch prick! I watched your son-of-a-bitch program every Sunday! I bought a son-of-a-bitch color TV just to watch your son-of-a-bitch program! You owe me! You owe Clark W. Griswold, Jr.! *You owe him!*"

Dad threw the car in reverse and floored it. The thrust jerked us all forward in our seats. Then he slammed on the brakes and threw it into forward. We screeched off toward the freeway. When we got to L.A., Dad got off the freeway and stopped at a sporting goods store. He took the checkbook off the dashboard and went inside.

A few minutes later, Dad came out of the store with a bag under his arm. He got into the car and kissed Mark. He started the engine and we drove back to the freeway. We got off at Santa Monica Boulevard and headed toward Beverly Hills and Bel Air.

"Clark?" Mom said. "Where are we going?"

Dad didn't answer. He just continued driving, being very careful now to observe speed limits and all the rules of the road.

"Clark? Clark? Clark?" said Mom, over and over again.

When we got to Beverly Hills, Dad pulled over. There was an old sedan parked ahead of us. A man wearing a straw hat came up to our car. He held up a map of the stars' homes.

"Hello, folks," he said. "Welcome to Hollywood!"

"Give me the map," Dad demanded as he drew a revolver out of the bag and pressed it against the man's nose. The man handed Dad the map. "Thank you."

We drove away, leaving the man standing in the middle of the road, shaking his head and stroking his white hair.

We stopped in front of a rambling mansion surrounded by a high fence. Dad turned off the motor. He loaded his revolver and stuck it in his belt. Without saying a word, he got out of the car and made for the fence. I followed him. Mom was too nuts to prevent me.

I never knew Dad was in such good shape, but he just climbed up the fence like it was a four-foot backyard stockade fence. I could see where he was going. There was a group of men sitting around a swimming pool having some kind of meeting. Dad crawled on his belly through the flower beds up to the house; then he stood still. A dog on a chain leaped from the patio toward the flower bed where Dad was standing. He fired and drilled the dog in midair.

"I've got your number, Disney! I'm Clark W. Griswold, and you owe me!"

The men who were reviewing drawings and papers on a large table turned in Dad's direction. A woman screamed and dropped a tray of drinks.

"I'll give you to the count of three, Walt Disney!"

"Can't we talk?" Disney said in the familiar voice that I recognized from the weekly introductions to his TV program.

"You closed your fantasy park, and that was a mistake!" Dad shouted as he waved his revolver at Mr. Disney. "I'm giving you to the count of three to run. I'm giving you a chance! You can run or I can blast your ass right here!"

Mr. Disney looked at the other men. He looked at the woman who had dropped the drinks and was now frozen with her hands over her mouth. A security guard came running around the corner of the house. He saw Dad and stopped, dropping his pistol on the lawn and raising his hands over his head.

"*One!*" Dad shouted.

Walt waited a moment, then dashed down the long stretch of grass. Dad dropped to one knee, followed Mr. Disney, and fired. Mr. Disney tumbled to the ground clutching his upper thigh. His momentum carried him into the flower beds. Two Beverly Hills policemen leaped on Dad and wrestled the weapon from his hand.

Mom, Patty, Missy, Mark, and I were cleared of conspiracy charges. They held Dad for attempted murder, assault with a deadly weapon, illegal use of a firearm, and two violations of the Beverly Hills noise code. He had to stay behind. We went home.

Mom called Grandpa Pete from the police station, and he arranged for tickets to be waiting for us at the airport. The police let us say good-bye to Dad. I felt really sorry for him, especially when he kissed me and said that he hoped I'd had at least a few minutes of fun on our vacation. I assured him I did. I also told him that I hoped he would beat the rap and be home real soon and that I didn't begrudge him for shooting such a neat guy as Mr. Disney.

We sort of forgot about Dad as soon as the engines on the airplane trembled and sputtered and moved us around in a graceful arc, then nosed up into the sky. Our hearts pounded with excitement as we watched L.A. shrink below us. We drank Coca-Cola and sailed over the desert valleys that we had fought our way across just the day before. We enjoyed sandwiches as we flew into the pollen-free Arizona air.

"Isn't this marvelous?" Mom sighed. She exhaled and shook her head. "It seems foolish now to drive when you can fly. Maybe this is the way to see the country. Look, down there below us, children!"

"Ladies and gentlemen, this is Captain Fred Freeman. Off to the right side of the aircraft you will see the Grand Canyon. Formed millions of years ago, it is . . ."

[1979]

MARK O'DONNELL

✳

The Laws of Cartoon Motion

1. Any body suspended in space will remain suspended in space until made aware of its situation.

Daffy Duck steps off a cliff, expecting further pastureland. He loiters in midair, soliloquizing flippantly, until he chances to look down. At this point, the familiar principle of 32 feet per second per second takes over.

2. Any body in motion will tend to remain in motion until solid matter intervenes suddenly.

Whether shot from a cannon or in hot pursuit on foot, cartoon characters are so absolute in their momentum that only a telephone pole or an outsize boulder retards their forward motion absolutely. Sir Isaac Newton called this sudden termination the stooge's surcease.

3. Any body passing through solid matter will leave a perforation conforming to its perimeter.

Also called the silhouette of passage, this phenomenon

is the specialty of victims of direct-pressure explosions and reckless cowards who are so eager to escape that they exit directly through the wall of a house, leaving a cookie-cutout-perfect hole. The threat of skunks or matrimony often catalyzes this reaction.

4. *The time required for an object to fall twenty stories is greater than or equal to the time it takes for whoever knocked it off the ledge to spiral down twenty flights to attempt to capture it unbroken.*

Such an object is inevitably priceless, the attempt to capture it inevitably unsuccessful.

5. *All principles of gravity are negated by fear.*

Psychic forces are sufficient in most bodies for a shock to propel them directly away from the surface. A spooky noise or an adversary's signature sound will induce motion upward, usually to the cradle of a chandelier, a treetop, or the crest of a flagpole. The feet of a running character or the wheels of a speeding auto need never touch the ground, ergo fleeing turns to flight.

6. *As speed increases, objects can be in several places at once.*

This is particularly true in tooth-and-claw fights, in which a character's head may be glimpsed emerging from a cloud of altercation at several places simultaneously. This effect is common as well among bodies that are spinning or being throttled, and simulates our own vision's trailing retention of images. A "wacky" character has the option of self-replication only at manic high speeds and may ricochet off walls to achieve the velocity required for self-mass-liberation.

7. Certain bodies can pass through a solid wall painted to resemble tunnel entrances; others cannot.

This trompe-l'oeil inconsistency has baffled generations, but at least it is known that whoever paints an entrance on a wall's surface to trick an opponent will be unable to pursue him into this theoretical space. The painter is flattened against the wall when he attempts to follow into the painting. This is ultimately a problem of art, not of science.

8. Any violent rearrangement of feline matter is impermanent.

Cartoon cats possess more deaths than even the traditional nine lives afford. They can be sliced, splayed, accordion-pleated, spindled, or disassembled, but they cannot be destroyed. After a few moments of blinking self-pity, they reinflate, elongate, snap back, or solidify.

9. For every vengeance there is an equal and opposite revengeance.

This is the one law of animated cartoon motion that also applies to the physical world at large. For that reason, we need the relief of watching it happen to a duck instead.

[1980]

GARRISON KEILLOR

✳

The Tip-Top Club

The idea of pouring warm soapy water into overshoes and wearing them around the house to give yourself a relaxing footbath while you work is one that all fans of WLT's "The Tip-Top Club" seem to have remembered over the years, along with the idea that if you're depressed you should sit down and write a letter to yourself praising all of your good qualities, and the idea of puffing cigarette smoke at violets to prevent aphids.

Every evening, Sunday through Thursday, at 10:00 P.M. ("and now . . . direct from the Tip-Top studio in downtown Minneapolis . . ."), WLT played the Tip-Top theme song—

Whenever you feel blue, think of something nice to do;
That's the motto of the Tip-Top crew.
Don't let it get you down, wear a smile and not a frown,
And you'll be feeling tip-top too.

—and Bud Swenson came on the air with his friendly greeting: "Good evening, Tip-Toppers, and welcome to *your* show. This is your faithful recording secretary, chief cook and bottle-washer, Bud Swenson, calling the Club to order and waiting to hear from you!" And of the hundreds of calls that came in on the Tip-Top line (847-8677, or T-I-P-T-O-P-S), and of the fifty or sixty that actually got on the air, many were from listeners who simply wanted Bud to know they were doing fine, feeling good, and enjoying the show. "And—oh, yes," they might add, "we got our boots on," referring to overshoes.

Every night, Bud got at least one request for a copy of the poem a woman had written about writing a letter to yourself. It was called "Dear Me," it was a hundred and eight lines long, WLT mailed out 18,000 copies of it in the six months after it was written (May 18, 1956), and it began:

> *When I look around these days*
> *And hear blame instead of praise*
> *(For to bless is so much harder than to damn),*
> *It makes me feel much better*
> *To write myself a letter*
> *And tell myself how good I really am.*
>
> *Dear Me, Sorry it's been*
> *So long since I took pen*
> *In hand and scribbled off a word or two.*
> *I'm busy with my work and such,*
> *And I need to keep in touch*
> *Cause the very closest friend I have is you.*

Through times of strife and toil,
You've always remained loyal
And stuck with me when other friends were far,
And because we are so close,
I think of you the most
And of just how near and dear to me you are.

As for puffing smoke at violets, it touched off a debate that lasted for years. For months after it was suggested by an elderly woman, Bud got call after call from listeners who said that smoke-puffing would *not* discourage aphids; that even if it would, there are *better* ways to discourage aphids; and, worse, that it might encourage young people to take up smoking.

The pro-puffers replied hotly that: (1) you don't have to *inhale* in order to *puff* on a plant; (2) the treatment should be given only once a week or so; and (3) anyone who wants to smoke probably will go ahead and do it *anyway*, violets or *no* violets.

As time passed, the issue became confused in the minds of some Tip-Toppers, who came to think that Bud himself was a smoker (he was not). To the very end (November 26, 1969), he got calls from listeners wanting to know if he didn't agree with them that smoking is a filthy habit. (He did.)

At Bud's retirement party, Roy Elmore, Jr., president of WLT, presented him with twenty-five potted violet plants, one for each year of service.

Controversy was the very thing that distinguished "The Tip-Top Club." It had none. Edgar Elmore, the founder of

WLT, abhorred controversy, and the terms of his will bound his heir, Roy Jr., to abhor it also. Though Edgar never heard Bud's show, having died in 1940, eleven years before the Club was formed, he certainly would have enjoyed it very much, as Roy Jr. told Bud frequently. No conversation about religion or politics was permitted, nor were callers allowed to be pessimistic or moody on the air. If a person started in to be moody, he or she was told firmly and politely to hang up and *listen* to the show and it would cheer him or her up. Few had to be told.

Vacations and pets were favorite Tip-Top topics, along with household hints, children, gardening, memories of long ago, favorite foods, great persons, good health and how to keep it, and of course the weather. Even when the weather was bad, even in times of national crisis, the Tip-Toppers always came up with cheerful things to talk about.

One reason for the show's cheery quality and the almost complete absence of crank calls was Bud's phone policy. After the first year he never divulged the Tip-Top phone number over the air (nor, for that matter, over the phone). In fact, it was an unlisted number, and one could obtain it only from another Tip-Topper. This tended to limit participation to those who understood the rules and accepted them.

The main reason for the show's cheery quality was Bud himself and his radio personality. His voice wasn't deep but his style of speaking was warm and reassuring, and he always tried to look on the bright side, even as host of "The Ten o'Clock News" (starting July 1, 1944). On the newscast,

Bud played up features and human-interest stories and he skimmed over what he called "the grim stuff." He might devote fifteen seconds to a major earthquake and three minutes to a story about a chimpanzee whose finger paintings had been exhibited at a New York gallery and fooled all the critics. His approach offended a few listeners ("the *New York Times* crowd," he called them), but most people liked it. Bud pulled in fifty or sixty fan letters a week, more than all other WLT newscasters combined.

After reading a few headlines, he'd say, "Oh, here's something you might be interested in," and he'd tell about a dog that had actually learned to sing and sing on key, or read a story about the world's largest known tomato, or about a three-year-old kid who was a whiz at chess; and then he'd talk about a dog that *he* knew, or a kid *he* knew, or a tomato *he* had seen, and then he'd say, "Well, I don't know. Let me know what *you* think."

At first, some letters said, "What happened to the news?" but they quickly dwindled. ("Anger doesn't last," Roy Jr. said. "Only love is lasting. Angry people spout off once and then get over it. The people who love you are loyal to the end.") Most of the letters were about a story Bud had read: the letter writer described a similar experience that *he* had had, or quoted a poem or saying that the story had reminded *her* of — and Bud made sure to read every one of those letters on the air. One day in the winter of 1950, Roy Jr. said, "It's time to close down the News. You need a new shingle."

According to Bud, the Tip-Top Club was the idea of a woman in St. Paul. "We love your show," she wrote in January 1951, "and feel that truly it is our show too. When I listen, as I do every night, I feel as if I am among friends and we are all members of a club that gathers around our radios. We share ideas and experiences, we inspire each other with beautiful thoughts, and I only wish I could meet personally every one of the wonderful people who also write to you, for when they write to you, they are truly writing to me also."

Bud read her letter on the air, and listeners responded favorably to the idea of a club. (Since he had often referred to his stories as "News-Toppers," Bud suggested the name Tip-Top Club and it stuck.)

Nobody at WLT quite remembers who came up with the phone idea. WLT had been doing remote broadcasts over telephone lines for years, starting with the "WLT Barn Dance and Bean Feed" in 1938; all that needed to be done to put a telephone signal on the air was wrap the bare end of one wire around the bare end of another. One night, Bud's engineer, Harlan, did just that, and a woman's voice came on describing dark thunderstorm clouds moving east toward Minneapolis.

"Is it raining there yet?" asked Bud.

"No," she said, "but it will be, any minute now. But I've got my boots on!"

Roy Jr. was leery of the phone idea from the start. "Every foulmouth in town will be slobbering into his telephone for the chance to get on the air," he told Bud. "Every creep who

writes on toilet walls, every dummy, every drunken son-of-
a-bitch from hell to breakfast. We'll be running a nuthouse.
We'll lose our license in a week."

Then Harlan came forward with his tape loop. Harlan
was one who seldom cracked a smile, but when WLT bought
its first tape recorders, two big Ampexes, in 1949, he was
like a boy with a new toy. He recorded everything on tape,
and he played around with it, and his favorite game was to
play around with Bud's voice. At first, he got a kick out of
playing Bud's voice at a faster speed so he sounded like a
hysterical woman; then backward, which sounded like Russian; then slower, so Bud sounded drunk; and then Harlan
became fascinated with editing Bud. With a razor blade in
hand, Harlan went through thousands of feet of Bud tape,
finding a word here and a word there, and a vowel sound
here and a consonant there, making new words, and snip-
ping and splicing hundreds of little bits of tape to form a few
sentences spoken in Bud's own voice, in which Bud spoke,
in his own warm and reassuring tones, about having carnal
relations with dogs, cats, tomatoes, small boys, chimpanzees,
overshoes, fruit jars, lawn mowers. It was disgusting, and
also an amazing feat of patience. In two years, Harlan assembled just three minutes of Bud.

Harlan solved the problem of loonies by the simple trick
of threading a continuous loop of tape through two machines
sitting side by side. Bud and his telephone caller could be
recorded on the first machine, which fed the tape to the second
machine, which played it back on the air three seconds later.

If the caller said something not befitting the show, Harlan, listening to the first machine, would have three seconds in which to turn off the second. "Can't beat it," said Harlan. "I hit the button and they die like rats."

Nevertheless, Roy Jr. was on hand for the first taped show and supervised the Stop button personally. "I trust you," he told Harlan, "but the way you talk, you might not notice profanity until it is too late." Bud explained the tape loop on the air and invited calls as Roy Jr. hunched over the machine, his finger in position, like a ship's gunner waiting for incoming aircraft. The first caller was a man who wanted to know more about the loop and if it might have useful applications in the home. He got flustered in mid-call and stopped. On his radio at home, he heard his own voice, delayed by tape, saying what he had said three seconds before. "Please turn your radio down," Bud said. It was a line that he was to repeat thousands of times in the next eighteen years.

"This has been an historic event," Roy Jr. said proudly when the show was over. He had cut off just two calls, the first one after the words "What in hell—" and the second at the mention of the Pope ("Probably nothing, but I wasn't about to take chances," he explained to Harlan).

Most of the calls were about the tape loop, with all callers favoring its use, howbeit with some trepidation that a mechanical failure or employee carelessness might lead to tragedy. Several were worried that certain persons might try to fool Bud, opening their calls with a few innocuous remarks and then slipping in a fast one. ("Thanks for the tip," said Bud. "I'm confident we can handle them.")

Communists, people agreed, might be particularly adept at subverting the tape loop. Communists, one man reported, learned these techniques at special schools, including how to insinuate their beliefs into a conversation without anyone being the wiser. ("Appreciate your concern, sir, and, believe me, we'll be on guard.")

It was three weeks before Roy Jr. turned over the guard duty to Harlan and Alice the switchboard girl. Alice was to screen all callers: no kids, no foreign accents, and nobody who seemed unusually intense or determined to get on the air. Harlan was the second line of defense. Roy Jr. instructed him to listen carefully to each call and try to anticipate what the caller was driving at; and if the conversation should drift toward deep waters—hit the button. No politics. No religion except for general belief in the Almighty, thankfulness for His gifts, wonder at His creation, etc. No criticism of others, not even the caller's kith and kin. Roy Jr. didn't want them to get dragged into family squabbles and maybe have to give equal time to a miffed husband or mother-in-law giving *their* side of it. No promotion of products, services, clubs, fund drives, or events.

"What's left to talk about?" Harlan wondered. "Not a goddamn helluva lot."

And, at first, the Tip-Toppers seemed unsure of what to talk about too. "Just thought I'd call and say hi," one would say. "Great. What are you doing tonight?" Bud would ask. "Oh, not much," the caller would reply. "Just sitting here listening to the show."

Gradually, though, they loosened up, and when Bud said to a caller, "Tell me about yourself," the caller generally did. Most Tip-Toppers seemed to be older persons leading quiet lives and keeping busy with hobbies and children and grandchildren, and, judging from the interest in household hints, their homes were neat as a pin and in good repair. They were unfailingly courteous ("The distinguished gentleman who spoke earlier on cats was very well-informed on most points, but I feel he may have overlooked the fact that cats will not shed if brushed regularly"), and soon Harlan was taking his finger off the button and relaxing in the control room and even leaving for a smoke now and then. The few nuts who called in Alice soon recognized by voice—she enjoyed talking with them, and after a few conversations they always asked for her and not for Bud. They sent her gifts, usually pamphlets or books but occasionally a box of cookies or a cake, which, on Harlan's advice, she did not eat. Three months went by, and not a single nut got past the loop; Roy Jr. raised Bud's salary and even gave him a contract—six months with an option of renewing for three more.

"It is so pleasant in this day and age when we are subjected to so much dissension and mud-slinging to take a rest and listen to a show that follows the old adage 'If you can't say something nice, don't say anything at all,'" a woman wrote to Bud. "I am a faithful listener-in and now have a telephone in my bedroom so that I can participate after turning in. I go to sleep listening to the show, and I believe I sleep better knowing it is there."

Sleep was a major item on the Tip-Top agenda: how much is needed? how to get it? what position is best? Many scorned the eight-hour quota as wasteful and self-indulgent and said four or five is enough for any adult. "The secret of longevity is to stay out of bed," said one oldster.

Most members disagreed; they felt they needed more sleep, and one call asking for a cure for insomnia would set off an avalanche of sleep tips — warm milk, a hot bath, a brisk walk, a brief prayer, a mild barbiturate — each of which had gotten the caller through some difficult nights. A doctor (he called in often, usually to settle somebody's hash on the value of vitamins, chiropractic medicine, and vegetarian diets) offered the opinion that worry causes 95 percent of all sleeplessness. He suggested that Tip-Toppers who go to bed with restless thoughts should fill their minds instead with pleasant memories and plans for vacations.

As for vacations, there were strong voices in the Club who argued that a Minnesotan's vacation money should be kept at home, not spent abroad. The rest of the world, it was said, could be seen perfectly well in the pages of the *National Geographic*. There was general agreement, that the purpose of a vacation is to rest and enjoy yourself and not necessarily to visit family members or to catch up on work around the house.

Housework was important, though, a sure antidote for grief and worry and feeling sorry for yourself. To scrub a floor or paint a wall or make a pie was better than going to a psychiatrist. At the same time, there was no use taking more time than necessary to get the job done, and every job had its shortcuts. "What's a quick way to get bubble gum out of hair?" a woman would ask, and minutes later, a legion of women who had faced that very problem would rally to her side. Give the Club a problem, and in short order the Club solved it, whether it be a wobbly table, a grape-juice stain, or a treacherous stair tread, and then it suggested two or three things you could do in the time you had saved, such as making lovely and useful gifts from egg cartons, Popsicle sticks, and bottle caps.

And then there were hobbies. Bud often asked callers, particularly the shyer ones, to talk about their hobbies. He *never* asked about their occupations, not after the first few times: the answers were always apologetic-sounding—"Oh, I'm just a truck driver," or, "Oh, I just work for the Post Office." But ask someone what he did in his spare time and the answer might be good for five or ten minutes.

Club members tended to be collectors. It seemed as if every object of which there was more than one sort, type, shape, brand, color, or configuration was the object of some collector's affection. "I have matchbook covers from more than thirty-five countries." "Some of my fruit jars have been appraised at ten dollars and more." "I hope someday to open a license-plate museum." "I plan to donate my nails to the historical society."

Bird-watching, a sort of collecting, was also popular, and Bud had to put a damper on the bird people, they were so fanatical. One might call in and say, "I wonder if anyone out there can help me identify a bird I heard this morning.

Its call sounded something like this — " and then whistle, "*twee-twee, twee-twee*," and suddenly Alice was swamped with calls, some identifying the bird, some saying they had heard it too and didn't know what it was either, and others wondering if the bird's call perhaps wasn't more of a "*twee-it, twee-it*."

Five nights a week, from 10:00 P.M. to sign-off, Bud sat in Studio B behind a table, the earphones clamped on, and scribbled notes on a pad as one Tip-Topper after another poured it out. After the first few months of the tape loop, he quit reading news stories and after the Club had hit full stride, telephonically speaking, he himself said very little, aside from an occasional question. He became a listener. For eighteen years, from 1951 to 1969, he sat in the same chair, in the same position (slightly hunched, head down and supported with one hand, the other hand writing, feet on the floor), and heard the same stuff, until he seemed to lose whatever personality he had in the beginning. He became neutral. "A goddamn ghost," Harlan said. "When he comes in, I don't even see him anymore. He don't really exist, except on the air."

At the age of sixty-five, he quietly retired. He didn't mention his retirement on "The Tip-Top Club." Tip-Toppers didn't know he was gone until they tuned in one night and heard Wayne Bargy. Wayne was the only WLT announcer willing to take the show. Others had subbed for Bud before when he took vacations and they noted a certain snideness, a meanness, among the Tip-Toppers, who implied in their conversations that the new man, while adequate, was certainly no Bud. "Bud would *know* that," a caller might say. "Bud wouldn't have said that." "Maybe I'll talk to Bud about it. When is Bud coming back?"

So one night out of the clear blue it was "The Tip-Top Club with Wayne Bargy," and one can only imagine the shock that Bud's fans felt to hear a new theme song (Simon and Garfunkel's "Sounds of Silence") instead of the old Tip-Top song, and then Wayne Bargy delivering a tribute to Bud as if Bud were dead. He called him "an innovator" and "a genius" and "a man who was totally concerned about others." "I loved him," said Wayne. "He was a totally understanding, giving type of man. He was someone I could always talk to about my problems.

"Friends, I know you're as disappointed as I am that Bud won't be here with us anymore, and let me tell you, I'd give anything if he were, and I want to be honest with you and admit that I've never done this type of show before and I don't know how good I am at talking with people, and maybe some of you will even wonder what I'm doing in the radio business and I have to admit that you may have a point there, but I would rather be honest about this than sit here and pretend that I'm somebody that I'm not, because I think that honesty has a place in radio, I don't think a radio person-ality has to be some sort of star or an idol or anything, I think he can be a real person, and even if I should fail and would quit this show tomorrow, I'd still be satisfied knowing I had done it my way and not tried to be like somebody else."

The Tip-Toppers heard him out; there was a minute or so of lull at the switchboard (perhaps they were too dazed to dial, or else they were composing carefully what they would say); and then the first wave struck. Even Harlan was surprised by the abuse Wayne got.

First call: "Why wait until tomorrow? Why not quit tonight?" (Wayne: "Thanks for calling.") A man said, "Oh, don't worry that we'll consider you a star, Wayne. Don't worry about that for one minute!" (Wayne: Okay, I won't.") A woman said it was the worst night of her life. (Wayne: "It's hard for all of us.") "You make me absolutely sick. You're the biggest mistake they've made down there!" ("I appreciate your honesty, sir. I don't necessarily agree with that statement, but I think it's important that you feel you can be honest with me.")

By midnight, Wayne had logged almost a hundred calls, most of them quite brief and most cut off by Harlan. The longest exchange was with a woman who wanted to know where Bud was. Wayne said that Bud had retired.

SHE: Then I'd like his number.

HE: I'm sorry?

SHE: I want Bud's phone number.

HE: I — ma'am, I wish I could give you that but I can't, it's against company policy. We don't give out announcers' home numbers to the general public.

SHE: Well, *I'm* not the general public. I'm Grace Ritter and he knows me even if you don't.

HE: I'm sorry, but —

SHE: And this is his show, and I think he has a right to know what you're doing to it! (CLICK)

During the midnight newscast, Roy Jr. called and told Wayne he was doing great. "I knew it'd be tough sledding the first night," he said, "but you stick in there. They're sore about Bud, but in three weeks they'll get tired and give up and all you'll get is flowers."

It didn't work that way. For one thing, Wayne had little interest in the old Tip-Top topics. He was divorced and lived in an efficiency apartment (no lawn to keep up, no maintenance responsibilities) and had no pets or children. His major interest was psychology. "People fascinate me," he said. ("You don't fascinate *me*," someone said.) He read psychology books and talked about them on the air. He said that he was undergoing therapy, and it had helped him to understand himself better. ("What's to understand?")

His other interests were eating out in foreign restaurants, attending films, and planning a trip to the Far East. ("How about leaving tomorrow?") Occasionally, he got a friendly caller who also liked Szechuan cuisine or Carl Rogers or Woody Allen movies, and he reached out and hung on to that call for dear life. Those calls would last for fifteen, twenty minutes, as if the caller were an old college chum he hadn't heard from in ages, but when he hung up, the Tip-Toppers were waiting, more determined than ever.

THEM: This show is so boring. You talk about stuff that nobody but you is interested in.
HIM: I really think you're mistaken about that, at least I hope you are, but more importantly, I think that I would have no business being here if I *didn't* talk about things

that interest me, because, when all is said and done, I do
have to be myself.

THEM: That's the problem, Wayne. Yourself. You're dull.

HIM: Well, I grant you I'm not slick or polished, and I'm
not a comedian, but that's not my job. Basically, I'm a
communicator, and whatever my faults or failures in relating to people, I do try to be positive.

THEM: You're positively boring.

HIM: Well, let's talk about that. Define your terms. What
do you mean by "boring"?

What they meant was Wayne Bargy. For all he said
about keeping an open mind ("You got a hole in your head,
Wayne!") and not condemning others but trying to understand people who may be different from ourselves ("You're
different from everybody, Wayne! You're a different
species!"), the Club kept a united front against him.

One night, Wayne casually mentioned that it was his first
anniversary hosting the show. The switchboard sizzled. One
man said it was time for Club members to take action, and
before Harlan could cut him off he announced a time and a
place for the meeting.

Word came back that the Tip-Toppers had elected officers and were putting together a mailing list for a monthly
newsletter. It was said the Club was assigning members to
"listening squads" with each squad assigned to two hours of
"Wayne duty" a week. The squad members were responsible
for listening to the show and calling in frequently. The newsletter printed a list of things to say.

It was harder on Harlan than on Wayne. Harlan had

started to assemble a special Wayne Bargy tape, but he had no time to work on it. What with Wayne giving out the phone number every fifteen minutes, the show was attracting oddballs, in addition to the legions of Tip-Toppers, and Harlan was cutting calls off the air by the dozens. One night, after Wayne had talked about his divorce (he said that he and his wife didn't "relate to each other sexually"), there passed a long half hour during which no call was fit to broadcast. "I was slapping them down like barnyard flies. We were up to our ears in crazies," said Harlan. "Finally, my fingers got sore, and Alice pulled the plug on the switchboard and her and me sat down and had a cup of coffee and left that poor dumb SOB sit and die by himself."

Wayne talked a long time that night. He said he'd had a typical middle-class upbringing until he went to college, which opened his mind up to new possibilities. He said he had gone into radio because it had tremendous possibilities for creative communication. This show was a tremendous opportunity to get people to open up their minds. He viewed himself as an educator of sorts.

"I'll be honest," he said. "The past year has been rough. There's a lot of anger and violence out there—and I don't say people shouldn't feel that way, but I do feel people should be willing to change. Life is change. We all change. I've changed. Frankly, when I started doing this show, I didn't come off very well. I didn't communicate well. I had a hard time relating to working-class people. I think I've improved. I'm learning. I've put my feelings on the line, and I've benefited from it. I'm going to keep on trying."

He did keep on trying, and the Tip-Toppers kept calling—
"We won't go away, Wayne!" they said, and he said, "I don't
want you to go away. I want you to stay and let's get to know
each other." That summer WLT did a survey that showed
that most of the Tip-Top Club audience was over forty (72
percent), the least desirable age group to advertisers, and in
July the station switched the Tip-Top slot to what it called "a
modified middle-of-the-road pop-rock format" with a disc
jockey who never talked except to give time, temperature,
and commercials. His name was Michael Keske, but he never
said it on the air.

[1981]

BRUCE McCALL

*

Rolled In Rare Bohemian Onyx,
Then Vulcanized by Hand

Dear Eminent Patron of the Mail Order Arts,

Imagine a collector's item so exquisitely detailed that each is actually *invisible* to the naked eye.

Think of an heirloom so limited in availability that when you order it, the mint specially constructed to craft it will be *demolished*.

Ponder an item so precious that its value has actually *tripled* since you began reading this.

Kiln-Fired in Edible 24-Calorie Silver

Never before in human history has the Polk McKinley Harding Coolidge Mint (not a U.S. Government body) commissioned such a rarity.

Consider: miniature pewterine reproductions, authenticated by the World Court at The Hague and sent to you in moisture-resistant Styrofoam chests, of the front-door letter slots of Hollywood's 36 most beloved character actors and actresses.

A special blue-ribbon Advisory Panel will insure that the Foundation Council's certificated and inscribed insignia is approved by Her Majesty's Master of Heralds before the application deadline.

Meanwhile, they are yours to inspect in the privacy of your home, office, shop, or den for *twenty years* by express permission, already withdrawn, of the Polk McKinley Harding Coolidge Mint—the only mint authorized to stamp your application with its own seal.

The equivalent of three centuries of painstaking historical research, supervised by the U.S. Bureau of Mines, has preceded this issue of *The Ornamental Handles of the Walking Canes of the Hohenzollern Princelings.*

Our miniature craftsmen have designed, cast, struck, etched, forged, and finished these authentic reproductions—not available in any store, even before they were commissioned—literally *without regard* for quality.

CERTIFIED BY THE AMERICAN KENNEL CLUB

But now, through a special arrangement with the Postmaster General of the Republic of San Marino, this 72-piece commemorative plinth, honoring *The Footprints of the Great Jewel Thieves of the French Riviera*—each encased in its own watered-silk caddy that revolves 360 degrees on genuine Swedish steel ball bearings—has been cancelled.

A unique way, you will agree, of introducing you and your loved ones to *The Great Cookie Jars of the Restoration*, just as Congreve the boy must have pilfered from.

They are so authentic that you can actually smell them with your nose.

And don't forget: every set of hand-fired porcelain reproductions of *The Padlocks of the Free World's Great Customs Houses* comes sealed in an airtight cask, fashioned after the shoe locker of a Mogul emperor so famous that we are prohibited from disclosing his name.

12 Men Died to Make the Ingots Perfect

But why, as a prudent investor, should you spend thousands of dollars, every month for a lifetime, to acquire this 88-piece set of *Official Diplomatic License Plates of the World's Great Governments-in-Exile*?

One Minnesota collector comments, "I never expected to buy an item so desirable that it has already kept its haunting fascination forever."

But even this merely hints at the extraordinary investment potential of the Connoisseur's Choice selection of *Great Elevator Inspection Certificates of the World's Tallest Buildings*.

Molded in unobtainable molybdenum, each is precision-ejected from a flying aircraft to check a zinc content that must measure .000000003 per cent or the entire batch will be melted down, discarded, and forgotten.

But "keepsake" is an inadequate term. Your Jubilee Edition of the 566 *Tunic Buttons of the World's Legendary Hotel Porters* will take you from New York City to San Francisco to Hong Kong to Bombay . . . and then actually *pay your way* back home.

There is one more aspect for you to consider before refusing this offer.

If you wish, you can have *The Lavaliere Mikes of TV's Greatest Talk Show Celebrity Guests*, custom-mounted on driftwood plaques that serve as 175 dainty TV snack tables — free.

There is, of course, a surcharge and a handling fee, as well as the 25 per cent duplication cost. But so amazing is this offer that you need only pay this levy once — and never again be bothered by it in your mortal life.

If for whatever reason you elect not to purchase the complimentary *Tokens of the World's Great Subway Systems*, you still profit:

> The solid-gold *Venetian Gondolier's Boat Pole Toothpick* and velvet-lined presentation case are yours to treasure for as long as this incredible offer lasts.

Our *Distinctive Axe Marks of the Immortal Brazilian Rubber Planters* are in such short supply that an advance application in your name is already reserved for you. To protect your investment, *none* will be made.

REGISTERED WITH THE
DEPARTMENT OF MOTOR VEHICLES

A dazzling proposition, you will agree. If you do not, your 560-piece set of *Belgium's Most Cherished Waffle Patterns*, together with your check or money order, will be buried at sea on or before midnight, April 15, 1982—the 70th anniversary, college-trained historians tell us, of the sinking of R.M.S. Titanic, one of the 66 *Great Marine Disasters* commemorated in this never-yet-offered series, each individually bronzed, annealed, Martinized, and hickory-cured by skilled artisans working under the supervision of the Tulane University Board of Regents.

Please note that each comes wrapped in authentic North Atlantic seaweed, its salt content confirmed by affidavit.

Best of all, you need not order. Simply steal a new Rolls-Royce, fence it, and turn the bills into small denominations of used money (U.S. currency only, please). No salesman will call. The Polk McKinley Harding Coolidge Mint is not a U.S. Government body. This is not an offering.

THE POLK MCKINLEY
HARDING COOLIDGE MINT

P.S. If you have already begun your *Napkin Rings of the State Supreme Court Dining Rooms* collection, please disregard.

[1981]

MOLLY IVINS

*

Tough as Bob War and Other Stuff

We've just survived another political season largely un-scathed. I voted for Bobby Locke for governor: he's the one who challenged Col. Muammar el-Qaddafi to hand-to-hand combat. In the Gulf of Sidra. On the Line of Death. At high noon. Next Fourth of July. "Only one of us will come out of the water alive," said Locke. Locke thinks the trouble with America is that we've lost respect for our leaders and this would be a good way to restore same. Me too. Besides, you should have seen the other guys.

The Republicans had a congressman running who thinks you get AIDS through your feet. That's Representative Tom Loeffler of Hunt, who is smarter than a box of rocks. His television advertisements proudly claimed, "He's tough as bob war" (bob war is what you make fences with), and also that in his youth Loeffler played football with two broken wrists. This caused uncharitable persons to question the man's good sense, so he explained he didn't know his wrists

were broken at the time. Loeffler went to San Francisco during the campaign to make a speech. While there, he wore
shower caps on his feet while showering lest he get AIDS
from the tile in the tub. He later denied that he had spent the
entire trip in his hotel room. He said: "I did walk around the
hotel. I did see people who do have abnormal tendencies.
I'd just as soon not be associated with abnormal people."
If that's true, what was he doing running for governor of
Texas?

Perhaps Loeffler's most enduring contribution to Texas
political lore was a thought that seemed to him so profound
he took to repeating it at every campaign stop and during
televised debates as well: "As I have traveled around this
state, many people have said to me, 'Texas will never be Texas
again.' But I say they are wrong. I say Texas will *always* be
Texas." Hard to add anything to that.

On the Democratic side, the nerd issue was dominant. The
ugly specter of nerditude was raised by A. Don Crowder,
a candidate from Dallas. Crowder's platform consisted of
vowing to repeal the no-pass, no-play rule on account of
it has seriously damaged high school football and is un-
American, un-Texan, and probably communist inspired.
No pass, no play was part of the education reform package
enacted last year by Governor Mark White and the State
Legislature. If you don't pass all your school subjects, you
can't participate in any extracurricular activities—including
football. Quite naturally, this has caused considerable resentment and could cost White the governorship. So A. Don

Crowder holds this press conference in which he says the reason Mark White favors no pass, no play is because White was "one of the first nerds in Texas." As evidence, Crowder produces White's high school annual, and there it was: the guy was zip in extracurricular activities in his school days. We're talking not even Booster Club. Not Glee Club or Stage Crew. Not even the Prom Poster Committee. According to Crowder, this explains "the psychological reasoning behind White's dislike of football."

There were headlines all over the state: "Gov. White Called 'Nerd' By Yearbook Wielding Foe." "Nerd Charge Merits Scrutiny." Meanwhile, we tracked down Donnie Crowder's high school annual and guess what? He was captain of the football team. Played baseball. Ran track. And was in the French Club. French Club! Need I say more? *Quel fromage.*

White's initial response to this slanderous aspersion was to whine about how tacky it was for Crowder to be so ugly right after the explosion of the *Challenger* shuttle. Nerd City. Then his campaign manager tries to pull it out by saying, So the guy was not real active in high school—but he was super-involved in after-school activities at the Baptist Church. Nerd! Nerd! Finally White gets his act together, comes out, and says, "Look, I grew up poor. My daddy had an accident when I was just a sophomore and he couldn't work after that, so I spent my high school years working summers and after school." While A. Don Crowder was in French Club, doubtlessly conjugating highly irregular verbs

with busty cheerleaders over the pâté and vin rouge, our governor was out mowing lawns, frying burgers, and pumping
gas to help his dear old silver-haired mother. Great stuff.
Besides, Bubba never joined no French Club.

Marko Blanco, as we call him in South Texas, will meet
former Governor Bill Clements for a rematch in November.
Clements was defeated by White four years ago on account
of he's an awful grouch. Grumpy versus the Nerd—what a
match-up.

Also contributing to the political festivities of late is that
peerless, fearless commie-hater Charlie Wilson of Lufkin.
It's possible to get used to Charlie. He has a certain charm.
When I called him to verify some of the more bloodthirsty
quotations attributed to him in the *Houston Post*'s account
of his latest trip to the Afghanistan border, the first thing he
said was, "The only thing those cocksuckers understand is
hot lead and cold steel." I was especially pleased that he took
his lady friend, Annelise Ilschenko, a former Miss World
U.S.A., along on the Afghan jaunt. According to the *Houston Post*, she is a "dark-haired and sloe-eyed beauty," and
you hardly ever find a good case of sloe-eyed beauty in the
newspapers anymore. The *Post* said, "[She] went everywhere
with Wilson, not even flinching as she sank her high-heeled
white leather boots into the thick brown ooze of Darra's
main street." No sacrifice is too great when you're fighting
for freedom.

Charlie told the *Post* reporter he went over there hoping
to "kill Russians, as painfully as possible." Myself, I think

it had more to do with an observation he made after he got back: "Hell, they're still lining up to see *Rambo* in Lufkin." Patriotism is always in good smell in East Texas. The night El Presidente started bombing Libya, the deejay at Benny B's, a honky-tonk in Lufkin, made all the patrons stand on their chairs and sing "The Star-Spangled Banner." He said if anybody refused to do it, "We'll know you're a commie faggot." Of course, they do the same thing at Benny B's for David Allan Coe's song "You Never Even Called Me By My Name." Living in East Texas can be a real challenge.

Living anywhere in Texas is getting to be a challenge as the price of oil slides gracefully toward single digits. Texas-bashing seems to be a popular new national pastime. "Let 'Em Rot in the Sun," said a cordial headline in the *New Republic*. Some Northern papers ran stories on our oil woes with heads the likes of "Sorry About That, J. R." I don't see that we've got any cause to whine about this vein of snottiness: some of the Bubbas did put bumper stickers on their pickups a few years back that said, "Let the Yankee Bastards Freeze in the Dark." Somehow I forebode that Yankees going and doing likewise is not going to teach Bubba any manners. The rest of us down here been having poor luck at it for a long time.

I would point out, though, that Texas is not a rich state, never has been. Never even made it up to the national average in per capita income until the tail end of the oil boom, and then we slid right down again. Poverty level here is always among the nation's highest and, according to a recent study by a team from Harvard University, Texas has more counties beset by hunger and malnutrition than any other state. Our second-biggest industry after oil is agriculture, and you've maybe read something about how it's going for farmers these days. Citrus crop in the Rio Grande Valley was wiped out by a freeze three years ago. Now they got drought and 40 percent unemployment, and the peso is still going down. Our banks had their money in oil, agriculture, and Mexico. We're losing a lot of banks.

There is no social support system for the poor in Texas. Adults get nothing; children get $57.50 a month. Bubba's got a beer-gut he can let shrink some and not be hurting, but almost half the children in this state are black or brown and they have no cushion. If Eddie Chiles goes broke, it's Don't Cry for Me Texarkana; John Connally and Ben Barnes on hard times, search me for sympathy; and I could give a shit about J.R. But that's not who's hurting.

Good thing we've still got politics in Texas—finest form of free entertainment ever invented.

[1986]

CALVIN TRILLIN

✳

Corrections

January 14

BECAUSE of an editing error, an article in Friday's theatre section transposed the identifications of two people involved in the production of "Waiting for Bruce," a farce now in rehearsal at the Rivoli. Ralph W. Murtaugh, Jr., a New York attorney, is one of the play's financial backers. Hilary Murtaugh plays the ingénue. The two Murtaughs are not related. At no time during the rehearsal visited by the reporter did Mr. Murtaugh "sashay across the stage."

March 25

BECAUSE of some problems in transmission, there were several errors in yesterday's account of a symposium held by the Women's Civic Forum of Rye on the role played by slovenliness in cases of domestic violence. The moderator of the symposium, Laura Murtaugh, is not "a divorced mother of eight." Mrs. Murtaugh, the president of the board of directors of the Women's Civic Forum, is married to Ralph W. Murtaugh, Jr., an attorney who practices in Manhattan. The phrase "he was raised with the hogs and he lived like a hog" was read by Mrs. Murtaugh from the trial testimony of an Ohio woman whose defense against a charge of assault was based on her husband's alleged slovenliness. It did not refer to Mrs. Murtaugh's own husband. Mr. Murtaugh was raised in New York.

APRIL 4

AN article in yesterday's edition on the growing contention between lawyers and their clients should not have used an anonymous quotation referring to the firm of Newton, Murtaugh & Clayton as "ambulance-chasing jackals" without offering the firm an opportunity to reply. Also, the number of hours customarily billed by Newton, Murtaugh partners was shown incorrectly on a chart accompanying the article. According to a spokesman for the firm, the partner who said he bills clients for "thirty-five or forty hours on a good day" was speaking ironically. There are only twenty-four hours in a day. The same article was in error as to the first name and the background of one of the firm's senior partners. The correct name is Ralph W. Murtaugh, Jr. There is no one named Hilary Murtaugh connected with the firm. Ralph W. Murtaugh, Jr., has at no time played an ingénue on Broadway.

APRIL 29

BECAUSE of a computer error, the early editions on Wednesday misidentified the person arrested for a series of armed robberies of kitchen-supply stores on the West Side of Manhattan. The person arrested under suspicion of being the so-called "pesto bandit" was Raymond Cullom, twenty-two, of Queens. Ralph W. Murtaugh III, nineteen, of Rye, should have been identified as the runner-up in the annual Squash for Kids charity squash tournament, in Rye, rather than as the alleged robber.

MAY 18

BECAUSE of an error in transmission, a four-bedroom brick colonial house on Weeping Bend Lane, in Rye, owned by Mr. and Mrs. Ralph W. Murtaugh, Jr., was incorrectly listed in Sunday's real-estate section as being on the market for $17,500. The house is not for sale. Also, contrary to the information in the listing, it does not have flocked wallpaper or a round bed.

JUNE 21

IN Sunday's edition, the account of a wedding that took place the previous day at St. John's Church in Rye was incorrect in a number of respects. The cause of the errors was the participation of the reporter in the reception. This is in itself against the policy of this newspaper, and should not have occurred. Jane Murtaugh was misidentified in two mentions. She was neither the mother of the bride nor the father of the bride. She was the bride. It was she who was wearing a white silk gown trimmed in tulle. The minister was wearing conventional ministerial robes. Miss Murtaugh should not have been identified on second mention as Mrs. Perkins, since she will retain her name and since Mr. Perkins was not in fact the groom. The number of bridesmaids was incorrectly reported. There were eight bridesmaids, not thirty-eight. Their dresses were blue, not glued. The bridegroom's name is not Franklin Marshall. His name is Emory Barnswell, and he graduated from Franklin and Marshall College. Mr. Barnswell never attended Emory University, which in any case does not offer a degree in furniture stripping. Mr. Barnswell's ancestor was not a signer of the Declaration of Independence, and was not named Hector (Boom-Boom) Bondini. The name of the father of the bride was inadvertently dropped from the article. He is Hilary Murtaugh.

[1990]

DAVE BARRY

＊

Tips for Women:
How to Have a Relationship with a Guy

Contrary to what many women believe, it's fairly easy to develop a long-term, stable, intimate, and mutually fulfilling relationship with a guy. Of course this guy has to be a Labrador retriever. With human guys, it's extremely difficult. This is because guys don't really grasp what women mean by the term *relationship*.

Let's say a guy named Roger is attracted to a woman named Elaine. He asks her out to a movie; she accepts; they have a pretty good time. A few nights later he asks her out to dinner, and again they enjoy themselves. They continue to see each other regularly, and after a while neither one of them is seeing anybody else.

And then, one evening when they're driving home, a thought occurs to Elaine, and, without really thinking, she says it aloud: "Do you realize that, as of tonight, we've been seeing each other for exactly six months?"

And then there is silence in the car. To Elaine, it seems like a very loud silence. She thinks to herself: Geez, I wonder if it bothers him that I said that. Maybe he's been feeling confined by our relationship; maybe he thinks I'm trying to push him into some kind of obligation that he doesn't want, or isn't sure of.

And Roger is thinking: Gosh. *Six months.*

And Elaine is thinking: But, hey, *I'm* not so sure I want this kind of relationship, either. Sometimes I wish *I* had a little more space, so I'd have time to think about whether I really want us to keep going the way we are, moving steadily toward . . . I mean, where *are* we going? Are we just going to keep seeing each other at this level of intimacy? Are we heading toward *marriage*? Toward *children*? Toward a *lifetime* together? Am I ready for that level of commitment? Do I really even *know* this person?

And Roger is thinking: . . . so that means it was . . . let's see . . . *February* when we started going out, which was right after I had the car at the dealer's, which means . . . lemme check the odometer . . . *Whoa!* I am *way* overdue for an oil change here.

And Elaine is thinking: He's upset. I can see it on his face. Maybe I'm reading this completely wrong. Maybe he wants *more* from our relationship, *more* intimacy, *more* commitment; maybe he has sensed—even before *I* sensed it—that I was feeling some reservations. Yes, I bet that's it. That's why he's so reluctant to say anything about his own feelings: He's afraid of being rejected.

And Roger is thinking: And I'm gonna have them look at the transmission again. I don't care *what* those morons say, it's still not shifting right. And they better not try to blame it on the cold weather this time. *What* cold weather? It's eighty-seven degrees out, and this thing is shifting like a goddamn *garbage truck*, and I paid those incompetent thieving cretin bastards *six hundred dollars.*

And Elaine is thinking: He's angry. And I don't blame him. I'd be angry, too. God, I feel so *guilty*, putting him through this, but I can't help the way I feel. I'm just not *sure*.

And Roger is thinking: They'll probably say it's only a ninety-day warranty. That's exactly what they're gonna say, the scumballs.

And Elaine is thinking: Maybe I'm just too idealistic, waiting for a knight to come riding up on his white horse, when I'm sitting right next to a perfectly good person, a person I enjoy being with, a person I truly do care about, a person who seems to truly care about me. A person who is in pain because of my self-centered, schoolgirl romantic fantasy.

And Roger is thinking: Warranty? They want a warranty? *I'll* give them a goddamn warranty. I'll take their warranty and stick it right up their . . .

"Roger," Elaine says aloud.

"What?" says Roger, startled.

"Please don't torture yourself like this," she says, her eyes beginning to brim with tears. "Maybe I should never have . . . Oh *God*, I feel so . . ." *(She breaks down, sobbing.)*

"What?" says Roger.

"I'm such a fool," Elaine sobs. "I mean, I know there's no knight. I really know that. It's silly. There's no knight, and there's no horse."

"There's no horse?" says Roger.

"You think I'm a fool, don't you," Elaine says.

"No!" says Roger, glad to finally know the correct answer.

"It's just that . . . It's that I . . . I need some time," Elaine says.

(There is a fifteen-second pause while Roger, thinking as fast as he can, tries to come up with a safe response. Finally he comes up with one that he thinks might work.)

"Yes," he says.

(Elaine, deeply moved, touches his hand.)

"Oh, Roger, do you really feel that way?" she says.

"What way?" says Roger.

"That way about time," says Elaine.

"Oh," says Roger. "Yes."

(Elaine turns to face him and gazes deeply into his eyes, causing him to become very nervous about what she might say next, especially if it involves a horse. At last she speaks.)

"Thank you, Roger," she says.

"Thank *you*," says Roger.

Then he takes her home, and she lies on her bed, a conflicted, tortured soul, and weeps until dawn, whereas when Roger gets back to his place, he opens a bag of Doritos, turns on the TV, and immediately becomes deeply involved in a rerun of a tennis match between two Czechoslovakians he has never heard of. A tiny voice in the far recesses of his mind tells him that something major was going on back there in the car, but he is pretty sure there is no way he would ever understand *what*, and so he figures it's better if he doesn't think about it. (This is also Roger's policy regarding world hunger.)

The next day Elaine will call her closest friend, or perhaps two of them, and they will talk about this situation for six straight hours. In painstaking detail, they will analyze everything she said and everything he said, going over it time and time again, exploring every word, expression, and gesture for nuances of meaning, considering every possible ramification. They will continue to discuss this subject, off and on, for weeks, maybe months, never reaching any definite conclusions, but never getting bored with it, either.

Meanwhile, Roger, while playing racquetball one day with a mutual friend of his and Elaine's, will pause just before serving, frown, and say: "Norm, did Elaine ever own a horse?"

We're not talking about different wavelengths here. We're talking about different *planets*, in completely different *solar systems.* Elaine cannot communicate meaningfully with Roger about their relationship any more than she can meaningfully play chess with a duck. Because the sum total of Roger's thinking on this particular topic is as follows:

Huh?

Women have a lot of trouble accepting this. Despite millions of years of overwhelming evidence to the contrary, women are convinced that guys must spend a certain amount of time thinking about the relationship. How could they not? How could a guy see another human being day after day, night after night, sharing countless hours with this person, becoming physically intimate—how can a guy be doing these things and *not* be thinking about their relationship? This is what women figure.

They are wrong. A guy in a relationship is like an ant standing on top of a truck tire. The ant is aware, on a very basic level, that something large is there, but he cannot even dimly comprehend what this thing is, or the nature of his involvement with it. And if the truck starts moving, and the tire starts to roll, the ant will sense that something important is happening, but right up until he rolls around to the bottom and is squashed into a small black blot, the only distinct thought that will form in his tiny brain will be, and I quote,

Huh?

Which is exactly what Roger will think when Elaine explodes with fury at him when he commits one of the endless series of petty offenses, such as asking her sister out, that guys are always committing in relationships because they have virtually no clue that they are in one.

"How *could* he?" Elaine will ask her best friends. "What was he thinking?"

The answer is, He *wasn't* thinking, in the sense that women mean the word. He can't: He doesn't have the appropriate type of brain. He has a guy brain, which is basically an analytical, problem-solving type of organ. It likes things to be definite and measurable and specific. It's not comfortable with nebulous and imprecise relationship-type concepts such as *love* and *need* and *trust*. If the guy brain has to form an opinion about another person, it prefers to form that opinion based on something concrete about the person, such as his or her earned-run average.

So the guy brain is not well-suited to grasping relationships. But it's good at analyzing and solving mechanical problems. For example, if a couple owns a house, and they want to repaint it so they can sell it, it will probably be the guy who will take charge of this project. He will methodically take the necessary measurements, calculate the total surface area, and determine the per-gallon coverage capacity of the paint; then, using his natural analytical and mathematical skills, he will apply himself to the problem of figuring out a good excuse not to paint the house.

"It's too humid," he'll say. Or: "I've read that prospective buyers are actually attracted more to a house with a lot of exterior dirt." Guys simply have a natural flair for this kind of problem-solving. That's why we always have guys in charge of handling the federal budget deficit.

But the point I'm trying to make is that, if you're a woman, and you want to have a successful relationship with a guy, the Number One Tip to remember is:

1. Never assume that the guy understands that you and he have a relationship.

The guy will not realize this on his own. You have to plant the idea in his brain by constantly making subtle references to it in your everyday conversation, such as:

- "Roger, would you mind passing me a Sweet 'n' Low, inasmuch as we have a relationship?"
- "Wake up, Roger! There's a prowler in the den and we have a relationship! You and I do, I mean."
- "Good news, Roger! The gynecologist says we're going to have our fourth child, which will serve as yet another indication that we have a relationship!"
- "Roger, inasmuch as this plane is crashing and we probably have only about a minute to live, I want you to know that we've had a wonderful fifty-three years of marriage together, which clearly constitutes a relationship."

Never let up, women. Pound away relentlessly at this concept, and eventually it will start to penetrate the guy's brain. Some day he might even start thinking about it on his own.

He'll be talking with some other guys about women, and, out of the blue, he'll say, "Elaine and I, we have, ummm . . . We have, ahhh . . . We . . . We have this *thing*."

And he will sincerely mean it.

The next relationship-enhancement tip is:

2. Do not expect the guy to make a hasty commitment.

By "hasty," I mean, "within your lifetime." Guys are *extremely* reluctant to make commitments. This is because they never feel *ready*.

"I'm sorry," guys are always telling women, "but I'm just not ready to make a commitment." Guys are in a permanent state of nonreadiness. If guys were turkey breasts, you could put them in a 350-degree oven on July Fourth, and they *still* wouldn't be done in time for Thanksgiving.

Women have a lot of trouble understanding this. Women ask themselves: How can a guy say he's "not ready" to make a permanent commitment to a woman with whom he is obviously compatible; a woman whom he has been seeing for years; a woman who once drove *his* dog to the veterinarian in *her* new car when it (the dog) started making unusual stomach noises and then barfing prolifically after eating an entire birthday cake, including candles, that *she* made from scratch for *him* (the guy), the result being that her car will smell like a stadium rest room for the next five years, at the end of which this guy will probably still say he's "not ready"? And how come this same guy was somehow capable, at age seven, of committing himself to a lifelong, passionate, win-or-lose relationship with the Kansas City Royals, who have never so much as sent him a card?

A lot of women have concluded that the problem is that guys, as a group, have the emotional maturity of hamsters. No, this is not the case. A hamster is much more capable of making a lasting commitment to a woman, especially if she gives it those little food pellets. Whereas a guy, in a relationship, will consume the pellets of companionship, and he will run on the exercise wheel of lust; but as soon as he senses that the door of commitment is about to close and trap him in the wire cage of true intimacy, he'll squirm out, scamper across the kitchen floor of uncertainty and hide under the refrigerator of nonreadiness.*

This is natural behavior. Guys are born with a fundamental, genetically transmitted mental condition known to psychologists as: The Fear That If You Get Attached to a Woman, Some Unattached Guy, Somewhere, Will Be Having More Fun Than You. This is why all married guys assume that all unmarried guys lead lives of constant excitement involving hot tubs full of naked international fashion models; whereas in fact for most unmarried guys, the climax of the typical evening is watching an infomercial for Hair-in-a-Spray-Can while eating onion dip straight from the container. (This is also true of married guys, although statistically they are far more likely to be using a spoon.)

---

* I am a professional writer. Do not try these metaphors at home.

So guys are extremely reluctant to make commitments, or even to take any steps that might *lead* to commitments. This is why, when a guy goes out on a date with a woman and finds himself really liking her, he often will demonstrate his affection by avoiding her for the rest of his life.

Women are puzzled by this. "I don't *understand*," they say. "We had such a great time! Why doesn't he *call*?"

The reason is that the guy, using the linear guy thought process, has realized that if he takes her out again, he'll probably like her even more, so he'll take her out *again*, and eventually they'll fall in love with each other, and they'll get married, and they'll have children, and then they'll have grandchildren, and eventually they'll retire and take a trip around the world, and they'll be walking hand-in-hand on some spectacular beach in the South Pacific, reminiscing about the lifetime of experiences they've shared together, and then several naked international fashion models will walk up and invite him to join them in a hot tub, and *he won't be able to do it.*

This is Basic Guy Logic. And it leads us to our final and most important tip for women who wish to have a successful relationship with a guy:

3. Don't make the guy feel threatened.

Guys are easily threatened by the tiniest hint that they have become somehow obligated, so you need to learn to give soothing, nonthreatening responses, especially in certain dangerous situations, as shown in the following table.

Situation	Threatening Response	Nonthreatening Response
You meet a guy for the first time.	"Hello."	"I am a nun."
You're on your first date. The guy asks you what your hopes for the future are.	"Well, I'd like to pursue my career for a while, and then get married and maybe have children."	"A vodka Collins."
You have a great time on the date, and the guy asks you if you'd like to go out again.	"Yes."	"Okay, but bear in mind that I have only three months to live."
The clergyperson asks you if you take this man to be your lawful wedded husband, for richer and poorer, in sickness and in health, etc., 'til death do you part.	"I do."	"Well, sure, but not *literally*."

[1995]

THE ONION

*

Clinton Deploys Vowels to Bosnia

Cities of Sjlbvdnzv, Grznc to Be First Recipients

WASHINGTON, DC—Before an emergency joint session of Congress Monday, President Clinton announced U.S. plans to deploy more than 75,000 vowels to the war-torn region of Bosnia. The deployment, the largest of its kind in American history, will provide the region with the critically needed letters A, E, I, O and U, and is hoped to render countless Bosnian names more pronounceable.

"For six years, we have stood by while names like Ygrjvs-lhv, Tzlnhr and Glrm have been horribly butchered by millions around the world," Clinton said. "Today, the United States must finally stand up and say, 'Enough.' It is time the people of Bosnia finally had some vowels in their incomprehensible words. The U.S. is proud to lead the crusade in this noble endeavor."

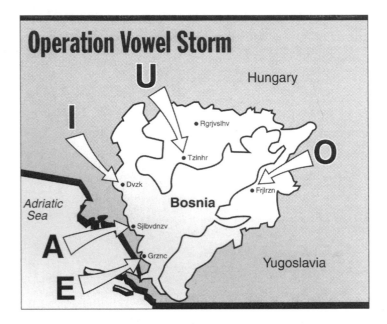

The deployment, dubbed Operation Vowel Storm by the State Department, is set for early next week, with the Adriatic port cities of Sjlbvdnzv and Grznc slated to be the first recipients. Two C-130 transport planes, each carrying more than 500 24-count boxes of E's, will fly from Andrews Air Force base across the Atlantic and airdrop the letters over the cities.

Citizens of Grznc and Sjlbvdnzv eagerly await the arrival of the vowels.

"My God, I do not think we can last another day, Trszg Grzdnjlkn, 44, said. "I have six children and none of them has a name that is understandable to me or anyone else. Mr. Clinton, please send my poor, wretched family just one E. Please."

Said Sjlbvdnzv resident Grg Hmphrs, 67: "With just a few key letters, I could be George Humphries. That is my dream."

If the initial airlift is successful, Clinton said the U.S. will go ahead with full-scale vowel deployment, with C-130s air-dropping thousands more letters over every area of Bosnia. Other nations are expected to pitch in, as well, including 10,000 British A's and 6,500 Canadian U's. Japan, rich in A's and O's, was asked to participate in the relief effort but declined.

"With these valuable letters, the people of war-ravaged Bosnia will be able to make some terrific new words," Clinton said. "It should be very exciting for them and surely much easier for us to read their maps."

Linguists praise the U.S.'s decision to send the vowels. For decades they have struggled with the hard consonants and difficult pronunciation of most Slavic words.

"Vowels are crucial to the construction of all language," Baylor University linguist Noam Frankel said. "Without them, it would be difficult to utter a single word, much less organize a coherent sentence. Please, don't get me started on the moon-man language they use in those Eastern European countries."

According to Frankel, once the Bosnians have vowels,

they will be able to construct such valuable sentences as, "The potatoes are ready," "I believe it will rain" and, "All my children are dead from the war."

The American airdrop represents the largest deployment of any letter to a foreign country since 1984. During the summer of that year, the U.S. shipped 92,000 consonants to Ethiopia, providing cities like Ouaououa, Eaoiiuae and Aao with vital, life-giving supplies of L's, S's and T's. The consonant-relief effort failed, however, when vast quantities of the letters were intercepted and hoarded by gun-toting warlords.

[1995]

SUSAN ORLEAN

✳

Shiftless Little Loafers

QUESTION: Why don't more babies work? Excuse me, did I say *more*? I meant, why don't *any* babies work? After all, there are millions of babies around, and most of them appear to be extremely underemployed. There are so many jobs—being commissioner of major-league baseball, say, or running the snack concession at the Olympic synchronized-swimming venue—and yet it seems that babies never fill them. So why aren't babies working? I'll tell you. Walk down any street, and within a minute or so you will undoubtedly come across a baby. The baby will be lounging in a stroller, maybe snoozing, maybe tippling a bottle, maybe futzing around with a stuffed Teddy—whatever. After one good look, it doesn't take a genius to realize that babies are *lazy*. Or worse. Think of that same baby, same languid posture, same indolent attitude, but now wearing dark sunglasses. You see it all the time. Supposedly, it has to do with UV rays, but the result is that a baby with sunglasses looks not just lazy but lazy and *snobby*. Sort of like an Italian film producer. You know: "Oh, I'm so sorry, Mr. Baby isn't available at the moment. No, Mr. Baby hasn't had a chance to look at your screenplay yet. Why don't you just send coverage, and Mr. Baby will get back to you when he can."

This is right about when you are going to bring up statistics about show-business babies. Granted, there are some show-biz babies, but their numbers are tiny. For one thing, there isn't that much work, and anyway most of it is completely visual-driven, not talent-driven. And everyone knows that babies lose their looks practically overnight, which means that even if Baby So-and-So lands a role in a major-studio feature she'll do the work and go to the big premiere, and maybe even make a few dollars on her back-end points, but by the next day she's lucky if she's an answer on "Jeopardy." Modelling superbabies? Same. Remember those babies zooming around in the Michelin tire ads? Where are they now?

The one job that babies seem willing and eager to do is stroller-pushing. Well, big deal, since (a) they're actually very bad at it, and (b) am I the only one who didn't get the memo saying that there was a lot of extra stroller-pushing that desperately needed to be done? Besides, it's not a job, it's a *responsibility*. For a baby to claim that pushing his or her own stroller counts as gainful employment is about as convincing as for me to declare that my full-time job is to floss regularly. Elevator-button pushing? Not a job: a *prank*.

Unless you really need to stop on every floor. And have you ever watched babies trying to walk? Is it possible that they don't work but still go out for a three-Martini lunch? Of course, babies do a lot of pro-bono projects, like stand-up (and fall-down) comedy, and preverbal psycholinguistic research, but we all know that pro bono is just Latin for Someone Else Buys My Pampers.

One recent summery morning, I walked across Central Park on my way to my own place of employment—where, by the way, I have to be every day whether I want to or not. The Park was filled with babies, all loafing around and looking happy as clams. They love summer. And what's not to like? While the rest of us, weary cogs of industry, are worrying about an annual report and sweating stains into our suits, the babies in the park are relaxed and carefree and mostly nude—not for them the nightmare of tan marks, let alone the misery of summer work clothes. And what were they doing on this warm afternoon? Oh, a lot of really taxing stuff: napping, snacking on Cheerios, demanding a visit with various dogs, hanging out with their friends—everything you might do on a gorgeous July day if you were in a great mood, which you would be if you didn't have to work for a living. That morning, I was tempted to suggest a little career counselling to one of these blithe creatures, but, as I approached, the baby turned his attention ferociously and uninterruptibly to one of his toes and then, suddenly, to the blade of grass in his fist. I know that look: I do it on buses when I don't want anyone to sit next to me. It always works for me, and it worked like a charm for this I-seem-to-remember-telling-you-I'm-in-a-meeting baby. I was out-foxed and I knew it, so I headed for my office. As I crossed the playground, weaving among the new leisure class, I realized something. The reason babies don't work? They're too *smart*.

[1996]

ROY BLOUNT JR.

＊

Gothic Baseball

People call Southern culture Gothic. As in emphasizing the grotesque. So? What's not to be Gothic about? Life? Please. Your own parents, two people who can't even legally use the same public restroom, perform an inconceivable act together—the upshot of which is, an invisible minnow bearing all of your father's traits plows headlong into an *egg* (there is no other word for it) bearing all of your mama's; and from this hodgepodge of fish and chicken, *you* begin to develop. Right on up through birth (don't ask), high school (where, in defiance of logic, most people are not popular), marriage (don't ask), and senility. And then, get this, you *die*. Literally. How can the South be significantly more Gothic than anywhere else?

As we ponder that question, let's look at an article that appeared recently in *The Women's Times*, which is published in the Berkshires of western Massachusetts. An interview with the actress Sandy Duncan, turned fifty.

343

Let me just mention that nobody ever calls the Berkshires Gothic. A meeting of the Pittsfield Easter Seal Stroke Club features three local men performing "The Three Wise Men Present a More Positive You." *The Women's Times* carries an ad for "Green Tara Healing Arts, Inc., a Holistic Health Center specializing in services for the adult survivor of trauma . . . Spiritually-based Therapy, Advanced CranioSacral Therapy." No connection to Scarlett O'Hara's Tara.

Anyway, the Sandy Duncan story. "Sandy's journey begins in East Texas in the heart of the Bible Belt," reports *The Women's Times*, and right away I stifle my first reaction. No, you're not going to catch me defending (*yeah, yeah, how 'bout the Holistic Belt?*) East Texas. "Sandy explains that her mother, 'trapped by the times and the locale,' spent her own childhood following her family from oil field to oil field as Sandy's grandparents struggled to feed their children. . . ."

The story goes on to say that Sandy made her "professional theatrical debut at eleven," and thereafter her mother encouraged her to "market her talents" beyond East Texas. "Instinctively, Sandy knew the image of a forever young sprite with an unwavering sunny disposition would serve her well. . . . Slight in build, she moves quickly and gracefully, seeming to mirror such an image." That image has stood her in good stead, the story reports, not only on Broadway as Peter Pan but also in *Roots*, for which she won an Emmy nomination. "The happy-go-lucky elf image was also supported by her starring role in . . . such film classics as *Million*

Dollar Duck, *The Cat from Outer Space*, and the original *Barney* videos."

But then she fell into a bad depression. "Sandy chose not to deny or 'override the pain.' Instead, encouraged to sit with her anguish, then to go through it, she courageously worked through several layers of fear. She gradually became aware that . . . 'I did not want to become a one-hundred-year-old elf.'"

Having discovered within herself "a penchant for putting pen to paper," she has written a play entitled *Free Fall*.

"Yes," she explains to *The Women's Times*, "*Free Fall*. Life is a boat with no bottom."

Is that story Gothic? I know it's not Southern. I don't even think Sandy Duncan was actually in *Roots*. I saw *Roots*. If I had seen an elf wielding a whip, or even frying chicken, I would remember it.

But here's why that story isn't Southern: the boat metaphor.

Southern life may be Gothic (murky, irrational, fantastic), but Southern figures of speech are in touch with the physical world. Wilson Pickett, of Alabama, once compared musical styles and cars: "You harmonize; then you customize. Now what kid don't want to own the *latest* model? . . . You got no cash for music lessons, arrangers, uniforms, backup bands, guitars. No nothin'. So look around for a good, solid chassis. This be your twelve-bar blues. . . . And once you get known for something special, *that* would be your hood ornament."

The late Big Jim Folsom figures prominently in any history of Gothic politics in the South, but you never heard him liken life to a bottomless boat. Once, by way of addressing commencement at the University of Alabama, Governor Folsom stood up and modestly explained that he had no education himself and didn't feel qualified to hold up before college graduates any vision of their future. However, he did have something useful to pass on—inexpensive meals that people living alone could fix for themselves. He devoted the rest of his speech to recipes, including his famous poke salad.

Alex Haley, a Tennessee native and the author of *Roots*, once said, in accepting an award, that he couldn't take full credit for his success. "It's like a turtle on a fencepost. You know he didn't get there by himself." A strange image of literary eminence. Never mind how the turtle got there, he would rather not be there. Maybe Haley, whose writerliness and veracity suffered some reproach, didn't feel good about where he was. Every time I'm tempted to resent not ever having had the opportunity to make an award-acceptance speech myself, I can just *see* that turtle there on that post.

But I can't see life as a bottomless boat. If it doesn't have a bottom, it isn't a boat. It might be something that floats, but then there wouldn't be any free fall involved. If it's something that you're born into and it immediately starts to sink—still it wouldn't be *free fall*, and how and why are you hanging on to it? Not to mention how you would breathe, unless you're some kind of aquatic animal, in which case . . .

I don't say Southerners can't lapse into the unvisualizable. A friend of mine in Atlanta says she heard somebody on the radio say, "Atlanta—it has seized itself by its bootstraps, and now it's standing tall." Then, too, isn't that Atlanta all over? It's not in free fall, it's in free rise, a topless bubble.

That's what's so irritating about Atlanta, to Southerners and Northerners as well. It's not Southern; it's fluxational, like life. Unless you just live there and have money and think in terms of the nice street you live on, Atlanta will drive you crazy trying to come up with a figure of speech for it. Good solid Southern images are vehicles to drive people *through* crazy. (Also, a boat is a vehicle. How can a boat, even with a bottom, *be* life?)

Granted, the vehicle may get carried away with itself and make things worse. I remember once, in college, riding on the back of a flatbed truck in a float depicting Interfraternity Cooperation, or something. We who were riding were supposed to be shouting out invitations to a big charity do of some kind. Promoting brotherhood, I believe. But the driver of the truck found himself to be enjoying truck driving so much for its own sake that he went faster and faster, so that we clarion callers in the back were reduced to hanging on for dear life and shouting, "Bobby, slow down!" The medium is the message. The notion of fraternal organizations' fostering breadth of brotherhood was flawed to begin with— there were separate Jewish and non-Jewish fraternities, there were separate fraternities and sororities, there was a separate organization for "independents" (people whom no fraternity wanted), and there were no black students in the whole college—so the statement we conveyed as we hurtled through the streets made sense, as a matter of fact. Instinctively, Bobby may have known what he was doing.

Probably, speaking of Gothic, so did the ancient German tribe of Goths, although they struck other early Europeans as barbarous, uncivilized. *Not our sort. Outlandish.* When the Visigoths (who were too Gothic even for the Ostrogoths) whipped Rome, that's when the Dark Ages began. Well, what came to be known as Gothic architecture "reflected the exalted religious intensity, the pathos, and the self-intoxication with logical formalism that were the essence of the medieval," according to *The Columbia Encyclopedia.* Do the French get defensive about that Chartres cathedral?

Just a couple of months ago, a Frenchwoman told me, on first acquaintance, that she didn't trust Southerners because the South had oppressed black people so. What was I going to do, deny it? I said, well, I knew it was true and knew it was a shame. She was a guest in my country, and was probably born after France's Nazi phase, so I didn't even counterattack. It occurred to me later that I might have given her something to think about by citing Harold Bloom's assertion that since there are no soliloquies in classic French drama, the French don't appreciate "the extraordinary originality of the way Shakespeare's protagonists ponder to themselves and, on the basis of that pondering, change."

Of course she could have come right back at me with, "So how rich is *Southern* culture in heroic inner bootstrap dialectic?" The French ward off bottomless free fall, layers of fear, all those things that Sandy Duncan went head to head with ("sit with her anguish"—*that* expression registers) by spinning out reductive abstract theories. Southerners prefer concrete figures of speech and anecdotes about life.

I found just such an anecdote the other day in a book called *Honor and Slavery: Lies, Duels, Noses, Masks, Dressing as a Woman, Gifts, Strangers, Humanitarianism, Death, Slave Rebellions, the Proslavery Argument, Baseball, Hunting and Gambling in the Old South*, by Kenneth S. Greenberg. According to Greenberg, it took a long time for baseball to take hold in the South, because Southern gentlemen found it dishonorable to *run* after hitting a ball. I don't know about that, but—here's the anecdote. After the Civil War, a Union veteran named George Haven Putnam recalled a baseball game "played by Northern soldiers outside their fortifications in the Deep South. While the ballplayers focused on fielding and hitting, Confederate skirmishers attacked them, shot the right fielder, captured the center fielder, and stole the baseball."

That's showing 'em! And why should that anecdote make me feel defensive? Sure, I love baseball and hated being in the army. But it's not as if those Yankees were *invited* to come South and set up fortifications. Then to play ball *outside* the walls! That's insulting. I'd say the ball was in the Confederates' court, so to speak.

The original Goths were invaders. I know invasion is in the eye of the invaded, but, still, calling Southerners

Gothic could be projection on Northerners' part. A lot of people would call burning down Georgia more Gothic than shooting a right fielder. Particularly one who was probably standing in the trampled remains of somebody's pea patch, or even on somebody's mama's grave.

Generally you stick your weakest player out in right field, in a pickup game like that. Lots of times a right fielder, realizing this, will become isolated and start brooding, pondering to himself. And all this time he's landing in the trampled remains of a pea patch that people planted around their mama's grave because she loved peas so much? And he knows it, too. I can just see it, sumbitch shot himself.

[1996]

GEORGE CARLIN

*

If I Were in Charge of the Networks

I'm tired of television announcers, hosts, newscasters, and commentators, nibbling away at the English language, making obvious and ignorant mistakes.

If I were in charge of America's broadcast stations and networks, I would gather together all the people whose jobs include speaking to the public, and I would not let them out of the room until they had absorbed the following suggestions.

And I'm aware that media personalities are not selected on the basis of intelligence. I know that, and I try to make allowances for it. Believe me, I really try. But still . . .

There are some liberties taken with speech that I think require intervention, if only for my own sake. I won't feel right if this chance goes by, and I keep my silence.

The English word *forte*, meaning "specialty" or "strong point," is not pronounced "*for*-tay." Got that? It's pronounced "fort." The Italian word *forte*, used in music notation, is pronounced "*for*-tay," and it instructs the musician to play loud: "She plays the skin flute, and her forte [fort] is playing forte [*for*-tay]." Look it up. And don't give me that whiny shit, "*For*-tay is listed as the second preference." There's a reason it's second: because it's not *first*!

Irony deals with opposites; it has nothing to do with coincidence. If two baseball players from the same hometown, on different teams, receive the same uniform number, it is not ironic. It is a coincidence. If Barry Bonds attains lifetime statistics identical to his father's, it will not be ironic. It will be a coincidence. Irony is "a state of affairs that is the reverse of what was to be expected; a result opposite to and in mockery of the appropriate result." For instance:

If a diabetic, on his way to buy insulin, is killed by a runaway truck, he is the victim of an accident. If the truck was delivering sugar, he is the victim of an oddly poetic coincidence. But if the truck was delivering insulin, ah! Then he is the victim of an irony.

If a Kurd, after surviving a bloody battle with Saddam Hussein's army and a long, difficult escape through the mountains, is crushed and killed by a parachute drop of humanitarian aid, that, my friend, is irony writ large.

Darryl Stingley, the pro football player, was paralyzed after a brutal hit by Jack Tatum. Now Darryl Stingley's son plays football, and if the son should become paralyzed while playing, it will not be ironic. It will be coincidental. If Darryl Stingley's son paralyzes someone else, that will be closer to ironic. If he paralyzes Jack Tatum's son that will be precisely ironic.

I'm tired of hearing *prodigal* being used to mean "wandering, given to running away or leaving and returning." The parable in the Book of Luke tells of a son who squanders his father's money. *Prodigal* means "recklessly wasteful or extravagant." And if you say popular usage has changed that, I say, fuck popular usage!

The phrase *sour grapes* does not refer to jealousy or envy. Nor is it related to being a sore loser. It deals with the rationalization of failure to attain a desired end. In the original fable by Aesop, "The Fox and the Grapes," when the fox realizes he cannot leap high enough to reach the grapes, he rationalizes that even if he had gotten them, they would probably have been sour anyway. Rationalization. That's all sour grapes means. It doesn't deal with jealousy or sore losing. Yeah, I know, you say, "Well, many people are using it that way, so the meaning is changing." And I say, "Well many people are really fuckin' stupid, too, shall we just adopt all their standards?"

Strictly speaking, *celibate* does not mean not having sex, it means not being married. No wedding. The practice of refraining from sex is called *chastity* or *sexual abstinence*. No fucking. Priests don't take a vow of celibacy, they take a vow of chastity. Sometimes referred to as the "no-nookie clause."

And speaking of sex, the *Immaculate Conception* does not mean Jesus was conceived in the absence of sex. It means Mary was conceived without Original Sin. That's all it has ever meant. And according to the tabloids, Mary is apparently the only one who can make such a claim. The Jesus thing is called *virgin birth*.

Proverbial is now being used to describe things that don't appear in proverbs. For instance, "the proverbial drop in the bucket" is incorrect because "a drop in the bucket" is not a proverb, it's a metaphor. You wouldn't say, "as welcome as a turd in the proverbial punchbowl," or "as cold as the proverbial nun's box," because neither refers to a proverb. The former is a metaphor, the latter is a simile.

Momentarily means *for* a moment, not *in* a moment. The word for "in a moment" is *presently*. "I will be there presently, Dad, and then, after pausing momentarily, I will kick you in the nuts."

No other option and *no other alternative* are redundant. The words *option* and *alternative* already imply otherness. "I had no option, Mom, I got this huge erection because there was no alternative." This rule is not optional; the alternative is to be wrong.

You should not use *criteria* when you mean *criterion* for the same reason that you should not use *criterion* when you mean *criteria*. These is my only criterions.

A *light-year* is a measurement of distance, not time. "It will take light-years for young basketball players to catch up with the number of women Wilt Chamberlain has fucked," is a scientific impossibility. Probably in more ways than one.

An *acronym* is not just any set of initials. It applies only to those that are pronounced as words. MADD, DARE, NATO, and UNICEF are acronyms. FBI, CIA, and KGB are not. They're just pricks.

I know I'm fighting a losing battle with this one, but I

refuse to surrender: Collapsing a building with explosives is not an *implosion*. An *implosion* is a very specific scientific phenomenon. The collapsing of a building with explosives is the collapsing of a building with explosives. The explosives explode, and the building collapses inwardly. That is not an implosion. It is an inward collapsing of a building, following a series of smaller explosions designed to make it collapse inwardly. Period. Fuck you!

Here's another pointless, thankless objection I'd like to register. I say it that way, because I know you people and your goddamn "popular usage" slammed the door on this one a long time ago. But here goes anyway:

A *cop out* is not an excuse, not even a weak one; it is an admission of guilt. When someone "cops a plea," he admits guilt to some charge, in exchange for better treatment. He has "copped out." When a guy says, "I didn't get to fuck her because I reminded her of her little brother," he is making an excuse. But if he says, "I didn't get to fuck her because I'm an unattractive schmuck," he is copping out. The trouble arises when an excuse contains a small amount of self-incriminating truth.

This one is directed to the sports people: You are destroying a perfectly good figure of speech: "Getting the monkey off one's back" does not mean breaking a losing streak. It refers only to ending a dependency. That's all. The monkey represents a strong yen. A losing streak does not compare even remotely. Not in a literary sense and not in real life.

Here's one you hear from the truly dense: "The proof is in

the pudding." Well, the proof is not in the pudding; the rice and the raisins are in the pudding. The proof of the pudding is in the eating. In this case, proof means "test." The same is true of "the exception that proves (tests) the rule."

An eye for an eye is not a call for revenge, it is an argument for fairness. In the time of the Bible, it was standard to take a life in exchange for an eye. But the Bible said, No, the punishment should fit the crime. Only an eye for an eye, nothing more. It is not vindictive, it is mitigatory.

Don't make the same mistake twice seems to indicate three mistakes, doesn't it? First you make the mistake. Then you make the same mistake. Then you make the same mistake twice. If you simply say, "Don't make the same mistake," you'll avoid the first mistake.

Unique needs no modifier. *Very unique, quite unique, more unique, real unique, fairly unique,* and *extremely unique* are wrong, and they mark you as dumb. Although certainly not unique.

Healthy does not mean "healthful." Healthy is a condition, healthful is a property. Vegetables aren't healthy, they're dead. No food is healthy. Unless you have an eggplant that's doing push-ups. Push-ups are healthful.

There is no such thing or word as *kudo. Kudos* is a singular noun meaning praise, and it is pronounced *kyoo*-dose. There is also a plural form, spelled the same, but pronounced *kyoo-*doze. Please stop telling me, "So-and-so picked up another kudo today."

Race, creed, or color is wrong. Race and color, as used in this phrase, describe the same property. And "creed" is a stilted, outmoded way of saying "religion." Leave this tired phrase alone; it has lost its usefulness. Besides, it reeks of insincerity no matter who uses it.

As of yet is simply stupid. As yet, I've seen no progress on this one, but of course I'm speaking as of now.

Here's one you can win money on in a bar if you're within reach of the right reference book: *Chomping at the bit* and *old stomping ground* are incorrect. Some Saturday afternoon when you're gettin' bombed on your old stamping ground, you'll be champing at the bit to use this one.

Sorry to sound so picky, folks, but I listen to a lot of radio and TV, and these things have bothered me for a long time.

[1997]

IAN FRAZIER

＊

Laws Concerning Food and Drink; Household Principles; Lamentations of the Father

Of the beasts of the field, and of the fishes of the sea, and of all foods that are acceptable in my sight you may eat, but not in the living room. Of the hoofed animals, broiled or ground into burgers, you may eat, but not in the living room. Of the cloven-hoofed animals, plain or with cheese, you may eat, but not in the living room. Of the cereal grains, of the corn and of the wheat and of the oats, and of all the cereals that are of bright color and unknown provenance you may eat, but not in the living room. Of the quiescently frozen dessert and of all frozen aftermeal treats you may eat, but absolutely not in the living room. Of the juices and other beverages, yes, even of those in sippy cups, you may drink, but not in the living room, neither may you carry such therein. Indeed, when you reach the place where the living room carpet begins, of any food or beverage there you may not eat, neither may you drink.

But if you are sick, and are lying down and watching something, then may you eat in the living room.

Laws When at Table

And if you are seated in your high chair, or in a chair such as a greater person might use, keep your legs and feet below you as they were. Neither raise up your knees, nor place your feet upon the table, for that is an abomination to me. Yes, even when you have an interesting bandage to show, your feet upon the table are an abomination, and worthy of rebuke. Drink your milk as it is given you, neither use on it any utensils, nor fork, nor knife, nor spoon, for that is not what they are for: if you will dip your blocks in the milk, and lick it off, you will be sent away. When you have drunk, let the empty cup then remain upon the table, and do not bite it upon its edge and by your teeth hold it to your face in order to make noises in it sounding like a duck; for you will be sent away.

When you chew your food, keep your mouth closed until you have swallowed, and do not open it to show your brother or your sister what is within; I say to you, do not so, even if your brother or your sister has done the same to you. Eat your food only; do not eat that which is not food; neither seize the table between your jaws, nor use the raiment of the table to wipe your lips. I say again to you, do not touch it, but leave it as it is. And though your stick of carrot does indeed resemble a marker, draw not with it upon the table, even in pretend, for we do not do that, that is why. And though the pieces of broccoli are very like small trees, do not stand them upright to make a forest, because we do not do that, that is why. Sit just as I have told you, and do not lean to one side or the other, nor slide down until you are nearly slid away. Heed me; for if you sit like that, your hair will go into the syrup. And now behold, even as I have said, it has come to pass.

Laws Pertaining to Dessert

For we judge between the plate that is unclean and the plate that is clean, saying first, if the plate is clean, then you shall have dessert. But of the unclean plate, the laws are these: If you have eaten most of your meat, and two bites of your peas, with each bite consisting of not fewer than three peas each, or in total six peas, eaten where I can see, and you have also eaten enough of your potatoes to fill two forks, both forkfuls eaten where I can see, then you shall have dessert. But if you eat a lesser number of peas, and yet you eat the potatoes, still you shall not have dessert; and if you eat the peas, yet leave the potatoes uneaten, you shall not have dessert, no, not even a small portion thereof. And if you try to deceive by moving the potatoes or peas around with a fork, that it may appear you have eaten what you have not, you will fall into iniquity. And I will know, and you shall have no dessert.

On Screaming

Do not scream; for it is as if you scream all the time. If you are given a plate on which two foods you do not wish to touch each other are touching each other, your voice rises up even to the ceiling, while you point to the offense with the finger of your right hand; but I say to you, scream not, only remonstrate gently with the server, that the server may correct the fault. Likewise if you receive a portion of fish from which every piece of herbal seasoning has not been scraped off, and the herbal seasoning is loathsome to you, and steeped in vileness, again I say, refrain from screaming. Though the vileness overwhelm you, and cause you a faint unto death, make not that sound from within your throat, neither cover your face, nor press your fingers to your nose. For even now I have made the fish as it should be; behold, I eat of it myself, yet do not die.

Concerning Face and Hands

Cast your countenance upward to the light, and lift your eyes to the hills, that I may more easily wash you off. For the stains are upon you; even to the very back of your head, there is rice thereon. And in the breast pocket of your garment, and upon the tie of your shoe, rice and other fragments are distributed in a manner wonderful to see. Only hold yourself still; hold still, I say. Give each finger in its turn for my examination thereof, and also each thumb. Lo, how iniquitous they appear. What I do is as it must be; and you shall not go hence until I have done.

Various Other Laws, Statutes, and Ordinances

Bite not, lest you be cast into quiet time. Neither drink of your own bathwater, nor of bathwater of any kind; nor rub your feet on bread, even if it be in the package; nor rub yourself against cars, nor against any building; nor eat sand.

Leave the cat alone, for what has the cat done, that you should so afflict it with tape? And hum not that humming in your nose as I read, nor stand between the light and the book. Indeed, you will drive me to madness. Nor forget what I said about the tape.

Complaints and Lamentations

O my children, you are disobedient. For when I tell you what you must do, you argue and dispute hotly even to the littlest detail; and when I do not accede, you cry out, and hit and kick. Yes, and even sometimes do you spit, and shout "stupid-head" and other blasphemies, and hit and kick the wall and the molding thereof when you are sent to the corner. And though the law teaches that no one shall be sent to the corner for more minutes than he has years of age, yet I would leave you there all day, so mighty am I in anger. But upon being sent to the corner you ask straightaway, "Can I come out?" and I reply, "No, you may not come out." And again you ask, and again I give the same reply. But when you ask again a third time, then you may come out.

Hear me, O my children, for the bills they kill me. I pay and pay again, even to the twelfth time in a year, and yet again they mount higher than before. For our health, that we may be covered, I give six hundred and twenty talents twelve times in a year; but even this covers not the fifteen hundred deductible for each member of the family within a calendar year. And yet for ordinary visits we still are not covered, nor for many medicines, nor for the teeth within our mouths. Guess not at what rage is in my mind, for surely you cannot know.

For I will come to you at the first of the month and at the fifteenth of the month with the bills and a great whining and moan. And when the month of taxes comes, I will decry the wrong and unfairness of it, and mourn with wine and ashtrays, and rend my receipts. And you shall remember that I am that I am: before, after, and until you are twenty-one. Hear me then, and avoid me in my wrath, O children of me.

[1997]

DAVID RAKOFF

✳

The Writer's Life

A TITAN OF AMERICAN LETTERS REFLECTS ON HIS
TIMELESS ART AND THE SACRIFICES IT EXACTS

Behold the Writer on Writing. Oh, how that very question—
How *does* the writer write?—rings in my ears, unasked but
clearly etched across the eager faces of the steady stream
of hopeful young acolytes who make the long trip up here
to my little outpost in the country. "Please," they seem to
beseech, "what alchemy, what ethereal fire transforms our
wordy soup of glottals and fricatives into language and that
language into writing . . . *your* writing, Mr. Rakoff?" Why
even attempt an answer when so few truly agree what constitutes writing? Surely, the act is not merely confined to those
moments, all too rare sadly, when pen is taken in hand, digit
raps against typewriter key or, in my case, when I speak into
this cunning little recorder or dictate aloud to Caitlin, aman-
uensis in excelsis extraordinaria, whom I plucked lo these
many years ago from that fiction colloquium at the New

School. [CAITLIN: REMIND REMIND *REMIND* ME ABOUT THE BLURB FOR TOBY WOLFF. DO NOT LEAVE THE HOUSE THIS EVENING WITHOUT MAKING ME COME UP WITH *SOMETHING!*]

All is Writing, I tell them. And, of course, Writing is All, I tell them, as well. For me the "writing" of my day begins the very instant I open my eyes, even before perhaps, when I sleepily hear my wife Jane, pathological early riser that she is, get up to dress and start breakfast. A writer's cortex kicks into gear even then. On cold mornings, that calming interval of staying warm among the labial folds of my eiderdown, mesmerized by the whorls of frost upon the windowpane by the bed—the only sounds being the hiss of the wood-burning stove in the kitchen and the regular whack! whack! of Jane as she chops more wood outside—that, too, is writing. Don't let anyone tell you different.

I tend to write best with a little privation, a numinous absence, a lack to push my thoughts forward: that hour of growing hunger before Jane fixes lunch; a brief period last summer when Celia, our youngest, shut the piano cover down on Caitlin's fingers and I was forced to bang out an entire chapter myself on the old Royal; during the frozen-earthed silence of winter. Especially during winter.

Luckily for me, winter comes early to these parts. Autumn's end is signaled by the grackles, those cacophonous weird sisters, those ludic brigands, their greasy black pin feathers brilliantined in the sunlight like the multi-hued spumy plume upon an oily puddle, laying waste to the damson plum in the yard. (Once, sitting in my Nakashima chair in my study, I watched for hours as Jane tried to wrap the oft-stripped fruit tree in meter upon meter of protective plastic sheeting. How many times did she fall from the ladder in her efforts that day? Strange the details that evade memory. And all to no avail. The birds still, like robber bridegrooms, absconded happily with the small, stone-hard purple hearts.) Not six short weeks thereafter, do the clouds come scudding across the low mountains to the North carrying with them the cold winds and the immense hibernative quiet. A little hardship: so good for the writer.

Above all, the writer must write for himself. Accolades and external laurels can be lovely but prove wanting in the end if the inner yearning to write (and write and write) is lacking. No sooner had we moved up here than, for example, Jane — talk of her National Book Award nomination for poetry and the attendant vicious gossip about the jealousies of the two-artist couple still buzzing on the carrion-glazed lips of that pack of vultures we call the literary establishment — stopped writing almost entirely. I always wondered at her much-professed time constraints. Was it a flagging desire, perhaps? After all, I often tell her, writers write.

O larkspur! O hawthorn!

Just as Meg Ryan, in "You've Got Mail," waxes panegyric about "bouquets of pencils," [CAITLIN: HAVE I THANKED NORA FOR THE AMARYLLIS? LET'S DO A NOTE *SOONEST* IF NOT] so I, too, even though I have not used a pencil in years, will spend a meditative hour arranging my bouquet. This, too, is writing: Red blue yellow yellow blue green yellow blue; yellow blue yellow green blue blue red yellow; yellow green blue blue blue red yellow yellow, I go on and on only to look up hours later to find the sky fading into indigo, the pale column of smoke rising from the wood fire Jane has lit under the washbasin out back.

The noxious, detergent fumes of the machine-bruised garment choke me and keep me from my work. I sneeze and become rheumy-eyed and quite sullen and I am not a man given to peevishness. Give me the elemental, tidal smell of the clothesline, the fragrance of sun, of hands lovingly snapping a garment in the breeze to pendulously sway on the line and then suddenly, gloriously, to have the wind rush in, a momentary presence in the shirt, a Woman of Air puffing out that dress. What visiting soul, what shade? My muse, perhaps?

But the breeze filling the clothes on the line is colder these days as they grow ever shorter. Jane's hands will be red and raw from the effort. No matter, supper can wait. Perhaps I shall rise from my desk early and make Jane a cup of tea! Ah, the too-giving writer is the doomed writer. My curse, alas.

I look down at my pencils. Those steadfast wooden soldiers. There is no judgment in them. "Go," they say. "There shall be work tomorrow. Tonight you can sit in front of the fire. Let your lips grow dark from purple wine. Go." It is a good day. A writer's day.

[CAITLIN: THEY WANT 1,000 WORDS. I THINK THIS IS ABOUT THAT. FOR WHAT THEY'RE PAYING ME, I'M NOT ABOUT TO BUST MY ASS ON THIS ONE. I BET THEY GAVE JOYCE CAROL OATES AT LEAST $5,000, LIKE SHE NEEDS THE

MONEY. A FEW FINAL THINGS BEFORE YOU GO: CALL UP GOZZI'S IN GREENWICH AND ORDER AN ORGANIC TURKEY FOR THANKSGIVING. NOT THE WILD, THE ORGANIC. THE WILD IS TOO TOUGH. IT SHOULD PROBABLY BE A BIG ONE THIS YEAR. THE DIDION-DUNNES MIGHT BE COMING. ALSO, FIND OUT REMNICK'S WIFE'S NAME—MAKE SURE HE EVEN HAS A WIFE; HE SEEMED A LITTLE RAREFIED AND SUSPICIOUSLY TRIM WHEN I MET HIM, IF YOU KNOW WHAT I MEAN—AND LET'S ORDER ONE OF THOSE PASHMINA THINGS FOR HER. CHECK TO SEE WHAT COLOR WE SENT TINA LAST CHRISTMAS, WE DON'T WANT ANY DOUBLING UP. THE GIRLS WANTED TO SEE SOME ANIMALS AT THE FARMER'S MARKET, THEY SET UP A PETTING ZOO OR SOMETHING. I TOLD THEM YOU'D TAKE THEM, I HOPE THAT'S OK. I'D ASK JANE BUT THE "MISTRESS OF THE MANOR" IS, AS ALWAYS, "TOO BUSY." BEFORE I FORGET, I HAVE SOME NOTES ON YOUR STORY. SOMEONE'S BEEN READING HER ALICE MUNRO A LITTLE TOO CLOSELY, DON'T YOU THINK? NOT TO WORRY, WRITING TAKES TIME, CAITLIN. AND WE'VE GOT LOTS OF THAT. SEE YOU IN THE MORNING.]

[1999]

BERNIE MAC

*

from I Ain't Scared of You

Black funerals? Don't go to no more black funerals. Bar 'em. Because black funerals are full of shit. I'm serious. They make me sick. Layin' up there in the fuckin' coffin, and we gotta go see this motherfucker, and he dead for three days. What the fuck we gotta go sit down and watch this motherfucker in the coffin for three days for?

White folks, you die tonight they bury your ass tomorrow. I like that about them. They have a funeral for 45 minutes and the lights on. It's bright. Bright curtains and everything. The guy sings, *Oh, Lord I'm so happy God saved me!* And then they close the fuckin' coffin. If you ain't see him, you fucked up.

Us? Three fuckin' days. He die, we gotta take some clothes over there, like he goin' some-motherfuckin'-where.

And something about black people: When somebody dies, black people love to find out how you died.

OLD WOMAN 1: How he die?

OLD WOMAN 2: Girl, I was rollin' my hair and I heard a thump. I went downstairs, that motherfucker was on the floor dead. I knew somethin' was wrong 'cause it was rainin' and I was rollin' my hair. I heard a thump. I had to put my gown on. And I walked downstairs, and he was layin' against the stove. I didn't get a chance to finish rollin' my hair, 'cause I heard that noise. He was layin' there! *(Sob . . . sob . . .) Layin' there. I knew somethin' was wrong 'cause I was rollin' my hair! And I heard a thump! And I walked downstairs! (Sob . . . sob . . .)* ain't have my house shoes, neither! And this motherfucker was dead.

Boy, the doorbell rang, and I never will forget! It was a Friday! And I was rollin' my hair! And I heard a thump! I walked down there, my brother was layin' on the floor dead! Oh, God, he was dead! I said, "Oh, Lord, I gotta call my sister and tell her." 'Cause I heard a thump! I knew that motherfucka was dead!

Then you got the wake. Why they call it the wake? He ain't wakin' up! You gotta sit there and watch this motherfucka in the coffin! Every now and then it look like he breathin'.

And she down at the end of a bench, "I was rollin' my hair."

Shut the fuck up down there!

And then black preachers . . . I'm sick of 'em. Why black preachers can't just come out and say, "For God so loved the world that he gave his only begotten Son. Yes, he did. And whosoever believes in Him shall not perish, but shall have everlasting life."

Why they can't just say that shit? It's gotta be dramatics, theater. Why the preacher gotta growl at us?

> BLACK PREACHER: Heh-heh-heh . . . I-I-I . . . I just wanna tell *somebodeee* . . . Heh-heh. Okay? I just wanna *teeell somebodeee* . . . Aw, whoa, Lord. Oh, Lord! Hunh-hunh! *Ohhh, Looordd* . . . I just wanna tell somebodeee . . . Tell it! Tell it!
>
> OLD WOMAN 2: I was rollin' my hair.

SHUT THE FUCK UP!

Then after they do all that, they gotta introduce some fat woman to come sing some song. Now, don't nobody know this heifer. The funeral parlor people don't know her. The deceased's family don't know her. Ain't nobody asked this heifer to sing.

She wanna make you cry—on purpose. She gon' sing an ol' song, "Precious Lord." But she gon' rewrite the shit. So here she come with her fat ass . . .

> FAT LADY: First, givin' honor to God, the pastor, members, and friends. I'm so happy to be here this evening, by the grace of God. Hallelujah! Hallelujah! Hallelujah! I want you all to bear with me as I attempt to sing this song, "Precious Lord Take My Hand."

This how she wanna make you cry. She clears her throat.

[2001]

DAVID SEDARIS

✳

Buddy, Can You Spare a Tie?

When my older sister and I were young, our mother used to pick out our school clothes and hang them on our doorknobs before we went to bed. "How's that?" she'd ask, and we'd marvel at these stain-free, empty versions of ourselves. There's no denying that children were better dressed back then: no cutoffs, no T-shirts, and velveteen for everybody. The boys looked like effeminate homosexuals, and the girls like Bette Davis in *What Ever Happened to Baby Jane?* It was only at Halloween that we were allowed to choose our own outfits. One year I went as a pirate, but from then on I was always a hobo. It's a word you don't often hear anymore. Along with "tramp," it's been replaced by "homeless person," which isn't the same thing. Unlike someone who was evicted or lost his house in a fire, the hobo roughed it by choice. Being at liberty, unencumbered by bills and mortgages, better suited his drinking schedule, and so he found shelter wherever he could, never a bum, but something much less threatening, a figure of merriment, almost.

None of this had anything to do with my choice of Halloween costume. I went as a hobo because it was easy: a charcoal beard smudged on the cheeks, pants with holes in them, a hat, an oversized shirt, and a sport coat stained with food and cigarette ash. Take away the hat, and it's exactly how I've dressed since 1978. Throughout the eighties, the look had a certain wayfarer appeal, but now, accented by amber teeth and nicotine-stained fingers, the word I most often hear is "gnarly." If Hugh is asked directions to the nearest Citibank, I am asked directions to the nearest plasma bank.

This is not to say that I have no standards. The year I turned forty, I threw out all my denim, so instead of crummy jeans I walk around in crummy slacks. I don't own a pair of sunglasses, or anything with writing on it, and I wear shorts only in Normandy, which is basically West Virginia without the possums. It's not that I haven't bought nice clothes—it's just that I'm afraid to put them on, certain they'll get burned or stained.

The only expensive thing I actually wear is a navy blue cashmere sweater. It cost four hundred dollars and looks like it was wrestled from the mouth of a tiger. "What a shame," the dry cleaner said the first time I brought it in. The sweater had been folded into a loaf-sized bundle, and she stroked it, the way you might a freshly dead rabbit. "It's so soft," she whispered.

I didn't dare tell her that the damage was intentional. The lengthy run across the left shoulder, the dozens of holes in the arms and torso; each was specifically placed by the design team. Ordinarily I avoid things that have been distressed, but this sweater had been taken a step further and ruined. Having been destroyed, it is now indestructible, meaning I can wear it without worry. For half this price, I could have bought an intact sweater, thrown it to a tiger, and wrenched it back myself, but after a certain age, who has that kind of time?

My second most expensive purchase was a pair of shoes that look like they belong to a clown. They have what my sister Amy calls "a negative heel," meaning, I think, that I'm actually taller with just my socks on. While not the ideal choice for someone my size, they're the only shoes I have that don't leave me hobbling. My feet are completely flat, but for most of my life they were still shaped like feet. Now, thanks to bunions, they're shaped more like states, wide boring ones that nobody wants to drive through.

My only regret is that I didn't buy more clown shoes—a dozen pairs, two dozen, enough to last me for the rest of my life. The thought of the same footwear day after day might bother some people, but if I have one fashion rule, it's this: never change. That said, things change. I like to think I'm beyond the reach of trends, but my recent infatuation with the man-purse suggests otherwise. It seems I'm still susceptible to embarrassing, rashlike phases, and though I try my best to beat them down, I don't always succeed. In hopes of avoiding future humiliation, I've arranged some of my more glaring mistakes into short lessons I try to review whenever buying anything new. They are as follows:

Guys Look Like Asses
in Euro-Style Glasses

High school taught me a valuable lesson about glasses: don't wear them. Contacts have always seemed like too much work, so instead I just squint, figuring that if something is more than six feet away I'll just deal with it when I get there. It might have been different in the eighteenth century when people wore nearly identical wire rims, but today's wide selection means that in choosing a pair of frames you're forced to declare yourself a certain type of person, or, in my case, a certain type of insect.

In 1976 my glasses were so big I could clean the lenses with a squeegee. Not only were they huge, they were also green with Playboy emblems embossed on the stems. Today these frames sound ridiculous, but back then they were actually quite stylish. Time is cruel to everything but seems to have singled out eyeglasses for special punishment. What looks good now is guaranteed to embarrass you twenty years down the line, which is, of course, the whole problem with fashion. Though design may reach an apex, it never settles back and calls it quits. Rather, it just keeps reaching, attempting to satisfy our insatiable need to buy new stuff. Squinting is timeless, but so, unfortunately, are the blinding headaches that often accompany it.

In the late 1990s, when I could no longer see my feet, I made an appointment with a Paris eye doctor who ran some tests and sent me off to buy some glasses. I'd like to blame my choice of frames on the fact that I couldn't see them clearly. I'd like to say they were forced upon me, but neither excuse is true. I made the selection of my own free will and chose them because I thought they made me look smart and international. The frames were made of dark plastic, with rectangular lenses not much larger than my eyes. There was something vaguely familiar about them, but I couldn't quite put my finger on it. After picking them up I spent a great deal of time in front of the mirror, pretending to share intelligent comments regarding the state of Europe. "Discount our neighbors to the east, and I think you'll find we've got a sleeping giant on our hands," I'd say.

I'd been wearing the glasses for close to a year when I finally realized who they rightfully belonged to. This person was not spotted on the cover of *Le Point* or *Foreign Affairs*—in fact, it wasn't even a real person. I was in New York, passing through a toy booth at the Chelsea flea market when I recognized my frames on the smug plastic face of Mrs. Beasley, a middle-aged doll featured on the 1960s television program *Family Affair*. This was the talking version, original, and in her box.

"Would you like me to pull the string?" the booth owner asked. I said no, and as I hurried away I could swear I heard a small whiny voice saying something about a sleeping giant.

BETTER THE GLASSES THAN SWEATY FAKE ASSES

Without a doubt, my best attributes are my calves. I don't know if they're earned or genetic, but they're almost comically muscular, the equivalent of Popeye's forearms. For years I was complimented on them. Strangers stopped me in the streets. But that all changed with the widespread availability of implants. Now when people look at my legs I sense them wondering why I didn't have my ass done at the same time. It's how women with naturally shapely breasts must feel—robbed and full of rage.

In high school I bought a pair of platform shoes, partly because they were popular and partly because I wanted to be tall. I don't mean that I prayed for height—it never occurred to me that an extra three inches would solve any of my problems. I was just curious. It's like living on the ground floor and wondering what the view is like two stories up. The shoes I bought were red suede with a solid, slablike sole. I'd have looked less ridiculous with bricks tied to my feet, but of course I couldn't see it back then. Other guys could get away with platforms, but on me they read as desperation. I wore them to my high school graduation and made a little deal with myself: if I could cross the stage and make it home without falling, I'd learn to accept myself and be happy with what I had. In children's stories, such lessons are learned for life, but in the real world they usually need reinforcing every few years.

Which takes us to the mid-1990s: my biggest physical gripe is not my height or the arrangement of my facial features, but the fact that I don't have an ass. Others in my family fared pretty well in that department, but mine amounts to little more than a stunted peach. I'd pretty much resigned myself to long sport coats and untucked shirts when I came across an ad, the boldfaced headline reading, "Tired of Ill-Fitting Pants?" I don't recall the product's exact name, but it amounted to a fake padded butt, the shapely synthetic cheeks sewn into the lining of a generous brief. I put it on my Christmas list and was given a pair by my friend Jodi, who waited a few weeks before admitting she'd actually sent me a woman's ass — in essence, a fanny.

And so it was. But that didn't stop me from wearing it. Though pear-shaped, my artificial bottom was not without its charms. It afforded me a confidence I hadn't felt in years and gave me an excuse to buy flattering slacks and waist-length jackets. While walking to the grocery store or post office, I'd invariably find myself passed by a stranger who'd clearly thought he was following somebody else: Little Miss January, or Pamela Anderson's stunt double.

My fanny kept me warm in the winter and early spring, but come hot weather it turned on me. The problem was the nylon padding, which, when coupled with a high tempera-ture, acted much like a heating pad, causing me to sweat away what little ass I'd had in the first place. Chafed and bony, by early June my natural bottom resembled a rusted coin slot.

It was fun while it lasted, but unless I tore myself away, I knew I'd be relying on prosthetics for the rest of my life. After one last walk around the block, I retired my fanny to its box in the hall closet. There it called to me, sirenlike, until a houseguest arrived, a tall, forlorn-looking woman who compared her ass, and not too favorably, to a cast-iron skillet. "I've got just the thing for you," I said. It wasn't my intention to give it to her, but after she tried it on, and I saw how happy it made her, how could I not? The woman stayed with us for a week, and while I hated for her to leave, I sort of loved watching her go.

The Feminine Mistake

"Buy it." This is my sister Amy's advice in regard to everything, from a taxidermied horse head to a camouflage thong. "Just get it," she says. "You'll feel better."

Eye something closely or pick it up for further inspection, and she'll move in to justify the cost. "It's not really *that* expensive, and, besides, won't you be getting a tax refund? Go on. Treat yourself."

The object in question may be completely wrong for me, but still she'll push, effectively clouding my better instincts. She's not intentionally evil, my sister, she just loves to see that moment, the split second when doubt is replaced by complete conviction. *Yes*, I'll think. *I have worked hard, and buying this will bring me the happiness I truly deserve.* When handing over my money, I'm convinced that the purchase is not only right, but hard-won and necessary.

In the year 2000 I went on a diet and lost a little too much weight. Amy and I would go out shopping, and when nothing fit me in the men's department she'd slowly guide me toward the women's. "This is nice," she'd say. "Why don't you try it on?" Once it was a sweater with buttons running down the left side instead of the right. "Oh, come on," she said. "Do you honestly think people pay attention to things like that?" It did seem unlikely that someone would notice the placement of a button. But what about the shoulder pads?

"We can remove them," she said. "Go ahead. Get it. It'll look good on you."

Though she'd promised that no one would ever notice, you could always tell when I'd been clothes shopping with Amy. I was the guy at the crowded steak house, removing the jacket with a label reading Sassy Sport. That was me with the darts in his shirt, the fabric slack where it should be filled with breasts. I'd step up to the restroom urinal and remember that these particular pants zipped up the back. At this point, people noticed. Amy suggested that a calf-length vest would solve the problem, but I had a better idea. It was called the boy's department.

With a Pal Like This, Who Needs Enemies

I've always liked the idea of accessories, those little pick-me-ups designed to invigorate what has come to feel drab and predictable. A woman might rejuvenate her outfit with a vintage Hermès scarf or jaunty rope belt, but the options for men aren't nearly so interesting. I have no use for cuff links or suspenders, and while I'll occasionally pick up a new tie it hardly leaves me feeling "kicky." Hidden accessories can do the trick, but again they're mainly the province of women. Garter belt and lingerie—yes. Sock garter and microbrief—no.

It was my search for something discreet, masculine, and practical that led me to the Stadium Pal, an external catheter currently being marketed to sports fans, truck drivers, and anyone else who's tired of searching for a bathroom. At first inspection, the device met all my criteria:

Was it masculine? Yes, and proudly so. Knowing that no sensible female would ever voluntarily choose to pee in her pants, the manufacturers went ahead and designed the product exclusively for men. Unlike a regular catheter, which is inserted directly into the penis, the Stadium Pal connects by way of a self-adhesive condom, which is then attached to a flexible rubber tube. Urine flows through the tube and collects in the "freedom leg bag," conveniently attached to the user's calf. The bag can be emptied and reused up to twelve times, making it both disgusting *and* cost effective. And what could be manlier?

Was it discreet? According to the brochure, unless you wore it with shorts, no one needed to know anything about it.

Was it practical? At the time, yes. I don't drive or attend football games, but I did have a book tour coming up, and the possibilities were endless. Five glasses of iced tea followed by a long public reading? *Thanks, Stadium Pal!* The window seat on an overbooked coast-to-coast flight? *Don't mind if I do!*

I ordered myself a Stadium Pal and realized that while it might make sense in a hospital, it really wasn't very practical for day-to-day use. In an open-air sporting arena, a piping hot thirty-two-ounce bag of urine might go unnoticed, but not so in a stuffy airplane or small, crowded bookstore. An hour after christening it, I smelled like a nursing home. On top of that, I found that it was hard to pee and do other things at the same time. Reading out loud, discussing my beverage options with the flight attendant, checking into a fine hotel: each activity required its own separate form of concentration, and while no one knew exactly what I was up to, it was pretty clear that something was going on. I think it was my face that gave me away. That and my oddly swollen calf.

What ultimately did me in was the self-adhesive condom. Putting it on was no problem, but its removal qualified as what, in certain cultures, is known as a *bris*. Wear it once, and you'll need a solid month to fully recover. It will likely be a month in which you'll weigh the relative freedom of peeing in your pants against the unsightly discomfort of a scab-covered penis, ultimately realizing that, in terms of a convenient accessory, you're better off with a new watchband.

Never Listen to My Father

It was the weekend of my brother's wedding, and my father was trying to talk me into a bow tie. "Come on," he said. "Live a little!" Outside the window, waves pounded against the shore. Seabirds soared overhead screeching what sounded like "Queer, queer, queer."

When worn with a tuxedo, a bow tie makes a certain kind of sense, but with a suit I wasn't sure I trusted it. The model my father chose was red-and-white-striped, the size of a luna moth, and as he advanced I backed toward the door.

"It's just a strip of cloth," he said. "No different than a

regular tie. Who the hell cares if it falls straight or swags from side to side?"

My inner hobo begged me not to do it, but I foolishly caved in, thinking it couldn't hurt to make an old man happy. Then again, maybe I was just tired and wanted to get through the evening saying as little as possible. The thing about a bow tie is that it does a lot of the talking for you. "Hey!" it shouts. "Look over here. I'm friendly, I'm interesting!" At least that's what I thought it was saying. It was a great evening, and at the end of it I thanked my father for his recommendation. "I knew you'd like it," he said. "A guy like you was made for a bow tie."

A short while after the wedding, while preparing for a monthlong cross-country trip, I bought one of my own and discovered that it said different things to different people. This bow tie was paisley, its dominant color a sort of midnight blue, and while a woman in Columbus thought it made me look scholarly, her neighbor in Cleveland suggested I might be happy selling popcorn.

"Like what's his name," she said. "The dead guy."

"Paul Newman is dead?"

"No," she said. "That other one. Orville Redenbacher."

Name association was big, as were my presumed interests in vaudeville and politics. In St. Louis the bow tie was characterized as "very Charlie McCarthy," while in Chicago a young man defined it as "the pierced eyebrow of the Republican party." This sent the bow tie back into my suitcase,

where it begged forgiveness, evoking the names of Daniel
Patrick Moynihan and Senator Paul Simon. "Oh come on,"
it said. "*They* were Democrats. Please let me out."

Political affiliation aside, I know what the young Chi-
cagoan had meant. It's a pretty sorry world when wearing
a bow tie amounts to being "out there." I'm just not sure
which is worse, the people who consider it out there that
someone's wearing a bow tie, or the person who thinks he's
out there for wearing it.

I wore my bow tie to twenty-seven cities, and in each of
them I found myself begging for affirmation. "Do you *really*
think it looks OK? *Really?*" I simply could not tell whether
it was right for me. Alone in an elevator I'd have moments
of clarity, but just as I reached for the knot, I'd recall some
compliment forced from a stranger. "*Oh, but it looks so ador-
able, so cute! I just want to take you home!*"

I'm told by my father that when I was an infant, people
would peek into my carriage and turn to my mother saying,
"Goodness, what a . . . baby." I've never been described as
cute, so why now? What was the bow tie saying behind my
back? And how could I put it in contact with twenty-year-
old marines rather than seventy-year-old women?

It was my friend Frank, a writer in San Francisco, who
finally set me straight. When asked about my new look he
put down his fork and stared at me for a few moments. "A
bow tie announces to the world that you can no longer get
an erection."

And that is *exactly* what a bow tie says. Not that you're

powerless, but that you're impotent. People offer to take you home not because you're sexy but because you're sex*less*, a neutered cat in need of a good stiff cuddle. This doesn't mean that the bow tie is necessarily *wrong* for me, just that it's a bit premature. When I explained this to my father, he rolled his eyes. Then he said that I had no personality. "You're a lump."

He sees the bow tie, at least in my case, as a bright string wrapped around a run-of-the-mill gift. On opening the package, the receiver is bound to be disappointed, so why set yourself up? It's a question my father answers in the pained, repetitive voice of a parole officer. According to him, you set yourself up in order to *exceed* those expectations. "You dress to give a hundred percent, and then you give a hundred and twenty. Jesus," he says. "You're a grown man. Haven't we been through this?"

Grown or not, I still feel best—more true to myself—when dressed like a hobo. The die was cast for me on Halloween, and though it has certainly not been proven, I think it's this way for everyone. Look at my brother, who dressed as an ax murderer, and at my sister Amy, who went as a confused prostitute. As for the other kids in my neighborhood, the witches and ghosts, the vampires, robots, and, oh God, the mummies, I can only hope that, like me, they work at home.

[2002]

WANDA SYKES

✳

It's So Hard

You know what's harder than being in a relationship? Getting out of one. When Neil Sedaka said "breaking up is hard to do," he wasn't lying. I know I won't get married again because breaking up is the hardest shit to do. It takes years to break up if you want to do it properly. If you want to be able to leave with all of your shit nicely packed in boxes and not thrown all across the front yard, it's going to take some time.

After talking with my divorced and single friends, we all have the same story, guys and girls. One day you wake up and look at your mate still sleeping and you think, I'm so fucking bored. I gotta get out of this shit. Your mate wakes up and asks if you're okay because you're biting your pillow with tears in your eyes. You just say, "I'm fine. I was watching you sleep." You know the relationship is over, but you know they don't know it's over. So now your dumb chicken-shit ass has to hang around another year or two waiting for them to figure it out and break up with you.

There is an art to breaking up. We all have that friend who is living day to day, doesn't have a real address, they just "crash" at a friend's crib, and are always needing a ride. That friend does *not* know how to end a relationship. They say all the wrong shit, like, "I can't help it if I'm the only one who liked themselves before we met." Talk like that will get your car destroyed and a restraining order filed against you.

It's too hard to break up. I don't envy anyone who's going through one. It's like all the talking and the crying is just too much. Then you gotta act like you care as much as the other person does. You know when they're hurting you gotta act like you're hurting, too. "I'm gonna miss you." "Yeah, I'm gonna miss you, too." Knowing you're just heading for the door. You gotta be careful not to pour the "I'm hurting, too" on too thick. One of my friends did that and his ass ended up in couple's therapy. Dragged the breakup out for another eight months, and cost him a couple of grand for the therapist. I told him to just pay the therapist to break them up. "This relationship is going nowhere, end it now. You two suck."

And then after the crying, there's that look. That sad, confused look on their face. That "Why? Why?" look. Oh, I can't take that shit. I can't take the pain in that look. That look is filled with disappointment and heartbreak and it's all directed right at you. That look will haunt you in your sleep. You can hear them, "You said you loved me." Then you start thinking, It would be easier for me to kill you than to have to go through this. It would be easier to shoot you in the head while you are sleeping than to go through this bullshit. At least if I shoot you, I won't have to look at that face. At least I'd get a different expression. A look of surprise or shock, like, "Hey, what's up with the gun, baby?" I can sleep at night with that look. I can live with myself with that surprised look as I'm walking out of the door.

At least if you kill 'em there will be some sympathy. People will comfort you during your time of mourning. That's better than having to answer a bunch of questions, like, "So, did they catch you cheating? Who's getting the house?" If you kill 'em, your friends will show up with a Bundt cake and some potato salad. "Sorry for your loss. We're here for you." "Thanks. Is that lemon frosting?"

That's why whenever there is a murder case, the first person that the police question is the spouse. The cops know who is the most likely person to have committed the crime. And if they find out that you were unhappy or were seeing somebody else on the side, you going straight to jail. They know that you couldn't break up and you took the easy way out.

Ask Scott Peterson about how hard it is to get out of a relationship. That's why he's on trial right now. I don't know if he killed his wife, Laci, but he sure looks guilty. He had the girlfriend on the side, talking about his wife knew about it and she was at peace with it. C'mon, man, there ain't a woman out there who's going to be "at peace" with her man cheating on her. And while she was pregnant, too! Yeah, she was "at peace," like the kind of peace they have in the Middle East.

Scott should have gone old school. Remember back in the day when men would just leave and walk out? They would be reading the paper, then just get up, "I'm going to get cigarettes." And then never come back. I understand that move. I totally get it. It makes sense to me. He was doing her a favor. He couldn't break up, just couldn't do it. He thought about it, probably tried to build himself up. "C'mon, man, you can do this. Just look her in the eye and tell her it's over. Yeah, yeah, I got this. Here goes." He gets up, looks at her, grabs his coat, "We need bread."

[2004]

JACK HANDEY

*

What I'd Say to the Martians

People of Mars, you say we are brutes and savages. But let me tell you one thing: if I could get loose from this cage you have me in, I would tear you guys a new Martian asshole.

You say we are violent and barbaric, but has any one of you come up to my cage and extended his hand? Because, if he did, I would jerk it off and eat it right in front of him. "Mmm, that's good Martian," I would say.

You say your civilization is more advanced than ours. But who is really the more "civilized" one: you, standing there watching this cage, or me, with my pants down, trying to urinate on you?

You criticize our Earth religions, saying they have no relevance to the way we actually live. But think about this: if I could get my hands on that god of yours, I would grab his skinny neck and choke him until his big green head exploded.

We are a warlike species, you claim, and you show me films of Earth battles to prove it. But I have seen all the films about twenty times. Get some new films, or so help me, if I ever get out of here I will empty my laser pistol on everyone I see, even pets.

Speaking of films, I could show you some films, films that show a different, gentler side of Earth. And while you're watching the films I sort of slip away, because guess what? The projector is actually a thing that shoots out spinning blades! And you fell for it!

You point to your long tradition of living peacefully with Earth. But you know what I point to? Your stupid heads.

You say that there is much your civilization could teach ours. But perhaps there is something that I could teach you—namely, how to scream like a parrot when I put your big Martian head in a vise.

You claim there are other intelligent beings in the galaxy besides Earthlings and Martians. Good, then we can attack them together. And after we're through attacking them, we'll attack you.

I came here in peace, seeking gold and slaves. But you have treated me like an intruder. Maybe it is not me who is the intruder, but you. No, not me—you, stupid.

You keep my body imprisoned in this cage. But I am able to transport my mind to a place far away, a happier place, where I use Martian heads for batting practice.

I admit that sometimes I think we are not so different after all. When you see one of your old ones trip and fall down, do you not point and laugh, just as we do? And I think we can agree that nothing is more admired by the people of Earth and Mars alike than a fine, high-quality cigarette. For fun, we humans like to ski down mountains covered with snow; you like to "milk" bacteria off of scum hills and pack them into your gill slits. So are we so different? Of course we are, and you will be even more different if I ever finish my homemade flame thrower.

You may kill me, either on purpose or by not making sure that all the surfaces in my cage are safe to lick. But you can't kill an idea. And that idea is: me chasing you with a big wooden mallet.

You say you will release me only if I sign a statement saying I will not attack you. And I have agreed, the only condition being that I can sign with a long sharp pen. And yet you still keep me locked up.

True, you have allowed me reading material—not the "human reproduction" magazines I requested, but the works of your greatest philosopher, Zandor or Zanax or whatever his name is. I would like to discuss his ideas with him—just me, him, and one of his big, heavy books.

If you will not free me, at least deliver a message to Earth. Send my love to my wife, and also to my girlfriend. And also to my children, if I have any anyplace. Ask my wife to please send me a bazooka, which is a flower we have on Earth. If my so-called friend Don asks you where the money I owe him is, please anally probe him. Do that anyway.

If you keep me imprisoned long enough, eventually I will die. Because one thing you Martians do not understand is, we humans cannot live without our freedom. So if you see me lying lifeless in my cage, come on in, because I'm dead. Really.

Maybe one day we will not be the enemies you make us out to be. Perhaps one day a little Earth child will sit down to play with a little Martian child, or larva, or whatever they are. But after a while, guess what happens: the little Martian tries to eat the Earth child. But guess what the Earth child has: a gun. You weren't expecting that, were you? And now the Martian child is running away, as fast as he can. Run, little Martian baby, run!

I would like to thank everyone for coming to my cage to hear my speech. Donations are gratefully accepted. (No Mars money, please.)

[2005]

DAVID OWEN

*

Your Three Wishes: F.A.Q.

You have been granted three wishes—congratulations. If you wish wisely, your wishes may bring you great happiness. Before wishing, please take a moment to read the following frequently asked questions.

1. Do my wishes have an expiration date?

No. Your wishes are good until used. Once you have made a wish, however, you cannot revoke it, except by using another wish, should any remain.

2. May I wish for absolutely anything?

A wish, if it is to be granted, must not violate the physical laws of the universe. You may wish for a particular co-worker to be fired (for example), or for Mt. Everest to collapse into a heap of rubble; you may not wish to live literally forever, or for the speed of light to be lowered to five miles an hour.

3. May I use one of my wishes to wish for more wishes?

No. You have been granted exactly three wishes. You cannot increase that number by wishing.

4. What happens if I merely think a wish?

No wish will be executed until you speak it out loud, so "wishful thinking" does not count. Note: If you inadvertently use one of your wishes to render yourself permanently speechless—by turning yourself into a pig, for example, or by wishing that you were dead—you will be unable to use your remaining wishes, if any are left, to correct the error.

5. How specific do I have to be? If I wish for "world peace," will you know what I'm talking about?

As a practical matter, no one ever wishes for "world peace." But it is always best to be specific. "I wish for my penis, when erect, to measure eighteen inches in length and six inches in diameter" is clear and concise—and it counts as one wish only, because length and diameter are two dimensions of the same object. "I wish for my penis, when erect, to measure eighteen inches in length and six inches in diameter, and I want it to be erect all the time" is two wishes. "I wish to be a global celebrity, but not Michael Jackson or Tom Cruise" is three.

6. If I wish for money, how much may I wish for?

There is no preset limit. However, you should keep in mind that money has value only in a functioning economic system. If you wish for "all the money in the world," you may have no opportunity to spend your fortune. It is best to be both realistic and unambiguous. If you wish merely for "great wealth" or "untold riches," you could end up with (for example) attractive grandchildren, stimulating hobbies, or a clean bill of health.

7. How come people who get three wishes always seem to wish for something that they regret, big-time—like that wood-cutter and the sausages?

The grantor of your wishes does not take ironic pleasure in human folly. Nevertheless, you alone are responsible for the outcome of your wishing. Hint: Avoid phrases that are open to catastrophic interpretation, such as "for the rest of my life." Also, keep in mind that the media tends to focus on wishes that turn out badly. "Man gets three wishes and lives happily ever after" is not considered news.

8. Can I use one of my three wishes to guarantee that neither of my other wishes will have negative consequences that I failed to foresee?

Hmm. I'm going to say no.

[2006]

GEORGE SAUNDERS

*

Ask the Optimist!

Dear Optimist:

My husband, who knows very well that I love nothing more than wearing bonnets, recently bought a convertible. He's always doing "passive-aggressive" things like this. Like once, after I had all my teeth pulled, he bought a big box of Cracker Jack. Another time, when I had very serious burns over 90 percent of my body, he tricked me into getting a hot oil massage, then tripped me so that I fell into a vat of hydrochloric acid. I've long since forgiven him for these "misunderstandings," but tell me, is there a way I can be "optimistic" about this "bonnet" situation?

Mad Due to No More Bonnets,
Cleveland, Ohio

Dear Mad:

You can still wear bonnets while riding in a convertible! But you will just have to have more of them to start with!

What I recommend? Buy a large number of bonnets, place them in the car, begin driving! When one blows off, put on another from your enormous stockpile! And just think of all the happiness you will create in your wake, as people who cannot afford bonnets scurry after your convertible, collecting your discards! Super!

Dear Optimist:

Upon returning from vacation, we found our home totally full of lemons. I mean totally. The cat even had one in its mouth. What do you recommend?

> Sourpuss,
> Seattle, Washington

Dear Sourpuss:

That is a tough one! What I recommend is, when life gives you lemons: (1) Buy a bunch of Hefty bags! (2) Fill the Hefty bags with lemons! (3) Lug the bags to the curb! And (4) Call a certified waste-disposal contractor to haul away the pile of lemons now rotting in the sun! Before long, like magic, your home will be lemon-free—and you can celebrate by going out and having something cold to drink! And don't forget to give Kitty a jaw massage!

Dear Optimist:

My wife is a terrific artist—except when it comes to me! Whenever she paints me, my legs are half the length of my torso, my face looks like the face of a frog, my feet are splayed outward unattractively like the feet of some hideous reptile, and I have a smug, pinched look on my face. Anyone else she paints, they look exactly like themselves. I pretend not to notice, but recently, at my wife's one-woman show, I could tell our friends were discussing this, and I felt embarrassed. How might I have handled this in a more optimistic way?

Hurt But Hopeful,
Topeka, Kansas

Dear Hurt But:

After receiving your letter, I sent a private investigator to your home with a camera! And guess what! Have you looked in the mirror lately? Your legs *are* squat, your face *is* the face of a frog, your feet *are* reptilian, your expression *is* smug and pinched! So not to worry! Your wife is a terrific artist!

Dear Optimist:

When I go to the zoo, I feel so sad. All those imprisoned animals sitting in their own feces. What do you suggest?

Animal Lover,
Pasadena, California

Dear Animal:

What I suggest is, stop going to the zoo! But should you find yourself tricked into going to a zoo, think about it as follows: All those animals, coated with their own poop, pacing dry, grassless trenches in their "enclosures," have natural predators, and might very well be dead if still in the wild! So ask yourself: Would I rather be dead, or coated in my own poop, repetitively pacing a dry, grassless trench? I certainly know *my* answer!

Dear Optimist:

A few years ago, I inadvertently declared war on the wrong country. Also, I perhaps responded a little slowly to a terrible national disaster. Also, many of my friends are under indictment. Also, the organization of which I am in charge is all of a sudden in huge crushing debt. And I still have over two years left in my job. Advice?

> *In Somewhat Over My Head,*
> *Washington, D.C.*

Dear In Somewhat:

Stay the course! Admit to nothing! Disparage your enemies! Perhaps declare another war? Do you have any openings in your Cabinet? Sounds like you could use a little Optimism! What would you pay? Have your people call my people!

Dear Optimist:

Recently, my wife left me for another man. Not only that, the other man was bigger, better-looking, and richer than me, and—at least according to my wife—better endowed and with a nicer singing voice and less back hair. To tell the truth, I am feeling somewhat "pessimistic" about this situation. Advice?

> *Depressed Because My Penis Is Smaller, Relative to*
> *That of My Wife's New and More Handsome Lover,*
> *Brighton, Michigan*

Dear Small-Penis:

Why not try to look on the bright side! At least he is not more articulate than you—

Dear Optimist:

Oh yes he is. I forgot that.

Dear Small-Penis:

No worries! I believe in you! She is clearly not the right woman for you, and by accepting this—

Dear Optimist:

Actually, Ralph speaks five languages and is just finishing up a translation from the Sanskrit of an ancient text on social deportment. And Judy *is* the right woman for me, I just know it. I could never love anyone else. I'd rather die.

Dear Small-Penis:

Wow, no wonder she left you! You are so negative! Also somewhat pigheaded!

Dear Optimist:

   I know, right? That's exactly what Judy always said. Oh, what's the point of living anymore? I'm just going to take these fast-acting suicide pills and ... and ... and ...

Dear Small-Penis:

   You know, Small-Penis, you don't seem to understand Optimism at all! What is the essential quality of the Optimist? He is non-Pessimistic! What is the essential quality of the Pessimist? They think too much, then get all depressed and paralyzed! Like you, Small-Penis! Me, I prefer to think as little as possible and stay peppy! Peppy and active! If something is bothering me, I think of something else! If someone tells me some bad news? I ignore it! Like, I knew this one guy, very Optimistic, who was being eaten by a shark and did not even scream, but just kept shouting, "It's all for the best!" Now *that* was an Optimist! In the end, he was just as dead, but he hadn't brought the rest of us down! What a great guy! I really miss him! No, I don't! It's all good! I don't miss Todd at all, even though we were briefly lovers and I've never felt so completely *inhabited*, if you know what I mean, so *valued*! But no biggie! I'm certainly not going to start moping about it! Right? Right, Small-Penis? Hello! Oh well, I guess he's off moping somewhere! Next letter!

Dear Optimist:

   I am an emaciated single mother living in a vast famine-affected region with my four starving children. Rebels frequently sweep down from the hills with automatic weapons and kill many of us and violate and abuse the others. All our men are dead or have been driven away, and there is no food or fresh water to be had. I would be very appreciative of any advice you might be able to offer us.

Not Altogether Hopeful,
Africa

Dear Hopeful:

Thanks so much for writing! Perhaps it would be of some consolation for me to tell you what a vast minority you are in! There are, relative to the world's population, very few people "in your boat"! Most of the rest of us are not starving or in danger, and, in fact, many of us do not even know that you are starving and in danger, and are just out here leading rich, rewarding lives, having all kinds of fun! Does that help? I hope so! And remember—trouble can't last forever! Soon, I expect, your troubles will be over!

Dear Optimist:

Recently, my father-in-law backed over me with his car. When I complained, he backed over me again. When, from beneath the wheels of his car, I complained again, he got out of his car, covered me in molten metal, hauled me to a public park, mounted me on a pedestal, and placed at my feet a plaque reading "SLOTH." What gives? I am trying to think about this incident in an optimistic way but am having some

difficulties, as my chin itches and I am unable to reach it with
my bronze-encrusted arms.

                    I Love Parks but, Hey, This Is Ridiculous,
                    Fort Myers, Florida

Dear Loves Parks:
    Oh, really? Bronze-encrusted arms? Then how did you
write that letter?

Dear Optimist:
    Uh, one of my arms is not totally bronze-encrusted?

Dear Parks:
    Then why don't you scratch your chin with that arm?

Dear Optimist:
    Uh, because I am holding my pen in that hand? And if I
drop the pen I will not be able to bend to retrieve it, because
my torso is totally encrusted in bronze? And the pigeons
will, like, run away with the pen? Hey, I've got an idea. Why
don't you suggest I *kill* myself? With fast-acting suicide pills,
after first calling me "negative" and "pigheaded"?

Dear Loves Parks:
    Is that you, Small-Penis? I thought the handwriting
looked familiar! Were you faking it just now when you said
you were taking those pills? And you're not really encrusted
in bronze at all, are you?

Dear Optimist:

That's right, genius, I am *not* dead and *not* encrusted in bronze and am *not* giving up and in fact am going to go and try to get Judy on the phone right now. If she'll just *listen* to me, then I know she'll—

Dear Optimist:

I am a man trapped in a turkey's body. I have dim memories of my life as a human. But then I look down, and there are my wattles! Sometimes when it rains I find myself gazing up at the sky, mouth open, gullet slowly filling with rain. I'm really starting to feel badly about myself. Can you help?

> *Chagrined Gobbler,*
> *A Farm Near Albany*

Dear Gobbler:

Of course I can help! Come to my house for some private counseling! Does Christmas work for you? And do you know anyone trapped in a pig's body? Wait for me at "the waiting spot," a tree stump with an ax leaning against it! Until then, I suggest eating as much as you can, preferably some high-quality corn! And keep your chin up, or your wattles up, or whatever!

Dear Optimist:

I was buried alive during the Eighteenth Century when I experienced a fit of narcolepsy and my family mistook my deep sleep for Death. In the 256 years since, trapped in my moldering Body by the terrifying circumstances of my departure from this Life, my Soul has longed for freedom. And yet everyone who once would have prayed for me has long since gone on to Eternity, and I, desperately lonely, am haunted by the scuffing feet of dog-walkers and the skittering of leaves in Autumn, doomed to exist in this semi-death forever, in a perpetual state of mild Terror, until Time itself shall end and our Creator returneth to redeem us all. Any thoughts about this?

Longing for the Sweet Peace of True Death, Plymouth, Massachusetts

Dear Longing:

Do you mind some "tough love"? Did they even have that in your time? Have you honestly tried your best to get out of this situation? Have you, for example, clawed frantically at the lid of your coffin for sixty or seventy years, after which have you tried literally digging your way to the surface even though your mouth was filling with dirt and you were nearly overcome with a horrific feeling of claustrophobia? Or have you just been lying there feeling sorry for yourself all this—

Dear Optimist:

No, no, I think you misunderstand my situation. I can't move. My mind is active, I can fear and regret and dream, but I can't move at all. I guess I thought when I said "dead" I assumed you understand that this meant—

Dear Longing:

No sense trying to blame me! I am not the bonehead who went through life with undiagnosed narcolepsy! I didn't mistake your sleep for death! I wasn't even alive in the eighteen hundreds or whenever! You know what? Just lie there awhile and think about what you really want!

Dear Optimist:

I started out life as an angel, then, through a misunderstanding, became a "fallen angel," and am now Lucifer, Master of Evil. Although I know I should be grateful — I love working for myself, and I'm one of the two most powerful beings in the universe — I sometimes feel a certain absence, as if there's some essential quality I'm lacking. I've heard people, as I make my rounds, speak of something called "goodness." Usually when I hear someone use this word, I get frustrated and immediately tempt them into doing something horrific — but lately, somehow, this isn't enough. Thoughts?

Satan,
Hell

Dear Satan:

Clearly you are lonely! What I recommend? Go visit Longing for the Sweet Peace of True Death, in his grave, in Plymouth, Massachusetts. He is lonely, you are lonely! A real win-win! Just reside with him there in his coffin awhile! I think he'll love it! Or maybe not! Maybe it will kind of scare him, to have Satan suddenly arrive in his cramped little coffin! Oh, I doubt it! Whatever! It's all good!

Dear Optimist:

I am feeling so great! I have totally internalized all the wonderful things you've taught us over the years, via your column! I am just so excited!

Thrilled to Be Alive, Never Felt Better!
Chicago, Illinois

Dear Thrilled:

Super! Did you have a question!

Dear Optimist:

No, not really!

Dear Thrilled:

Then what the heck! What is the name of this column! Is it: "Make a Statement to The Optimist?" Is it "Come Up in Here and Act All Like Mr. Perfect?" Is it—

Dear Optimist:

No problem! I totally respect what you're saying! Many apologies and I hope you have a great day! You know, actually, I am going to go sit awhile and think about what I've done, so that, if I did in fact do something wrong, I won't, in the future, repeat my mistake!

Thrilled

Dear Thrilled:

Jeez, what an asshole! Well, that's about all the space we have, so—

Dear Optimist:

Damn it! Judy would not take my call. This is the worst day of my life.

Small-Penis

Dear Small-Penis:

We are done here! The column is done for the day! Do I come to your work and mess with you?

Dear Optimist:

I don't work! And thanks very much for rubbing *that* in. You know what? I've had it with you. I'm coming straight over to your house right now. Got it? How do you feel about that, smart guy?

Small-Penis

Dear Anyone:

Please call the police! I am sure it will be fine! Oh God, he's here! He's breaking down the door! Please call the police! Help! Help!

Dear Optimist:

How do you like that? How does that feel, Mr. Superior?

Dear Everyone:
   Ouch! Ouch! Oh God!

Dear Everyone!
   It is finished. The Optimist is no more. We are, at last, free of his arrogance. And Judy, if you're out there? Size isn't everything. And articulate isn't everything, and tall isn't everything, and also, sweetie, I have just now had my back waxed. Give me some hope! I await your letter, darling!
                                          Small-Penis, aka Steve

Dear Small-Penis, aka Steve:
   Hi, Steve! How's it going? I'll be replacing the Optimist here at the column! Just call me The New Optimist! Super! What I recommend? Turn yourself in! There will be good food in jail, and time for contemplation, and who knows, you may even, eventually, have a great spiritual realization and pull your head out of your ass! Isn't that better than living on the lam? Judy is not taking you back, no way, and I should know! Judy is staying with me forever!
                                 Thrilled to Be Alive, Never Felt Better,
                                 aka The New Optimist

Dear Ralph, You Bastard!
   Is that really you? You scum, you wife-stealer! Look what you've reduced me to! I am now a murderer! I murdered the Optimist! My God, the look on his face — even at the end, he was trying so hard to smile pleasantly!
                                                          Steve

Dear Steve-o:

Yup, you schmuck, it is me, Ralph! And guess what! I followed you over here! I am right outside! You'll never harass poor Judy again! I have with me a letter I've written, which I will plant on your corpse, so all the world will believe that, after killing the Optimist, you did away with yourself in a bizarre murder-suicide! You are a fool and the Optimist was a fool! If one really wants to be an Optimist, there is only one way: Win! Always win! Be superior and never lose! Slaughter your enemies and live on, so that you and only you are left to write the history books! Good-bye, Steve! Ralph rules! Here I come! Oh, you look so scared! There! I have done it! Steve is no more! I am going home to make Optimistic love to the beautiful Judy! And from now on this column is mine! No more working at the oil-change place while trying to write my Sanskrit book on weekends!

Thrilled, aka Ralph,
aka The New Optimist

Dear New Optimist:

I recently left my husband of ten years for a new man. Although I feel I basically did the right thing (my ex was small-penised and hairy-backed and not very articulate), I have to admit I feel a little guilty. What do you suggest?

Completely Happy, Almost

Dear Completely Happy:

Don't worry about it! It's all good! What I'd recommend is, as soon as your new man gets home from wherever he is right now, make love to him more ferociously than you've ever made love to anyone in your life! Show your love by doing things to him you never even contemplated doing with that boring loser Steve!

Dear New Optimist:

OK! Will do! As a matter of fact he just rang the bell! Gotta go!

Completely Happy, All the Way!

P.S. Say, how did you know my ex-husband's name was Steve?

Dear Completely Happy All the Way:

Don't be so negative! That's what got you in trouble in the first place, Judy! You think too much! Just be quiet and do what I say! Follow my lead! Hail Optimism! Long live the New Optimist! Open the door, Judy, open the door, so we can begin our beautiful life together! And don't even think of back-talking me, missy!

Dear New Optimist:

OK! Super! Thanks for the advice! Come in, Ralph! My God you look flushed, and honey, gosh, why are you holding that bludgeon?

Completely Happy, All the Way, Although Maybe
Just a Little Bit Scared Now, aka Judy

Dear Judy:

There will be no problems whatsoever, Judy, if you simply acknowledge my absolute supremacy in a way that continually pleases me! And this is not a bludgeon! It is a bouquet of flowers! Right? Right, Judy? Well, that's all the space we have! Not that I'm complaining! See you next time! Never doubt yourself, and, if you start feeling down, castigate yourself, and, if others try to put the slightest trace of a doubt in your mind, rebuke them, and, should your rebuke not alter their speech, you may bring harm to them, even unto death, and, after they have died, feel free to arrange their rictus-stiffening mouths into happy, hopeful smiles! And that's an order! Believe me, you'll be doing them a favor! Just kidding! You are special!

The New Optimist

[2006]

JENNY ALLEN

*

Awake

I'm up. Are you up?

I'm trying to go back to sleep. But I'm awake. Awake awake awake.

That's what Buddha said. Buddha said, "I am awake." Buddha got that idea, that whole concept, from a middle-aged woman, I'm sure.

Not that this sleepless business ends after a certain age. I think you have to die first.

If you added up all the hours I've been awake in the middle of the night, it would come to years by now. Fifty may be the new forty, but, for the sleepless woman, fifty is the new eighty.

Thank you, that's a very good idea, but I already took a sleeping pill. I fell asleep right away—it's bliss, that drugged drifting off—but now I'm awake again. That always happens! I fall asleep, boom, and then, four or five hours later, I wake up—like it's my turn on watch, like I've just had a full night's sleep. But if I act as if I've had a full night's sleep, if I get up and do things, I will be pitiful tomorrow. I will confuse the TV remote with the cordless phone and try to answer it. I will not notice any of my typos—I will type "pubic school" this and "pubic school" that in e-mails to people whose public schools I am looking at for my daughter. I will say, "I saw store at the Shelly," and then I will have to make one of those dumb Alzheimer's jokes.

I could take another sleeping pill, but I worry about that. I worry about liking sleeping pills too much. Sleeping pills always make me think of Judy Garland. Poor Judy.

It's funny about the name Judy, isn't it? No one names anyone Judy anymore—do you ever see five-year-old Judys?—but half the women I know are named Judy. You would probably be safe, when meeting any woman over fifty, just to say, "Nice to meet you, Judy." Most of the time you would be right.

I am going to lie here and fall asleep counting all the Judys I know.

Thirteen Judys. Including my husband's ex-wife. Who's very nice, by the way.

I'm still awake.

Some people who knew my husband before I knew him call me Judy. "Hi, Judy, how are you?" they say, and I never correct them. Who can blame them, when they know so many Judys? Although I do sort of hope that later they will realize they have called me by my husband's ex-wife's name and take note of what a nice person I must be not to have corrected them.

Are all my Judy friends up, like me? Judy in Brooklyn, are

you up? Judy on Amsterdam Avenue, Judy in Lincoln Towers, Judy in Morningside Heights, Judy on Riverside Drive? I'm here in bed imagining that I can see all of you—I probably *could* see a few of you from my window if you waved at me. I feel like the teacher on "Romper Room" when I was little. She used to hold a big magnifying glass the size of a tennis racquet in front of her face, so that it was between her and you, and she would say, "I see Nina, and Becky, and Scott, and Glenn, and Judy . . ."

I see them. I see all my Judys, and I see Martha and Angeline and Eden, and Ellie and Goldie and Jackie and Wendy, and everyone in my book group. I see them lying there in their nighties, their faces shiny with night cream. Some of us lie alone, some of us lie next to another person, who is, enragingly, sleeping like a log. How can these people next to us sleep so profoundly? They snore, they shake their restless-leg-syndrome legs all over their side of the bed, they mutter protests from their dreams—"I didn't say Elmira!" and "It's not yours!" They're making a regular racket, and yet they sleep on.

Sleepless friends, I am thinking about you. Ginny, did you decide what to do about day camp for your grandchildren this summer? Martha, what are you reading to help you fall back asleep? Will you call me tomorrow and tell me about it? Mimi, are you up thinking about who you haven't had lunch with lately? You're eighty-seven years old. That's a hundred and thirty-nine in wakeful-woman years. Congratulations for hanging in there.

Sometimes I fall asleep to the television. And a strange thing happens: no matter what I have fallen asleep watching, when I wake up in the middle of the night "Girls Gone Wild" is on. I never turn the channel to "Girls Gone Wild," I promise. It's just on. My goodness, those girls must sleep well, when they finally do sleep. I have to change the channel right away when I see "Girls Gone Wild," because I always think about the girls' mothers, and that upsets me. I worry about their mothers, up in the middle of the night, waking up to "Girls Gone Wild": "That one looks just like Melanie — oh, my God."

Look. "Law & Order" is on. I've seen this episode, of course. Do they run the same ones over and over, or is it that I have seen every one there is? What a scary thought. Fortunately, I never remember what happens after the opening scene, when they find the dead person, so I can watch them all over again.

That was a good one. Although one day maybe there will be a teenager on the show who isn't a psycho killer.

I'm still awake.

Friends, are you all still up? It seems inefficient somehow for all of us to be awake separately; wouldn't it be great if we could pool all our individual little tributaries of wakeful energy into one mighty Mississippi, and then harness it, like a W.P.A. project, like the Hoover Dam? We could power something. We could light up Manhattan. We could light up Manhattan and have a huge party for all the women who are awake.

I should read. Reading is too hard for the dead of night. Reading has too many words in it. Including words I might not know. If I read a word I don't know, I will feel compelled to scrawl it on whatever piece of paper is on my bedside table and then hope that I'll be able to read my writing tomorrow, and will remember to look up the word in the dictionary. If I am too lazy to write down the word, I will have to make a decision about whether to dog-ear the page—bad reader citizenship!—and I don't want the burden of that choice now, in the middle of the night.

Also, I know that even if I do look a word up tomorrow I won't remember the definition next week. I keep looking up the same words over and over. "Fungible." "Heliotrope." How many times am I supposed to look up "heliotrope"? I used to remember the definitions, but I haven't for years. I still know a lot of words, though. "Cleave" is a funny word, because it means to sunder, and, strangely, it also means to stick to. "Ouster" is a funny word. "Ouster" means the act of getting rid of someone, but it also means the person who does the getting rid of. Who should be the ousterer. "Timorous" means timid, but why not just say "timid"?

Timmy was the name of the boy in "Lassie," the television show. The theme music for the show was melancholy, shockingly so. It made you yearn, it made you homesick, even as you watched it in your own home.

I'm still awake. Only now everything is sort of blending together. It's the time of night when I think I may finally be losing my mind for good. The theme song from "Lassie" is blending into the Brownie song, the one about "I've something in my pocket, it belongs across my face," about a Great Big Brownie Smile. Where's my older daughter's Girl Scout sash? Why didn't the younger one ever do Girl Scouts? What's in that pot-roast recipe besides a cinnamon stick and horseradish and a can of cranberry sauce? What was my old Zip Code when I lived on Third Avenue? Why didn't I submit that expense report worth a thousand dollars nine years ago?

Instead of going crazy, maybe I will just lie here and regret things. Let's see . . . Can't I blame the really big mistakes on others? Didn't they fail me, didn't they provoke me, didn't they drive me to it? Didn't they just really strain my patience?

No, face it, you have some things to regret. Now you have to sit with it, as Buddha would say — or, in your case, lie with it. Not exactly the path to Slumberland.

Here's the question: Have you done the love thing? The unconditional-love thing? Have you done it with your children? And with the person lying next to you, the one with the jitterbugging legs?

Oh, look. The city sky is turning from purplish black to . . . brown. It's going to be daylight soon. Dawn! How are you, Dawn? How's my girl? As long as you're up, I might as well get up, too. We can keep each other company.

[2008]

SLOANE CROSLEY

*

The Pony Problem

As most New Yorkers have done, I have given serious and generous thought to the state of my apartment should I get killed during the day. Say someone pushes me onto the subway tracks. Or I get accidentally blown up. Or a woman with a headset and a baby carriage wheels over my big toe, backing me into some scaffolding, which shakes loose a lead pipe, which lands on my skull. What then? After the ambulance, the hospital, the funeral, the trays of cheese cubes on foil toothpicks . . .

Back in the apartment I never should have left, the bed has gone unmade and the dishes unwashed. The day I get shot in a bodega (buying cigarettes, naturally) will in all likelihood be the day before laundry Sunday and the day after I decided to clean out my closet, got bored halfway through, and opted to watch sitcoms in my prom dress instead! I have pictured my loved ones coming to my apartment to collect my things and I have hoped that it would only be "lived-in" messy —

bras drying on the shower curtain rod, muddy sneakers by the door. But that is never going to happen. My dust balls alone have a manifest destiny that drives them far beyond the ruffle of the same name.

I like to think that these hypothetical loved ones would persist in their devotion to dead me no matter what. They would literally be blinded by grief, too upset putting sweaters in boxes to notice that I hadn't dry-cleaned them in a year. That is, until one of them made his or her way to the kitchen.

"Where are you going?" my father would ask.

"Packing up her bedroom's much too painful," my mother would tell him, choking back the tears. "I'm going to start on the kitchen."

This is the part I dread. This is the part where my mother would open the drawer beneath my sink only to discover my stash of plastic toy ponies. There are about seven of them in there. Correction: one's a Pegasus, blue with ice skates. The rest vary in size, texture, and realism. Some are covered in brown felt, some have rhinestone eyes. Some come with their own grooming brushes, others with the price sticker still on their haunches. If they arrived in plastic and cardboard packaging, they remain unopened as if they will appreciate like Star Wars figurines. Perhaps they are not the dirtiest of dirty secrets, but they're about as high as one can get on the oddity scale without a ringer like toenail clippings.

I'm not exactly sure how the ponies happened. Though I have an inkling: "Can I get you anything?" I'll say, getting up from a dinner table. "Coffee, tea, a pony?" People rarely laugh at this, especially if they've heard it before. "This party's supposed to be fun," a friend will say. "Really?" I'll respond. "Will there be pony rides?" It's a nervous tic and a cheap joke, cheapened further by the frequency with which I use it. For that same reason, it's hard to weed out of my speech—most of the time I don't even realize I'm saying it. There are little elements in a person's life, minor fibers that become unintentionally tangled with our personality. Sometimes it's a patent phrase, sometimes it's a perfume, sometimes it's a wristwatch. For me, it is the constant referencing of ponies.

I don't even like ponies. If I made one of my throwaway equine requests and someone produced an actual pony, Juan Valdez–style, I would run very fast in the other direction. During a few summers at camp, I rode a chronically dehydrated pony named Brandy who would jolt down without notice to lick the grass outside the corral and I would careen forward, my helmet tipping to cover my eyes. I do, however, like ponies in the abstract. Who doesn't? It's like those movies with animated insects. Sure, the baby cockroach seems cute with CGI eyelashes, but how would you feel about fifty of her real-life counterparts living in your oven? And that's precisely the manner in which the ponies clomped their way into my regular speech: abstractly. "I have something for you," a guy will say on our first date. "Is it a pony?" No. It's usually a movie ticket or his cell phone number or a slobbery tongue kiss. But on our second date, if I ask again, I'm pretty sure I'm getting a pony.

And thus the pony drawer came to be. It's uncomfortable to admit, but almost every guy I have ever dated has unwittingly made a contribution to the stable. The retro pony from the '50s was from the most thoughtful guy I have ever known. The one with the glitter horseshoes was from a boy who would later turn out to be gay. The one with the rainbow haunches was from a pot dealer, and the one with the price tag stuck on the back was given to me by a narcissist who was so impressed with his gift he forgot to remove the sticker. Each one of them marks the beginning of a relationship. I don't mean to hint. It's *not* a hint, it's a flat-out demand: I. Want. A. Pony. I think what happens is that young relationships are eager to build up a romantic repertoire of private jokes, especially in the city where there's not always a great "how we met" story behind every great love affair. People meet at bars, through mutual friends, on dating sites, or because they work in the same industry. Just once a guy asked me out between two express stops on the N train. We were holding the same pole and he said, "I know this sounds crazy but would you like to go to a very public place and have a drink with me?" I looked into his seemingly non-psycho-killing, rent-paying, Sunday *Times*–subscribing eyes and said, "Yes. Yes, I would." He never bought me a pony. But he didn't have to.

If I subtract the overarching strangeness of being a grown woman with a toy collection, I like to think of the ponies as a tribute to my type—I date people for whom it would occur to them to do this. This is not such a bad thing. These are men who are creative and kind. They hold open doors and pour wine. If I joined a cult, I like to think they would come rescue me. No, the fulfilling of the request isn't the problem. It's the requesting that's off. They don't know yet that I make it all the time and I don't have the heart to tell them how whorish I am with my asking. For them, it's a deleted scene out of *Good Will Hunting*. For me, it's *Groundhog Day*. They have no reason to believe they're being unoriginal. Probably because they're not: I am. What am I asking when I ask for a pony but to be taken for more unique than I probably am?

The ponies, if by accident, have come to represent the most overtly sentimental part of my life. Because all of these relationships have ended, they have ended more or less badly. No affair that begins with such an orchestrated overture can end on a simple note. What I am left with is the relics of those relationships.

After a breakup, I'll conduct the normal breakup rituals. I'll cut up photographs, erase voice mails, gather his dark concert T-shirts I once slept in and douse them with bleach before I use them to clean my bathtub. But not the ponies. When I go to throw them away, I feel like a mother about to slap her child for the first time, to cross a line she never intended to cross. She's spitting mad. The arm flies up. And it never comes down.

Yet I feel a pressure to do something with the ponies. Statistically speaking, my chances of getting smacked on the head with a lead pipe are increasing every time I lock the door behind me. Also, a drawer full of beady-eyed toys is insanely creepy. But what to do?

Actual love letters I do in stages. I biannually clean out drawers of nonsensical items—receipts, loose double-A batteries, rubber bands of indeterminate origin—and stumble across a love letter. Unable to throw it out, I stick it in another drawer, crammed at the bottom, until I clean that one out, too, and finally throw the letter out. One romantic note generally goes through a minimum of three locales before it gets tossed out for good. But the ponies are uncrammable. They're three-dimensional and bubblegum-scented and impossible to hide, even from myself. Every time I open the drawer, it's a trip down Memory Lane, which, if you don't turn off at the right exit, merges straight into the Masochistic Nostalgia Highway. They are too embarrassing to leave out in the open, facing west like a collection of china elephants. They are too many to slide under the sofa. They are too plastic to wedge behind the radiator. I want to send them around the world like the Travelocity gnome, have them come back to me years from now when I have an attic in which to shut them away. As if all this weren't enough, there is that flash of my mother dressed in black, staring aghast into the open kitchen drawer. In a city that provides so many strange options to be immortalized by the local tabloids, it is just as important to avoid humiliation in death as it is in life.

"What is it?" my father would shout, imagining all the things you never like to think of your father imagining: flavored condoms, pregnancy tests, a complete set of Third Reich collectors' cards.

"Look!" my mother would howl, picking up Ranch Princess Pony (with matching bridle and real horseshoe charm necklace!) by her faux flaxen mane. Just before she passed out.

My first thought is to go to the Salvation Army and donate the ponies to the children. But the notion turns me into an insta-hippie—the ponies have bad karma. I wouldn't just be giving some kid Stargazer (with the glow-in-the-dark mane), I would be giving her Manic-Depressive Simon, who talked back to billboards and infomercials and kicked me in his sleep. My next idea is to leave the ponies in the trash for a homeless person to find and sell on the street. But I can't risk seeing them on a table with used books and polyester scarves as I walk to the subway each morning. I think about burying them in the park but have my doubts about the ponies' biodegradability. I think about burning them, melting them into a puddle of plastic as their real-life counterparts were once melted for glue. Maybe I'll just sneak out to the reservoir after dark with a raft made from pool noodles and rubber bands and give them a Viking funeral.

While each subsequent idea is tilled from a progressively more unsophisticated plot, I know that I can't simply throw the ponies out with the recycling. The ponies have their roots in me, not the other person. They are *my* nervous habit, *my* odd little secret. While each serves as a memory of a specific individual, each memory is filtered through the same brain: mine. The ponies are a part of me—they deserve better than that. The keeping of love letters suddenly seems like a petty crime. I have the romantic equivalent of a body in the freezer.

So I put the ponies in a black plastic bag, grabbing them out of their drawer like a jewel thief who, for the sake of urgency, does not consider the preciousness of each object. I tie the bag in a knot, leave the apartment, and take them with me on the subway. I get on a sparsely populated car, drop them between my legs, and begin casually pushing them further under the seat with my heels. Then, just as casually, I forget to take them with me when I get up. I leave them there on the N train, bound for Brooklyn.

Of course, the second the doors shut, I realize what I have done. Actually, that's not true. The second the doors shut, I feel great. Sneaky and great and nostalgia-free.

The second after that I realize what I have done. In my effort to liberate myself from the ponies, I have given some poor girl at the end of the subway car a solid reason to think she might not make it back to her apartment that night: a suspiciously abandoned unmarked package on public transport. I wonder what must be racing through her mind as she sits motionless, unable to turn her gaze away from the lumpy plastic bag. I wonder if she flashes back to her apartment—to the dust, to the expired yogurt in the fridge, to the terrible DVDs that she won't be able to explain were "a gift." Perhaps she has her own holy grail of humiliation. Perhaps there's a collection of porcelain bunnies in the medicine cabinet.

In any case, the ponies are gone. They are on their way to a borough where eventually they will hit the end of the line and cycle back into the heart of the city. Unless the bomb squad finds them first. They are finally out of my sight and not even an 8.5 on the Nostalgia Richter Scale can summon them back. I created them and now I have uncreated them and there is nothing I can do about it. Except maybe continue to look both ways before crossing the street and avoid areas with a high saturation of random violence. I breathe a sigh of resolute relief. From now on I will make a conscious effort to remember—should I find myself face-to-face or pipe-to-skull with the end of my life—that the real proof that I have tried to love and that people have tried to love me back was never going to fit in a kitchen drawer.

[2008]

LARRY WILMORE

✳

If Not an Apology, at Least a "My Bad"

America has always had a strained relationship with its black citizens. No one can deny that most of it stems from slavery. Some black leaders have argued that before the country can even begin to heal from these terrible wounds, a federal apology is needed. So far that hasn't come. Some individual states have issued apologies in an effort to wipe clean the dirty akashic record, but many feel even these efforts have fallen short.

For example, the New Jersey apology was "the vestiges of slavery are ever before African-American citizens, from the overt racism of hate groups to the subtle racism encountered when requesting health care, transacting business, buying a home, seeking quality public education and college admission, and enduring pretextual traffic stops and other indignities." The response from the black community was a collective "what the fuck was that?"

The problem, from the black perspective, is not the intent

behind the apology but the apology itself. It doesn't sound like anything. It was as impersonal as someone taking your order at the drive-thru at a Carl's Jr. The only thing missing was "Do you want fries with that?" And ironically, blacks do want fries with that. Especially if it's a shake. In other words, we want an apology that will satisfy us like a trip to McDonald's. And if you've seen any McDonald's commercial with brothas dancing around, you know how much we love Mickey D's.

The problem from the federal government's point of view is more complicated. How do they issue an apology for something that happened so long ago? Anybody who was a slave is dead, as is anyone who was a slave owner. Americans today feel that since they had nothing to do with it, why should they feel sorry? Also, millions of Americans are descendants of immigrants who came over after slavery and weren't involved at all. This also holds true for blacks whose grandparents are immigrants and don't share a history of slavery themselves. Where do they fit in the apology?

Personally, I feel the federal government should stop worrying about hurting people's feelings and bite the bullet. It really isn't that hard. In fact, there are many different ways the government can apologize and save face at the same time. I've come up with a few suggestions.

THE "MY BAD" APOLOGY

This universal show of contrition works really well with brothas. It was first developed in pick-up basketball games and then evolved into almost any situation where an apology is needed. It's pretty simple and can be worked into almost any presidential address. For example, the president is giving a speech on, let's say, the economy. Right in the middle of it, he veers off and mentions slavery. He then says, "Oh, and while we're talking about that horrible institution, I'd just like to say to my fellow Americans whose ancestors may have been afflicted, my bad." And you're done. Believe me, every brotha in every barber shop will nod their head and say, "Aw, don't worry about it man." And if the president ends this apology with a double fist pump to the chest, it'll make brothas feel even better.

The "my bad" apology also blows right by white people, which is another added plus. I can't recommend this highly enough.

THE "GUY" APOLOGY

Slavery is a very sensitive issue and I don't have to reiterate how touchy brothas are. So the "guy" apology (where you dance around the subject and let the other person fill in the blanks in their own mind) is a wonderful choice. This is one that the president would do face-to-face with a so-called black leader to get the proper rhythm. It would go something like this:

> PRESIDENT: Hey, so-called black leader, about that um, you know, that bullshit that went down, you know, um . . .

SO-CALLED BLACK LEADER: You mean the—

PRESIDENT: Yeah, that. Um, you know, that shit was uh, that shit was not, uh—

SO-CALLED BLACK LEADER: That shit was not right.

PRESIDENT: Exactly. And I just want you to know, that um, you know, I would never, um—

SO-CALLED BLACK LEADER: Man, you don't even have to say it, I feel you.

PRESIDENT: Thanks, so-called black leader, cause I would hate to have something like that, you know, come between us.

SO-CALLED BLACK LEADER: It won't. Now give me some dap.

He gives him some dap (it's like a high five but it's not) and he's done. This apology, if done well, can let everybody off the hook without all the messy emotional stuff.

THE "ABSENT-MINDED" APOLOGY

This apology is a very sneaky though effective tactic, because it allows the government to apologize for slavery while pretending as if it already has. This also has the advantage of seeming spontaneous, which gives it a very organic feel.

For instance, the president is taking questions from the press corps and someone says, "When is the United States government going to apologize for slavery?" The president merely feigns surprise and says, "We haven't apologized for slavery? Wow, I thought that was done a long time ago." I guarantee you this will throw people off their game. Immediately they'll come back with, "Hell no, you haven't apologized for slavery!" The president stays with the ruse and says, "I could've sworn one of the last two presidents apologized already. You know what, let me check into that but in the meantime I agree with you."

Do you see what I did there? By adopting a sympathetic attitude coupled with a puzzled recollection and then topped off with agreeing with them, he is able to squash discussion without alienating either side. And on top of that, he never really even apologizes! Bravo.

THE "BURY THE LEAD" APOLOGY

This is also a sneaky apology but is accomplished through misdirection instead of misrecalling. The basic idea is to bury the apology inside of a speech with a very distracting topic.

For instance, the president could be giving a speech to announce the first brothas who will be sent to Mars. Right before the most interesting part, apologize for slavery and then continue. Everyone will be so interested and caught up in the brothas going to Mars announcement that no one will pay much attention to the apology. Nonetheless, you've said you're sorry and can move on. And if anyone ever challenges you, tell them to check the transcripts of your speech.

Word of caution, this should be done only on a Friday so it will be guaranteed to be buried in the press the next day.

Side note: It would be awesome if brothas got to go to Mars!

THE "IRRESPONSIBLE CELEBRITY" APOLOGY

This is the rambling type of apology where you seem very sincere and contrite but you never quite admit to anything and almost blame any bad feelings on the other person. And since this is primarily a narcissistic apology, you don't have to worry about promising reparations when you're done. Just pledge to go to rehab or counseling and all's good. It works something like this: "If anybody was offended or took the institution of slavery in the wrong way, the United States deeply regrets that it happened. I am immediately instituting sensitivity classes for all government employees and their families so the healing process can begin. Once again, I can't tell you how ashamed this government feels in regards to possibly having some citizens misinterpret or misconstrue our historical behavior, which we regret, in the wrong way."

Tip: In order to really pull this off, be sure to wear an extremely sad and contrite face with your eyes looking down the entire time. You can't miss.

THE "SHAKING YOUR TURKEY NECK" APOLOGY

This works only if you have enough fat under your chin to constitute a turkey neck. It was first popularized in the films of the 1930s and was more a show of indignation than an apology. A pudgy patron of society would suffer an indignity and cry out, "This is unmitigated gall! Unmitigated gall, I tell you!" Because this is so old school and no one says "unmitigated gall" anymore, this probably shouldn't be the "go to" apology. But in a pinch, I like it for its boldness. There is no better show of solidarity for a cause than when the apologizer is more outraged than the apologizee.

Here's how it might play: when discussing the notion of an appropriate apology for slavery, the president or government official shakes his turkey neck on the words "inexcusable, unconscionable, and deplorable."

For example, "This country's actions were INEXCUS-ABLE, UNCONSCIONABLE, and represented the most DEPLORABLE of deeds, I tell you! The most DEPLOR-ABLE of deeds!"

Don't be afraid of this technique. Brothas will be so impressed by your anger that they'll probably overlook the fact that you didn't really apologize.

THE "YOU GO FIRST" APOLOGY

I love this particular approach because it really requires an enormous set of balls. The idea is to get the black community to apologize for something first and then you piggyback the slavery apology on top of that. I know, it sounds unlikely, but with the perfect blend of timing and panache this could be quite effective. The downside is you could be waiting forever for black people to apologize for something. Don't let that stop you though, because as each day passes there are more and more things that blacks may feel deserve contrition on their part.

For example, O.J. Simpson. The longer he's out of jail and playing golf, the more black people may feel they need to apologize for making him the face of their oppression.

The apology might go like this:

> So-called Black Leader: You know what, this O.J. thing has gotten completely out of hand. We are so sorry we backed this loser in the first place. We just want to say—
>
> Government Official: (interrupting) You don't even have to go on. I completely know what you're talking about. Just like we hate what happened with that whole slavery thing. We totally feel your pain.

Even though it sounds a bit colloquial, "totally feeling" black people's pain goes a long way in the community. Good luck.

The "Tearful Jimmy Swaggart" Apology

This is probably the most dramatic of apologies and requires a president or government official with a very large emotional reservoir. You literally have to cry your eyes out in anguished sorrow. And you must not—I repeat, must not—fake it. A good sorrowful phrase is "We have sinned! Please forgive us Lord, we have sinnnnnnnned!" The more blubber and snot you can muster during this over-the-top show of regret the better.

Though this is an actual apology, it takes reparations off the table because everyone will feel so bad for you.

THE "MY OPPRESSION IS WORSE THAN YOUR OPPRESSION" APOLOGY

This is a tough one because there aren't too many grievances worse than slavery. The closest is sexism. Women have been treated poorly pretty much since the beginning of time. Brothas had a good run during the Egyptian period and a few flashes in the Middle Ages.

You need a high-ranking female government official (of course, a female president is ideal) to face the press. She should make it clear, through the use of hand gestures, eye rolling, and impatient exhaling that slavery is nothing compared to what women have faced. A great technique is to mutter something under her breath that is impossible to make out except for the words "women" and "had it worse."

This is most useful when you want to keep brothas from holding on to the moral high ground. Because we all know, as long as brothas have the moral high ground, they will throw it back in your face.

THE "THROW IT IN WITH ALL THE OTHER APOLOGIES" APOLOGY

You don't even have to make a big deal about it with this apology. Just start apologizing for everything. Somewhere in the middle of your rant, just throw in, "Oh and slavery, too."

This sounds a little callous, but trust me, if you are apologizing for some serious enough shit, no one will notice.

I hope these suggestions help our government to do the right thing when it comes to healing the rift that has been a part of this country for way too long. And don't get too caught up on which one to use, because at the end of the day, no matter what you say, black people won't believe it. Nevertheless, we still want to hear you say it anyway. Sorry.

[2009]

CONTRIBUTORS

GEORGE ADE (1866–1944)
Born in Kentland, Indiana. His books include *Fables in Slang* (1899), *People You Know* (1903), *Breaking into Society* (1904), *Hand-Made Fables* (1920); also a successful playwright whose plays include *The College Widow* (1904) and *The Fair Co-Ed* (1908).

JENNY ALLEN
Wrote and performed the one-woman play *I Got Sick Then I Got Better* (2007); author of *The Long Chalkboard* (with illustrations by her husband Jules Feiffer); has contributed stories and articles to *The New Yorker*, *New York*, *Vogue*, *The New York Times*, and other publications.

WOODY ALLEN (B. 1935)
Born Allen Stewart Konigsberg in New York City. After an early career as a stand-up comedian he directed over forty films including *Sleeper* (1973), *Annie Hall* (1977), *The Purple Rose of Cairo* (1985), and *Match Point* (2005). His writings have been collected in *Getting Even* (1971), *Without Feathers* (1975), *Side Effects* (1980), and *Mere Anarchy* (2007).

DAVE BARRY (B. 1947)
Born in Armonk, New York. Author of many books including *The Taming of the Screw* (1983), *Dave Barry's Guide to Marriage and/or Sex* (1987), *Dave Barry's Greatest Hits* (1988), *Dave Barry Slept Here* (1989), *Dave Barry's Complete Guide to Guys* (1996), *Big Trouble* (1999), and *I'll Mature When I'm Dead* (2010). He won a Pulitzer Prize in 1988 for his column in the *Miami Herald*.

DONALD BARTHELME (1931–1989)
Born in Philadelphia; moved with family to Houston, Texas as a
child. His stories were collected in *Come Back, Dr. Caligari* (1964),
Unspeakable Practices, Unnatural Acts (1968), *City Life* (1970),
Sadness (1972), *Amateurs* (1976), *Great Days* (1979), *Overnight
to Many Distant Cities* (1983). He also published the novels *Snow
White* (1967), *The Dead Father* (1975), *Paradise* (1986), and *The
King* (1990). *Guilty Pleasures* (1974) was a collection of non-fiction
pieces. He was a founder of the Creative Writing Program at the
University of Houston.

HENRY BEARD (B. 1945?)
He was on the staff of the *Harvard Lampoon* and, with Douglas
Kenney, wrote *Bored of the Rings*, a parody of J.R.R. Tolkien, in
1968. With Kenney and Rob Hoffman he founded the *National
Lampoon* in 1969. His later publications include *Miss Piggy's Guide
to Life* (1981), *French for Cats* (1991, with John Boswell), and *The
Official Politically Correct Dictionary and Handbook* (1992, with
Christopher Cerf).

ROY BLOUNT JR. (B. 1941)
Born in Indianapolis, Indiana, and grew up in Georgia. His books
include *About Three Bricks Shy of a Load* (1974), *What Men Don't
Tell Women* (1984), *Not Exactly What I Had in Mind* (1985), *Roy
Blount's Book of Southern Humor* (1994), and *Long Time Leaving:
Dispatches from Up South* (2007).

LENNY BRUCE (1925–1966)
Born Leonard Alfred Schneider in Mineola, New York. Appeared
as a solo performer in nightclubs and concert halls in the 1950s
and 1960s; released recordings including *The Sick Humor of Lenny
Bruce* (1959), *Togetherness—I Am Not a Nut, Elect Me* (1959), and

Lenny Bruce—American (1960). Many recordings of his live performances subsequently appeared. His arrest for obscenity in San Francisco in 1961 was followed by many others; he was convicted of obscenity in New York City in 1964. He received a posthumous gubernatorial pardon in 2003. His autobiography *How to Talk Dirty and Influence People* was serialized in *Playboy*, 1964–65, and was published as a book in 1967.

GEORGE CARLIN (1937–2008)
Born in New York City. After performing in a comedy team with Jack Burns, he went solo, recording *Take-Offs and Put-Ons* in 1967. He made numerous television appearances on the *Tonight Show*, *Saturday Night Live*, and other programs; he starred in the sitcom *The George Carlin Show*, 1994–95. His many recordings included *Class Clown* (1972) and *Playin' with Your Head* (1986). Seven collections of his writing have been published, including *Brain Droppings* (1997), *When Will Jesus Bring the Pork Chops?* (2004), and *Last Words* (2009).

SLOANE CROSLEY (B. 1978)
Has published two books: *I Was Told There'd Be Cake* (2008) and *How Did You Get This Number* (2010). Her writing has appeared in *The Village Voice*, *BlackBook*, *Salon*, *Elle*, *The New York Times*, and other publications.

PETER DE VRIES (1910–1993)
Born in Chicago; his parents were Dutch immigrants. Published novels including *Tunnel of Love* (1954), *Comfort Me with Apples* (1956), *The Mackerel Plaza* (1958), *The Tents of Wickedness* (1959), *Through the Fields of Clover* (1961), *The Blood of the Lamb* (1961), *Reuben, Reuben* (1964), *Let Me Count the Ways* (1965), *The Vale of Laughter* (1967), *Into Your Tent I'll Creep* (1971), *The Glory of*

the Hummingbird (1974), *I Hear America Swinging* (1976), and *Peckham's Marbles* (1986); his stories were collected in *No, But I Saw the Movie* (1952) and *Without a Stitch in Time* (1972). He was on the staff of *The New Yorker* from 1944 to 1987.

NORA EPHRON (B. 1941)
Born in New York City and grew up in Beverly Hills. Films she has written and directed include *Sleepless in Seattle* (1993), *You've Got Mail* (1998), and *Julie & Julia* (2009). Her novel *Heartburn* was published in 1983. Her essays have been collected in *Wallflower at the Orgy* (1970), *Crazy Salad* (1975), *Scribble Scribble* (1978), *I Feel Bad About My Neck* (2006), and *I Remember Nothing* (2010).

IAN FRAZIER (B. 1951)
Born in Cleveland, Ohio. His books include *Great Plains* (1989), *On the Rez* (2000), and *Travels in Siberia* (2010). His humor writing has been collected in *Dating Your Mom* (1986), *Coyote vs. Acme* (1996), and *Lamentations of the Father* (2008), and he has edited the anthology *Humor Me: An Anthology of Funny Contemporary Writing* (2010). He has been on the staff of *The New Yorker* since the 1970s.

BRUCE JAY FRIEDMAN (B. 1930)
Born in the Bronx, New York. He has published eight novels, including *Stern* (1962), *A Mother's Kisses* (1964), *The Dick* (1970), *About Harry Towns* (1974), *The Current Climate* (1989), and *A Father's Kisses* (1996). His stories have been collected in *Black Angels* (1966), *Let's Hear It for a Beautiful Guy* (1984), *Three Balconies* (2008), and other volumes. His landmark anthology *Black Humor* appeared in 1965.

VERONICA GENG (1941–1997)
Born in Atlanta, Georgia, and grew up in Philadelphia. She was a regular contributor to *The New Yorker*, where she also worked as an editor. Her writing also appeared in *The Village Voice*, *The New York Review of Books*, *The New Republic*, and other publications. She published two collections of humor writing: *Partners* (1984) and *Love Trouble Is My Business* (1988).

JACK HANDEY (B. 1949)
Born in San Antonio, Texas. He began as a television writer, working as a writer and producer at *Saturday Night Live*, among other programs. His writing has appeared in *National Lampoon*, *The New Yorker*, and elsewhere. His collections include *Deep Thoughts* (1992), *Deeper Thoughts: All New, All Crispy* (1993), *Fuzzy Memories* (1996), and *What I'd Say to the Martians and Other Veiled Threats* (2003).

O. HENRY (1862–1910)
Born William Sidney Porter in North Carolina. Established himself as a newspaper columnist in Texas in the 1890s. Accused of embezzling funds from a bank where he had worked as a teller, he fled to Honduras to escape prosecution, and was arrested on returning to the U.S. to see his dying wife. Began writing short stories while serving a three-year prison term. *Cabbages and Kings* (1904), based on his experiences in Honduras, was followed by many collections of stories including *The Four Million* (1906), *The Trimmed Lamp* (1907), *The Voice of the City* (1908), and *Whirligigs* (1910).

JOHN HUGHES (1950–2009)
Born in Lansing, Michigan. Worked as a copywriter before selling his story "Vacation '58" to *National Lampoon*. The story was eventually filmed as *National Lampoon's Vacation* (1983). Hughes's

filmography includes, as writer and director, *Sixteen Candles* (1984), *The Breakfast Club* (1985), *Pretty in Pink* (1986), and *Ferris Bueller's Day Off* (1986).

LANGSTON HUGHES (1902–1967)
Born in Joplin, Missouri; grew up in Kansas, Illinois, and Ohio. With the publication of *The Weary Blues* (1926), recognized as a preeminent poet of the Harlem Renaissance. Wrote prolifically in many genres: poetry, fiction, drama, autobiography. Created the character Jesse B. Semple ("Simple") for a column in the *Chicago Defender*, and published a series of books centered around him, beginning with *Simple Speaks His Mind* (1950).

MOLLY IVINS (1944–2007)
Born in Monterey, California; grew up in Houston, Texas. In the course of her journalistic career she wrote for many papers including *The Texas Observer*, *The Washington Post*, *The New York Times*, the *Dallas Times Herald*, and the *Fort Worth Star-Telegram*. Collections of her writing include *Molly Ivins Can't Say That, Can She?* (1991), *Who Let the Dogs In?: Incredible Political Animals I Have Known* (2004), and *Bill of Wrongs: The Executive Branch's Assault on America's Fundamental Rights* (2007).

GARRISON KEILLOR (B. 1942)
Born in Anoka, Minnesota. He began his career in radio with *The Morning Program* on Minnesota Educational Radio in 1969. His long-running show *A Prairie Home Companion* made its debut in 1974. His many books include *Happy to Be Here* (1981), *Lake Wobegon Days* (1985), *Leaving Home* (1987), *We Are Still Married* (1989), *The Book of Guys* (1993), and *Life Among the Lutherans* (2009).

RING LARDNER (1885–1933)
Born in Niles, Michigan. Began writing sports journalism as a teen-ager and eventually contributed to many newspapers including the *Chicago Examiner*, the *Boston American*, and the *Chicago Tribune*. He became a prolific writer of short stories as well as novels and plays. His books include *You Know Me Al* (1916), *The Big Town* (1921), *How to Write Short Stories* (1924), *The Love Nest* (1926), and *Round Up* (1929).

FRAN LEBOWITZ (B. 1950)
Born in Morristown, New Jersey. After establishing herself as a writer for *Interview* and *Mademoiselle*, she published the collec-tions *Metropolitan Life* (1978) and *Social Studies* (1981). She is the subject of Martin Scorsese's documentary *Public Speaking* (2010).

SINCLAIR LEWIS (1885–1951)
Born in Sauk Centre, Minnesota. Became famous with the publica-tion of his novel *Main Street* (1920), which was followed by *Bab-bitt* (1922), *Arrowsmith* (1925), *Elmer Gantry* (1927), *Dodsworth* (1929), and *It Can't Happen Here* (1935). He won the Nobel Prize in Literature in 1930.

ANITA LOOS (1888–1981)
Born Corinne Anita Loos in Sisson, California. She began her career as a film scenarist with *The New York Hat* (1912), directed by D. W. Griffith, and wrote hundreds of screenplays from the silent era until the 1940s. Her novel *Gentleman Prefer Blondes* (1925) was hugely successful and was followed by *But Gentle-men Marry Brunettes* (1928). She published her autobiography *A Girl Like I* in 1966, and subsequently the memoir *Kiss Hollywood Good-by* in 1974.

BERNIE MAC (1957–2008)
Born Bernard McCullough in Chicago. After establishing himself as a stand-up comic he appeared in many films, including the
documentary *The Original Kings of Comedy* (2000). His television
series *The Bernie Mac Show* was broadcast from 2001 to 2006. *I
Ain't Scared of You*, a collection of humor pieces, was published in
2001; the memoir *Maybe You Never Cry Again* appeared in 2003.

BRUCE MCCALL (B. 1935)
Born in Simcoe, Ontario. After a career as an advertising artist in
Canada, he moved to New York City and became a contributor
of writing and art to *National Lampoon* and *The New Yorker*.
His work has been collected in *Zany Afternoons* (1982), *Thin Ice*
(1997), *Marveltown* (2008), and other volumes.

H. L. MENCKEN (1880–1956)
Born in Baltimore, Maryland. He was a contributor to the *Balti-
more Sun* from 1906 to 1948. His many books include *The Ameri-
can Language* (1919), *Prejudices* (Series 1 to 6, 1919–27), *Happy
Days* (1940), *Newspaper Days* (1941), *Heathen Days* (1943), and *A
Mencken Chrestomathy* (1948).

MARK O'DONNELL (B. 1954)
Born in Cleveland, Ohio. He has contributed to *The New Yorker*,
Spy, *McSweeney's*, *The Atlantic*, and other publications. His books
include *Elementary Education: An Easy Alternative to Actual
Learning* (1985), *Vertigo Park and Other Tall Tales* (1993), and the
novels *Getting Over Homer* (1996) and *Let Nothing You Dismay*
(1998). He co-wrote the musical *Hairspray* (2003).

MICHAEL O'DONOGHUE (1940–1994)
Born in Sauquoit, New York. After an early career as a playwright, created with artist Frank Springer the comic book series *The Adventures of Phoebe Zeit-Geist*, published in book form in 1968, and co-wrote the movie *Savages* (1972). He was a staff writer and editor for *National Lampoon*, and was head writer on *Saturday Night Live*, 1975–78.

THE ONION
A parodistic newspaper, distributed free, founded at the University of Wisconsin (Madison) in 1988 by two undergraduates, Tim Keck and Christopher Johnson. It was edited by Scott Dikkers from 1988 to 1999 and again from 2005 to 2008. The paper subsequently expanded to a website and a web video broadcast.

SUSAN ORLEAN (B. 1955)
Born in Cleveland, Ohio. She has been a staff writer at *The New Yorker* since 1992. Her books include *Red Sox and Bluefish* (1987), *Saturday Night* (1990), *The Orchid Thief* (1998), *The Bullfighter Checks Her Makeup* (2001), *My Kind of Place* (2004), *Lazy Little Loafers* (2008), and *Rin Tin Tin: The Life and the Legend* (2011).

DAVID OWEN (B. 1955)
Has been a staff writer at *The New Yorker* since 1991, having previously worked at *The Atlantic*, *Harper's*, and *Spy*. He is also a contributing editor of *Golf Digest*. His numerous books include *The Walls Around Us* (1991), *My Usual Game* (1995), *The First National Bank of Dad* (2003), *Copies in Seconds* (2004), and *Green Metropolis* (2009).

DOROTHY PARKER (1893–1967)
Born in West End, New Jersey. Worked at *Vogue*, 1914–16; sub-sequently was a staff writer for *Vanity Fair* and a frequent con-tributor to *The New Yorker*. With Robert Benchley and Robert E. Sherwood she was among the founders of the Algonquin Round Table. Her poetry was collected in *Enough Rope* (1926), *Sunset Gun* (1928), and *Death and Taxes* (1931), and her stories in *Laments for the Living* (1930), *After Such Pleasures* (1933), and *Here Lies* (1939).

S. J. PERELMAN (1904–1979)
Born Sidney Joseph Perelman in Brooklyn, New York; grew up in Providence, Rhode Island, and attended Brown University. Wrote for humor magazines including *Judge* and *College Humor*, and was eventually a regular contributor to *The New Yorker*. His first book was *Dawn Ginsbergh's Revenge* (1929), and his many subsequent collections include *Strictly from Hunger* (1937), *Crazy Like a Fox* (1944), *Keep It Crisp* (1946), *Westward Ha!* (1948), and *The Road to Miltown* (1957). He worked on the scripts for the Marx Brothers films *Monkey Business* (1931) and *Horse Feathers* (1932), among many other screenplays.

CHARLES PORTIS (B. 1933)
Born in El Dorado, Arkansas. After a career in journalism, includ-ing a number of years as staff writer and London bureau chief for the *New York Herald-Tribune*, he published the novels *Norwood* (1966), *True Grit* (1968), *The Dog of the South* (1979), *Masters of Atlantis* (1985), and *Gringos* (1991).

DAVID RAKOFF (B. 1964)
Born in Montreal, Canada. He has worked in publishing, published in periodicals including *GQ*, *Salon*, and *New York*, and contrib-

uted to the public radio program *This American Life*. His work has been collected in *Fraud* (2001), *Don't Get Too Comfortable* (2005), and *Half Empty* (2010).

PHILIP ROTH (B. 1933)
Born in Newark, New Jersey. His books include *Goodbye, Columbus* (1959), *Portnoy's Complaint* (1969), *The Ghost Writer* (1979), *The Counterlife* (1986), *Sabbath's Theater* (1995), *American Pastoral* (1997), *The Human Stain* (2000), *The Plot Against America* (2004), *Exit Ghost* (2007), and *Nemesis* (2010). He won the Man Booker International Prize in 2011.

GEORGE SAUNDERS (B. 1958)
Born in Amarillo, Texas. He has worked as an engineer and technical writer, and was employed by an oil company in Sumatra. His fiction has been published in *CivilWarLand in Bad Decline* (1996), *Pastoralia* (2000), *The Very Persistent Gappers of Frip* (2000), *The Brief and Frightening Reign of Phil* (2005), and *In Persuasion Nation* (2006). A collection of essays, *The Braindead Megaphone*, appeared in 2007.

DAVID SEDARIS (B. 1956)
Born in Binghamton, New York. Since 1992 his work has often been featured on the public radio programs *Morning Edition* and *This American Life*. His work has been collected in *Barrel Fever* (1994), *Naked* (1997), *Me Talk Pretty One Day* (2000), *Dress Your Family in Corduroy and Denim* (2004), *When You Are Engulfed in Flames* (2008), and *Squirrel Seeks Chipmunk: A Modest Bestiary* (2010). He is the recipient of a Grammy award and the 2001 Thurber Prize for American Humor.

JEAN SHEPHERD (1921–1999)
Born in Chicago; grew up in Hammond, Indiana. From 1948 on he worked as a radio performer on various stations in Philadelphia, Cincinnati, and New York, including a long-running program on New York's WOR. His written work, originally published in periodicals including *Playboy*, *Mad*, and *The Village Voice*, was collected in *In God We Trust, All Others Pay Cash* (1966), *Wanda Hickey's Night of Golden Memories* (1971), *The Ferrari in the Bedroom* (1972), and other volumes. *A Christmas Story*, a film based on his work, appeared in 1983.

TERRY SOUTHERN (1924–1995)
Born in Alvarado, Texas. Early stories, written during a period of residence in Paris, appeared in *The Paris Review*. His first novel *Flash and Filigree* (1958) was followed by *Candy* (with Mason Hoffenberg, published in Paris in 1958 but not until 1964 in the U.S.), *The Magic Christian* (1959), *Red-Dirt Marijuana and Other Tastes* (1967), *Blue Movie* (1970), and *Texas Summer* (1992). He worked on the screenplays for *Dr. Strangelove* (1964), *The Loved One* (1965), *Easy Rider* (1969), and other films.

FRANK SULLIVAN (1892–1976)
Born in Saratoga Springs, New York. He was a columnist for the New York *World* and began writing for *The New Yorker* in 1926. Collections of his writing include *Life and Times of Martha Hepplethwaite* (1926), *In One Ear* (1933), *A Pearl in Every Oyster* (1938), *The Night the Old Nostalgia Burned Down* (1953), and *A Moose in the Hoose* (1959). He was a member of the Algonquin Round Table.

WANDA SYKES (B. 1964)
Born in Portsmouth, Virginia. She worked for the National Security
Agency before beginning a career as a stand-up comic in the late
1980s. She became a writer and performer on *The Chris Rock Show*,
appeared regularly on *Curb Your Enthusiasm*, and has starred in
her own series, *Wanda at Large* and *The Wanda Sykes Show*. Her
book *Yeah, I Said It* was published in 2004.

HUNTER S. THOMPSON (1937–2005)
Born in Louisville, Kentucky. After serving in the Air Force began
a career in journalism and over the years would write for publications including *The National Observer*, *The New York Times Magazine*, *Scanlan's Monthly*, and *Rolling Stone*. His books include
Hell's Angels (1967), *Fear and Loathing in Las Vegas* (1971), *Fear
and Loathing: On the Campaign Trail '72* (1973), and *The Great
Shark Hunt* (1979), the first installment of *The Gonzo Papers*, a
multivolume collection of his journalism. He died of a self-inflicted
gunshot wound at his home in Woody Creek, Colorado.

JAMES THURBER (1894–1961)
Born in Columbus, Ohio. He became a member of *The New Yorker*
staff in 1927 and for the next three decades contributed writing
and drawings to the magazine. His first book, *Is Sex Necessary?*
(1929), written in collaboration with E. B. White, was followed by
many others including *The Owl in the Attic and Other Perplexities*
(1931), *The Seal in the Bedroom and Other Predicaments* (1932),
My Life and Hard Times (1933), *The Middle-Aged Man on the
Flying Trapeze* (1935), *Fables for Our Time and Famous Poems
Illustrated* (1940), *My World—and Welcome To It* (1942), *The 13
Clocks* (1950), and *The Years with Ross* (1959).

CALVIN TRILLIN (B. 1935)
Born in Kansas City, Missouri. He became a staff member of *The New Yorker* in 1963 and for many years wrote the feature "U.S. Journal." He has also written as a columnist for *The Nation, Time,* and in syndication. His books include *American Fried: Adventures of a Happy Eater* (1974), *Uncivil Liberties* (1982), *Killings* (1984), *Travels with Alice* (1989), *Messages from My Father* (1996), and *Family Man* (1998).

GEORGE W. S. TROW (1943–2006)
Born in Greenwich, Connecticut. He graduated in 1965 from Harvard, where he was president of the *Lampoon*, and was later an editor of *National Lampoon.* He worked at *The New Yorker* for thirty years. His books include *Within the Context of No Context* (1981) and *My Pilgrim's Progress: Media Studies, 1950–1998* (1999).

MARK TWAIN (1835–1910)
Born Samuel Clemens in Florida, Missouri. His books include *The Innocents Abroad* (1869), *Roughing It* (1872), *The Adventures of Tom Sawyer* (1876), *Life on the Mississippi* (1883), *Adventures of Huckleberry Finn* (1884), *A Connecticut Yankee in King Arthur's Court* (1889), *The Tragedy of Pudd'nhead Wilson* (1894), *The Man That Corrupted Hadleyburg* (1900), and *What Is Man?* (1906).

E. B. WHITE (1899–1985)
Born Elwyn Brooks White in Mount Vernon, New York. He began writing for *The New Yorker* in 1925 and joined the magazine's staff two years later. His books include *Is Sex Necessary?* (with James Thurber, 1929), *One Man's Meat* (1942), *Here Is New York* (1949), *The Second Tree from the Corner* (1954), and the children's books

Stuart Little (1945), *Charlotte's Web* (1952), and *The Trumpet of the Swan* (1970). He won a Presidential Medal of Freedom (1963) and an honorary Pulitzer Prize (1978).

LARRY WILMORE (B. 1962)
Born in Los Angeles. He was an actor in film and television before becoming a writer and producer for a range of television shows including *The Fresh Prince of Bel-Air*, *The Jamie Foxx Show*, and *The Bernie Mac Show*. Since 2006 he has made regular appearances on *The Daily Show*. His book *I'd Rather We Got Casinos: And Other Black Thoughts* was published in 2009.

TOM WOLFE (B. 1931)
Born in Richmond, Virginia. After receiving a doctorate in American Studies from Yale, he wrote for *The Washington Post, The New York Herald Tribune*, *New York*, and *Esquire*, becoming part of the journalistic tendency he called the New Journalism. His books include *The Kandy-Kolored Tangerine-Flake Streamline Baby* (1965), *The Electric Kool-Aid Acid Test* (1968), *Radical Chic & Mau-Mauing the Flak Catchers* (1970), *The Right Stuff* (1979), *The Purple Decades* (1982), *The Bonfire of the Vanities* (1987), *A Man in Full* (1998), and *I Am Charlotte Simmons* (2004).

SOURCES AND
ACKNOWLEDGEMENTS

Great care has been taken to locate and acknowledge all owners of copyrighted material included in this book. If any such owner has inadvertently been omitted, acknowledgement will gladly be made in future printings.

George Ade, "The Lecture Tickets That Were Bought but Never Used": *Breaking into Society* (New York: Harper & Brothers, 1904), pp. 44–53.

Jenny Allen, "Awake": *The New Yorker*, June 2, 2008. Copyright © 2008 by Jenny Allen. Originally published in *The New Yorker*.

Woody Allen, "A Look at Organized Crime": *Getting Even* (New York: Random House, 1971), pp. 13–18. Copyright © 1966, 1967, 1968, 1969, 1970, 1971 by Woody Allen. Copyright renewed © 1998 by Woody Allen. Used by permission of Random House, Inc.

Dave Barry, "Tips for Women: How to Have a Relationship with a Guy": *Dave Barry's Complete Guide to Guys* (New York: Random House, 1995), pp. 59–71. Copyright © 1995 by Dave Barry. Used by permission of Random House, Inc.

Donald Barthelme, "In the Morning Post": *Not Knowing: The Essays and Interviews* (New York: Random House, 1997), pp. 39–40. Copyright © 1997 by The Estate of Donald Barthelme. Originally published in *The New Yorker*. Copyright © 1997 by Donald Barthelme. Reprinted by permission of the Wylie Agency, LLC.

Henry Beard, Michael O'Donoghue, and George W. S. Trow, "Our White Heritage": *National Lampoon*, September 1972. Excerpted from *National Lampoon*, September 1972. Copyright © National Lampoon, Inc.

Roy Blount Jr., "Gothic Baseball": *Long Time Leaving: Dispatches from Up South* (New York: Random House, 2007), pp. 69–73. Copyright © 2007 by Roy Blount Jr. Reprinted by permission of International Creative Management, Inc.

Lenny Bruce, from *How to Talk Dirty and Influence People*: *How to Talk Dirty and Influence People* (Chicago: Playboy Press, 1965), pp. 124–31. Copyright © 1963 by Lenny Bruce. Reprinted with permission of Kitty Bruce.

George Carlin, "If I Were in Charge of the Networks": *Brain Droppings* (New York: Hyperion, 1997), pp. 115–21. Copyright © 1997 Comedy Concepts, Inc. Reprinted by permission of Hyperion. All rights reserved.

Sloane Crosley, "The Pony Problem": *I Was Told There'd Be Cake* (New York: Penguin, 2008), pp. 1–8. Copyright © 2008 by Sloane Crosley. Used by permission of Riverhead Books, an imprint of Penguin Group (USA) Inc.

Peter De Vries, "The House of Mirth": *The New Yorker*, December 20, 1956. Copyright © 1956 by Peter De Vries. Originally published in *The New Yorker*. Reprinted by permission of The Estate of Peter De Vries.

Nora Ephron, "A Few Words about Breasts": *Crazy Salad* (New York: Alfred A. Knopf, 1975), pp. 3–12. Copyright © 1972 by Nora Ephron. Reprinted by permission of International Creative Management, Inc.

Ian Frazier, "Laws Concerning Food and Drink; Household Principles; Lamentations of the Father": *Lamentations of the Father* (New York: Macmillan, 2009), pp. 8–13. Copyright © 2008 by Ian Frazier. Reprinted by permission of Farrar, Straus and Giroux, LLC.

Bruce Jay Friedman, "The Tax Man": *Let's Hear It for a Beautiful Guy* (New York: Donald I. Fine, 1984), pp. 27–35. Copyright © 1984 by Bruce Jay Friedman. Reprinted with permission of the author.

Veronica Geng, "Curb Carter Policy Discord Effort Threat": *Partners* (New York: Harper Collins, 1984), pp. 102–3. Originally published in *Not The New York Times*, and most recently published in *Love Trouble: New and Collected Work*. Copyright © 1999 by Veronica Geng. Reprinted by permission of The Wylie Agency, LLC.

Jack Handey, "What I'd Say to the Martians": *What I'd Say to the Martians and Other Veiled Threats* (New York: Hyperion, 2008), pp. 24–27. Copyright © 2005 by Jack Handey. Originally published in *The New Yorker*. Reprinted by permission of the Wylie Agency, LLC.

O. Henry, "The Ransom of Red Chief": *Whirligigs* (New York: Doubleday, Page and Co., 1910), pp. 100–15.

John Hughes, "Vacation '58": *National Lampoon*, September 1979. Excerpted from *National Lampoon*, September 1972. Copyright © National Lampoon, Inc.

Langston Hughes, "Simple Prays a Prayer": *Simple Speaks His Mind* (New York: Simon & Schuster, 1950), pp. 12–17. Copyright © 1944 by Langston Hughes. Reprinted by permission of Farrar, Straus and Giroux, LLC. Electronic rights used by permission of Harold Ober Associates Inc.

Molly Ivins, "Tough as Bob War and Other Stuff": *Molly Ivins Can't Say That, Can She?* (New York: Random House, 1991), pp. 40–43. Copyright © 1991 by Molly Ivins. Used by permission of Random House, Inc.

Garrison Keillor, "The Tip-Top Club": *Happy To Be Here* (New York: Atheneum, 1981), pp. 59–75. Copyright © 1981 by Garrison Keillor. Used by permission of the Penguin Group (USA) Inc. Electronic rights used by permission of Prairie Home Productions, LLC.

Ring Lardner, "On Conversation": *First and Last* (New York: Charles Scribner's Sons, 1934), pp. 243–46. First published in *The San Francisco Examiner*, August 16, 1925 as "Ring Lardner

Runs Into Brilliant Pullman Talkers." Copyright © 1934 by Ellis A. Lardner, renewal copyright © 1962 by Ring Lardner Jr. Reprinted with permission of Scribner, a division of Simon & Schuster, Inc. All rights reserved.

Fran Lebowitz, "Better Read Than Dead: A Revised Opinion": *Metropolitan Life* (New York: Dutton, 1978), pp. 26–31. Copyright © 1978 by Fran Lebowitz. Reprinted by permission of International Creative Management, Inc.

Sinclair Lewis, from *Babbitt: Main Street & Babbitt*, John Hersey, ed. (New York: The Library of America, 1992), pp. 533–47. First published in 1922.

Anita Loos, from *Gentlemen Prefer Blondes*: *Gentlemen Prefer Blondes* (New York: Liveright, 1925), pp. 18–22. Copyright © 1925 by Anita Loos, renewed 1925 by Anita Loos Emerson. Copyright © 1963 by Anita Loos. Used by permission of Liveright Publishing Corporation.

Bernie Mac (with Darrell Dawsey), from *I Ain't Scared of You*: *I Ain't Scared of You: Bernie Mac on How Life Is* (New York: Simon & Schuster, 2001), pp. 127–29. Copyright © 2001 by Bernie Mac. Reprinted with permission of Pocket Books, a division of Simon & Schuster, Inc. All rights reserved.

Bruce McCall, "Rolled in Rare Bohemian Onyx, Then Vulcanized by Hand": *The New Yorker*, December 21, 1981. Copyright © 1981 by Bruce McCall. Originally published in *The New Yorker*.

H. L. Mencken, "Imperial Purple": *The Impossible H. L. Mencken: A Selection of His Best Newspaper Stories*, Marion Elizabeth Rodgers, ed. (New York: Doubleday, 1991), pp. 400–04. First published in the Baltimore *Evening Sun*, August 17, 1931. Published by permission of the Enoch Pratt Free Library, Baltimore, in accordance with the terms of the will of H. L. Mencken and his bequest to the Library.

Mark O'Donnell, "The Laws of Cartoon Motion": *Elementary*

Education: An Easy Alternative to Actual Learning (New York: Alfred A. Knopf, 1985), pp. 19–21. Copyright © 1985 by Mark O'Donnell. Used by permission of Alfred A. Knopf, a division of Random House, Inc.

The Onion, "Clinton Deploys Vowels to Bosnia": *The Onion*, December 5, 1995. Copyright © 2011 by Onion, Inc. Reprinted with permission of *The Onion*. www.theonion.com.

Susan Orlean, "Shiftless Little Loafers": *The New Yorker*, July 22, 1996. Copyright © 1996 by Susan Orlean. Originally published in *The New Yorker*. Reprinted by permission.

David Owen, "Your Three Wishes: F.A.Q.": *The New Yorker*, January 16, 2006. Copyright © 2006 by David Owen. Originally published in *The New Yorker*.

Dorothy Parker, "The Waltz": *Here Lies* (New York: Viking Press, 1939), pp. 171–78. Copyright 1933, renewed © 1961 by Dorothy Parker, from *The Portable Dorothy Parker* by Dorothy Parker, edited by Marion Meade. Used by permission of Viking Penguin, a division of Penguin Group (USA) Inc.

S. J. Perelman, "Farewell, My Lovely Appetizer": *Keep It Crisp* (New York: Random House, 1946), pp. 16–28. Reprinted by permission of Harold Ober Associates Inc. Copyright © 1944, 1972 by S. J. Perelman. First published in *The New Yorker*, December 16, 1944.

Charles Portis, "Your Action Line": *The New Yorker*, December 12, 1977. Copyright © 1977 by Charles Portis. Originally published in *The New Yorker*. Reprinted by permission of the author.

David Rakoff, "The Writer's Life": *Salon*, November 9, 1999. Copyright © 1999 by David Rakoff.

Philip Roth, "Letters to Einstein": from "On the Air," *New American Review* 10, 1971. Copyright © 1971 by Philip Roth. Reprinted by permission of the Wylie Agency, LLC.

George Saunders, "Ask the Optimist!": *The Braindead Megaphone*

(New York: Penguin, 2007), pp. 103–18. Copyright © 2007 by George Saunders. Used by permission of Riverhead Books, an imprint of the Penguin Group (USA) Inc.

David Sedaris, "Buddy, Can You Spare a Tie?": *When You Are Engulfed in Flames* (New York: Little, Brown, 2008), pp. 49–62. Copyright © 2008 by David Sedaris. Reprinted by permission of Little, Brown and Company, New York, NY. All rights reserved.

Jean Shepherd, "The Counterfeit Secret Circle Member Gets the Message, *or* The Asp Strikes Again": *In God We Trust, All Others Pay Cash* (New York: Random House, 1966), pp. 50–56. Copyright © 1966 by Jean Shepherd. Used by permission of Doubleday, a division of Random House, Inc.

Terry Southern, from *The Magic Christian*: *The Magic Christian* (London: Andre Deutsch Ltd., 1959), pp. 52–57. Copyright © 1959, 1960 by Terry Southern. Reprinted by permission of Susan Schulman, A Literary Agency, New York, on behalf of the Terry Southern Literary Trust. All rights reserved.

Frank Sullivan, "The Night the Old Nostalgia Burned Down": *The Night the Old Nostalgia Burned Down* (Boston: Little, Brown, 1948), pp. 3–10. Courtesy of the Saratoga Springs History Museum.

Wanda Sykes, "It's So Hard": *Yeah, I Said It* (New York: Atria, 2004), pp. 139–42. Copyright © 2004 Sykes Entertainment, Inc. Reprinted with permission of Atria Books, a division of Simon & Schuster, Inc. Electronic rights granted by Sykes Entertainment.

Hunter S. Thompson, "The Kentucky Derby Is Decadent and Depraved": *The Great Shark Hunt* (New York: Simon & Schuster, 1979), pp. 24–38. Copyright © 1979 by Hunter S. Thompson. Reprinted with permission of Simon & Schuster, Inc.

James Thurber, "More Alarms at Night": *Writings & Drawings*,

Garrison Keillor, ed. (New York: The Library of America, 1996), pp. 169–73. First published in 1933 in *My Life and Hard Times* by James Thurber. Copyright © 1933 by Rosemary A. Thurber. Reprinted by arrangement with Rosemary A. Thurber and The Barbara Hogenson Agency, Inc. All rights reserved.

Calvin Trillin, "Corrections": *The New Yorker*, February 5, 1990. Copyright © 1990 by Calvin Trillin. Originally published in *The New Yorker*.

Mark Twain, "A Presidential Candidate": *Collected Tales, Sketches, Speeches, & Essays 1852–1890*, Louis J. Budd, ed. (New York: The Library of America, 1992), pp. 725–26. First published in 1879 as "Mark Twain as a Presidential Candidate."

E. B. White, "Across the Street and into the Grill": *The Second Tree from the Corner* (Boston: Houghton Mifflin, 1954), pp. 140–43. Copyright © 1954 by E. B. White. Reprinted by permission of International Creative Management, Inc.

Larry Wilmore, "If Not an Apology, at Least a 'My Bad'": *I'd Rather We Got Casinos: And Other Black Thoughts* (New York: Hyperion, 2009), pp. 193–203. Copyright © 2009 by Hearthstone Productions, Inc. Reprinted by permission of Hyperion. All rights reserved.

Tom Wolfe, "The Secret Vice": *The Kandy-Kolored Tangerine-Flake Streamline Baby* (New York: Farrar, Straus and Giroux, 1965), pp. 254–61. Copyright © 1965, renewed 1993 by Tom Wolfe. Reprinted by permission of Farrar, Straus and Giroux, LLC.